Competition among States and Local Governments

SOCIAL & BEHAVIORAL SCIENCES   *Political Science*   *U.S. Politics*

29-4781   JK325   91-12344 CIP

Competition among states and local governments: efficiency and equity in American federalism, ed. by Daphne A. Kenyon and John Kincaid. Urban Institute, 1991. 285p index atp ISBN 0-87766-517-6, $52.75; ISBN 0-87766-516-8 pbk, $24.25

During the past 15 years, competition among state and local governments within the US has intensified significantly. As federal aid shrank and economic growth lagged, subnational governments fought fiercely for a better slice of the private sector pie. Using a wide range of weapons, ranging from tax breaks to outright grants, these governments wooed and pursued businesses within the US and, in more recent times, throughout the world. What has been the impact of this interjurisdictional competition on, inter alia, the quality and quantity of state and local public services, tax equity, economic efficiency, and the American federalist system? This volume enlists some of the leading specialists on these matters. In a generally clear and consistently sophisticated fashion, they provide an interim assessment on the pros and cons of heightened intergovernmental competition. Highly recommended for all libraries.—*E. T. Jones, University of Missouri-St. Louis*

DAPHNE A. KENYON
AND JOHN KINCAID
Editors

Albert Breton
John E. Chubb
Daniel J. Elazar
Ronald C. Fisher
R. Scott Fosler
Steven D. Gold
Therese J. McGuire
Dick Netzer
Nonna A. Noto
Wallace E. Oates
Robert W. Rafuse, Jr.
Andrew Reschovsky
Robert M. Schwab
John Shannon
Robert Tannenwald

Competition among States and Local Governments

Efficiency and Equity in American Federalism

THE URBAN INSTITUTE PRESS
Washington, D.C.

In cooperation with the Advisory Commission on
Intergovernmental Relations

Library of Congress Cataloging in Publication Data

Competition among States and Local Governments: Efficiency and Equity in American Federalism

1. Federal government—United States.   2. Intergovernmental fiscal relations—United States.   I. Kenyon, Daphne A.   II. Kincaid, John, 1946–

JK325.C57   1991   91-12344
321.02'0973--dc20   CIP

ISBN 0-87766-517-6 (alk. paper)
ISBN 0-87766-516-8 (alk. paper; casebound)

Urban Institute books are printed on acid-free paper whenever possible.

Printed in the United States of America.

9   8   7   6   5   4   3   2   1

Distributed by:
            University Press of America
4720 Boston Way   3 Henrietta Street
Lanham, MD 20706   London   WC2E 8LU   ENGLAND

ACKNOWLEDGMENTS

Early drafts of the papers in this volume were presented at a conference entitled "Interjurisdictional Tax and Policy Competition: Good or Bad for the Federal System?" held at The Urban Institute, March 23–24, 1988. The conference was cosponsored by the U.S. Advisory Commission on Intergovernmental Relations, Washington, D.C., and the State Policy Center of The Urban Institute. Funding was provided by the J. Howard Pew Freedom Trust.

Participants in the conference included many prominent scholars in economics, political science, and public finance. In addition to the authors represented in this volume, speakers included: Roy W. Bahl, Georgia State University, Atlanta; Warren T. Brookes, *Detroit News*; Robert D. Ebel, U.S. Advisory Commission on Intergovernmental Relations; Fred Ferguson, Price Waterhouse; Helen F. Ladd, Duke University, Durham; E. Blaine Liner, State Policy Center, The Urban Institute; William Niskanen, Cato Institute, Washington, D.C.; Frederick D. Stocker, National Tax Association–Tax Institute of America, Columbus, Ohio; and Deil S. Wright, University of North Carolina, Chapel Hill.

Many people deserve thanks for making the conference a success and for realizing the potential of this volume. The U.S. Advisory Commission on Intergovernmental Relations placed the topic of tax and policy competition near the top of its 1988 research agenda. E. Blaine Liner and Robert D. Ebel originated the idea for the conference. Mary Mingo and Martha Nicholson coordinated the details of the conference. Susan Braman and Ruthamae Phillips also provided essential help in producing this volume.

CONTENTS

Figures

Tables

American state and local governments are the focus of increasing attention as we near the end of the 20th century. Retrenchment of the federal government, which began in the 1970s under President Jimmy Carter, has placed more expenditure responsibilities and fiscal burdens on our 50 states and nearly 40,000 general-purpose local governments. Since 1978, real federal aid has declined, and more federal mandates have been imposed, while state and local policymakers have faced continuing citizen concern about taxes as well as periodic tax revolts.

Interest in the effects of competition among states and local governments has been sparked by these and other changes in our federal system as well as by an interest in how future quasi-federal systems, such as post-1992 Europe, might function. As stated in the Introduction to this volume, competition among states and local governments can be defined as "rivalrous behavior in which each government attempts to win some scarce beneficial resource" (e.g., new corporate headquarters) "or avoid a particular cost" (e.g., responsibility for hosting a hazardous waste site.) Governments make use of public service, tax, and regulatory policies in their efforts to compete with each other.

The authors contributing to this volume take a fresh look at the effects of competition among states and local governments and how certain federal policies can moderate or exacerbate the negative consequences of such rivalry. Two decades ago, policymakers and analysts were nearly uniform in decrying the detrimental effects of interjurisdictional competition on public service levels and tax systems. This volume reflects the growing realization that such competition can, under certain circumstances, have beneficial effects, such as promoting responsiveness of governments to their citizens.

Questions addressed in the volume include how competition among states and local governments affects the taxing, spending, and redistributive behavior of governments. The effects of interstate competition on state tax policy are analyzed, as is the special case of state and local competition for economic development.

This volume is the outcome of a cooperative endeavor of the U.S. Advisory Commission on Intergovernmental Relations and The Urban Institute, and represents a useful expansion of resources made possible by such cooperation. Each institution strives to provide information, through publications such as this, that can improve understanding of America's governments and ultimately improve their policies. However, the views expressed in this volume do not necessarily represent those of the Commission or of the Institute.

William Gorham
The Urban Institute
Washington, D.C.

Robert B. Hawkins, Jr.
U.S. Advisory Commission on
Intergovernmental Relations

Chapter One

INTRODUCTION

Daphne A. Kenyon and John Kincaid

Competition among states and local governments has come to the public's attention in many ways. News stories have described competition for foreign and domestic investment, job-producing industry, corporate headquarters, military bases, sports teams, and tourists. In addition, states and localities sometimes compete to avoid costs—for example, to exclude hazardous waste sites and power plants, or to discourage in-migration of homeless persons and welfare recipients.

Because state and local governments are semiautonomous decision-making units, a certain amount of competition among them is probably inherent in our federal system. However, manifestations of that competition have changed over the years. More than 200 years ago, states competed to control western territories and to avoid footing the bills incurred during the Revolutionary War. In the 19th century, states and localities competed for immigrants, public works projects, and railroads. Two decades ago, state and local governments competed for federal grants-in-aid. Analysts also worried about suburban "exploitation" of central cities as local governments in metropolitan areas vied for high-income citizens and tax-base resources.

Competition among governments can be defined as rivalrous behavior in which each government attempts to win some scarce beneficial resource or to avoid a particular cost.[1] There are two types of competition among governments in a federal system: intergovernmental and interjurisdictional. Intergovernmental competition, which some observers call vertical competition, encompasses competition between governments having different powers—namely, competition between the national government and the states, between a state and its local governments, between a county and other local governments within its territory, and between general-purpose and special-purpose local governments. Intergovernmental competition is an important issue in the federal system, but it is not the primary focus of this volume.[2]

Interjurisdictional competition, which some observers call horizontal competition, entails competition between governments having comparable powers in the federal system—namely, competition among states and among similar types or classes of local governments—in short, interstate and interlocal competition.[3] This type of competition is the primary focus of this volume. Furthermore, most of the authors in this book examine interjurisdictional competition from an economic perspective, although several place that competition in a broader historical and political science perspective.

Governments may use fiscal (i.e., tax or expenditure) or regulatory powers to compete with other governments. Governments may increase their relative attractiveness by adopting certain general policies, such as imposing relatively low tax burdens or maintaining high-quality education systems. Alternatively, state and local governments may compete by offering specific incentives, such as special tax packages designed to attract particular business firms.

The prevailing popular and academic consensus has long been that competition among states and local governments has predominantly negative effects. Various analysts have argued that such competition leads to inadequate state and local spending, reduced reliance on ability to pay taxes, too low a reliance on taxes borne directly by business, and a waste of resources as government efforts to attract businesses from other jurisdictions result in a zero-sum game.[4] Consequently, cooperation among governments, or cooperative federalism, has been the dominant normative model of American federalism in the 20th century.

Within the last two decades, however, the negative view of interjurisdictional competition has been challenged on a number of fronts. Instead, there is a growing realization of the potential benefits that competition can provide for the citizens of the competing governments. The chapters in this volume, therefore, reflect efforts to reassess interjurisdictional competition.

KEY POLICY IMPLICATIONS

Interjurisdictional competition has many policy implications. For example, certain forms of this competition, such as competition for economic development, have generated much public attention and many state and local government programs. To assess interjurisdictional competition, one must also address values and attitudes regarding the appropriate degree of national income redistribution and the appropriate locus of responsibility for such redistribution. Interjurisdictional competition furthermore has fundamental implications for the division of power and authority among governments in a federal system. In addition, certain federal policies toward state and local governments, although not specifically designed to affect interjurisdictional competition, can only be adequately evaluated in light of both their effects on interjurisdictional competition and the benefits and costs of that competition. By the same token, certain state policies toward local governments can only be properly evaluated if the effects of interlocal competition are understood. Finally, those who assert that competition among states and local governments affects the nation's international competitiveness have offered their own policy proposals. The paragraphs following explore each of these policy contexts briefly.

Policymakers and analysts have long had strong concerns about state and local competition for economic development. A wide range of economic development incentives is currently offered—so many that a recent 50-state survey of financial incentives totaled almost 800 pages (National Association of State Development Agencies 1991). Nevertheless, many questions are raised about their effectiveness. From the nation's standpoint, the key question is whether such incentives merely shift the location of business activity within the United States, constituting a zero-sum game. There are also questions about whether these incentives are cost effective for the offering governments.[5] For example, a recent study of financial incentives used by state and local governments to attract new automobile plants concluded that the "incentive cost per job created" for certain plants was extremely high—in some cases exceeding $100,000 (Fiordalisi 1989). Suggestions for curtailing such wasteful competition run the gamut from outright prohibition to proposals for changing the "rules of the game," such as requiring officials to publish cost estimates of economic development incentives. Chapters 13 through 15 in this volume, by Dick Netzer, R. Scott Fosler, and Nonna A. Noto, respectively, discuss the effects of state and local competition for economic development as well as policies for improving its efficacy.

The theme of the relationship of interjurisdictional competition to policies intended to redistribute income arises several times in this volume. Federal, state, and local governments redistribute income through expenditure programs (e.g., Aid to Families with Dependent Children) and taxes (e.g., relatively progressive income taxes). Most of the authors in this book find that interjurisdictional competition limits the extent to which state and local governments can effectively carry out such redistributive policies. Some authors conclude that federal limits on interjurisdictional competition are then called for. Others argue that redistribution of income by state and local governments is inappropriate, and that the federal government should take on this responsibility. For that reason, they eschew recommendations for limiting interjurisdictional competition.

Perhaps the most fundamental policy issues affected by an assessment of interjurisdictional competition involve the structure of the federal system and the division of power and authority among the different governments. The key question is whether we operate federalism as a system of multiple centers of power in which state and local governments have broad authority to enact policies of their own choice, or whether we operate federalism as a system of administrative decentralization in which state and local governments essentially implement uniform national policies. If interjurisdictional competition has predominantly beneficial effects, then it is important to preserve independent spheres of power and authority for state and local governments. On the other hand, if interjurisdictional competition is predominantly harmful, then federal preemption of state and local authority is not so worrisome.

Federal mandates on state and local governments have become a contentious issue for state and local government officials, especially during the last decade. Such mandates can blunt interjurisdictional competition when they require all states and/or localities to conform to the same federal rules or to provide specified services at certain minimum or maximum levels. The more pervasive such federal preemption of state and local authority, the more our federal system takes on the character of a unitary system, and the greater the degree to which state and local governments are transformed from independent governments into administrative divisions of the central government.[6]

A number of federal fiscal and regulatory policies have potentially important effects on interjurisdictional competition. Put another way, federal policies form a framework within which state and local governments compete. Federal policies can affect the "rules of the game" for interjurisdictional competition, change the distribution of resources among governments and thus affect their relative abilities to compete, or modify state and local incentives to engage in competition.

For example, either federal grants-in-aid or tax expenditures aiding states and localities can alter the distribution of resources among governments, with the potential for improving or worsening the competitive positions of the less-well-off state and local governments. The federal tax-exemption for industrial development bonds (IDBs) is an example of a policy that encourages interjurisdictional competition. The federal government bears the cost of this economic development incentive, which encourages state and local governments to use this device, and indirectly stimulates state and local competition for economic development.

Three chapters in this volume consider federal policies in the light of interjurisdictional competition. After examining the evidence that interjurisdictional competition might be unstable, Albert Breton, in chapter 2, suggests that federal grants targeted to low-income jurisdictions might alleviate the instability. Therese J. McGuire, in chapter 9, describes two models of interjurisdictional competition and questions whether either one provides an additional rationale for federal grants to state and local governments. And Robert Tannenwald, in chapter 11, asks how the changes in federal tax law made by the Tax Reform Act of 1986 affected the relative competitive position of the 50 state-tax systems.

Just as federal fiscal and regulatory policies affect competition among states and local governments, state policies affect interlocal competition. Proposals to loosen or tighten state limitations on local government tax and debt policies should consider the benefits and costs of the interlocal competition that is likely to be affected by such changes. One policy proposal for which an understanding of the effects of interjurisdictional competition is important is the perennial recommendation that small local governments be consolidated into larger governments. To the extent that interlocal competition has beneficial effects, the case for such government reorganization is weakened.[7] None of the papers in this volume explicitly reviews state policies affecting interlocal competition; however, analyses of the effects of interjurisdictional competition throughout the volume are partly relevant for interlocal as well as interstate competition.

Finally, one can consider the international implications of competition among states and localities. On the one hand, state and local officials may do a better job of competing for economic development in an international setting than officials of the federal government. On the other hand, competition among states and local governments may damage the competitive standing of the U.S. economy. Such competition can produce diversity as different governments respond to the preferences of different groups of citizens. Fiscal and regulatory diversity among the 50 states and almost 40,000 general-purpose local governments may be a stumbling block to attracting businesses from other countries. For that reason, some observers argue that greater harmonization among the states (and thus less competition) must occur for the United States to be economically competitive with the European Economic Community.[8]

Having thus considered a range of policies for which interjurisdictional competition is relevant, we next present two frameworks for understanding such competition.

ALTERNATIVE CONTEXTS FOR UNDERSTANDING INTERJURISDICTIONAL COMPETITION

The chapters in this volume can be viewed through two lenses. Some state and local government analysts, including most political scientists, base their understanding of competition among governments on a particular theory of federalism. Other analysts, including most economists, base their understanding of competition among states and local governments on a particular theory of the effects of competition in a market economy. In other words, competition among states and localities can be understood within the context of: (1) a model of federal government structure or (2) a theory of competition among firms in a market economy.

The usual economic approach assumes that the role of governments is analogous to the role of business firms, and that the role of citizens is analogous to the role of consumers. That is, governments supply goods and services demanded and paid for by citizens. Furthermore, economists assume that governments may form either competitive or monopolistic markets. For example, a metropolitan area with four general-purpose local governments would generally be considered to have a monopolistic structure, whereas a metropolitan area with 40 general-purpose local governments would be considered to have a competitive structure. Economic theories of the effects of competitive versus monopolistic market structures are modified to apply to the relations among governments. The famous Tiebout model, in which citizen-taxpayers "vote with their feet," is a well-known example of an economist's application of the market analogue to relations among local (and, to some degree, state) governments (Tiebout 1956).

Political scientists are more likely to analyze interjurisdictional competition within the context of the principles of federalism espoused by the founding fathers or of alternative theories of federalism that have evolved over the last 200 years. A federal system can be defined as a governmental system in which there are two or more primary orders of government (e.g., state and federal), each of which possesses significant and constitutionally independent powers.[9] Because the states and the federal government are the primary constitutional entities in the United States, theories of federalism tend to focus on the relationship between the federal government and the states, and only secondarily on interstate or interlocal relationships.

A political scientist also is apt to take a more historical approach than the economist, emphasizing the different theories and practices of federalism that have prevailed during different periods of American history—from dual federalism to cooperative federalism and, perhaps now, to coercive or competitive federalism. A political scientist also is likely to question the assumptions underlying economic conceptions of federalism. For example, do individuals behave like consumers with respect to government? Is economic rationality central to citizen behavior with respect to public services? Do family, friendship, and neighborhood ties inhibit mobility, and are such ties therefore irrational from the perspective of a consumer-voter model of federalism?

The disciplinary division between the federalism theory and market analogue paradigms is not absolute, however. Even though political scientists have contributed most of the rationales for a federal system of government, one economic theory of federalism, generally known as fiscal federalism, has also been influential. On the other side, some political scientists have used the market analogy to analyze interjurisdictional relations. Both economists and political scientists have contributed to the development of theories of "competitive federalism," which rely heavily on the market analogy.

Alternative Theories of Federalism

COOPERATIVE FEDERALISM

Cooperative federalism has been the preeminent theory of American federalism, at least since the New Deal.[10] This model has been used both to describe and to prescribe the character of the relationships among the various governments in our federal system. According to cooperative federalism, the primary characteristic of intergovernmental relationships is and should be sharing and mutual accommodation (e.g., comity) achieved through bargaining and mutual respect for constitutional allocations of authority. Although this theory focuses mainly on the relationship between the federal government and the states, it implies that cooperative relationships among state and local governments, as well as between the federal government and the states, are the norm.

The U.S. Advisory Commission on Intergovernmental Relations (ACIR), the federal government's permanent bipartisan commission charged with examining intergovernmental relations in the United States, was established in 1959 on principles of cooperative federalism. The commission's enabling legislation stipulates that one of the ACIR's tasks is to work toward "a more orderly and less competitive fiscal relationship between the levels of government . . . ." (Public Law 86-380, 1959.) Throughout most of the commission's history, its research has tended to favor cooperation in both interjurisdictional and intergovernmental relations. A 1981 ACIR report, for example, examined interstate tax competition, focusing on competition among the states to attract and hold industry. The major question raised by the report was "whether federal intervention is needed because interstate competition for industry has reached a point that is demonstrably adverse to the economic health of the states and the nation" (U.S. Advisory Commission on Intergovernmental Relations 1981b).[11]

Daniel J. Elazar has been one of the most influential contributors to the theory of cooperative federalism. His paper in this volume (chapter 4) places cooperative federalism in a historical context and summarizes key elements of the theory.

FISCAL FEDERALISM

An alternative theory of federalism, one based on economic principles, is fiscal federalism.[12] This theory attempts to provide a rationale for a federal system of government and to establish guidelines for an appropriate division of responsibilities among governments. The theory focuses on the characteristics of the public goods and services provided by governments. First, the variation in the demand for public goods and the geographical distribution of their benefits are taken into account. Next, the costs of production, particularly potential economies of scale, are considered. (When economies of scale are important, costs per unit of production fall as the scale of production increases.)

Proponents of fiscal federalism argue that a federal system allows citizens to obtain the advantages of both centralization (such as economies of scale in the production of certain public goods) and decentralization (such as variety in the provision of local public goods in accordance with the preferences of different groups of citizens.) The optimal number and size of governments ultimately depends on a trade-off between benefit and cost characteristics. For example, whether a particular state should establish 4 or 40 crime-control districts would depend on such factors as the variation in citizens' crime-control needs and preferences (which would tend to argue in favor of greater decentralization) and economies of scale in providing crime control (which would tend to argue for greater centralization.)

COMPETITIVE FEDERALISM

In recent years, a number of studies by both economists and political scientists have explored the concept of competitive federalism.[13] Because this literature explicitly considers competition among states and local governments, and takes a generally benign view of such competition, competitive federalism is of particular relevance for this volume.

A primary motivation for the interest in competitive federalism is concern with government failure, specifically, the potential for federal, state, and local governments to be less than ideally responsive to their constituents. Thomas R. Dye (1990: 1–3) strongly emphasized this point:

> All governments, even democratic governments, are danger-
> ous. . . . Democratic political processes alone cannot restrain Levi-
> athan. . . . Among the most important "auxiliary precautions" the
> founders devised to control government is federalism, which they
> viewed as a source of constraint on Leviathan. . . . Federalism is not
> only competition between the national government and the states, the
> topic of most modern scholarship on federalism; it is also competi-
> tion between the states. Indeed, it is also, by extension, competition
> among the nation's eighty-three thousand local governments.

To some extent, competitive federalism is also a reaction to prob lems with cooperative federalism, especially the notion of collusion, in which federal, state, and local officials "cooperate" to enhance their power and reelection opportunities by circumventing the competitive dynamics of federalism. Changing the focus to competitive federalism may help achieve a better balance between cooperation and competition in our federal system. John Kincaid (1988) has recently argued that both competition and cooperation among governments are inherent in our federal system. He views increased intergovernmental and interjurisdictional competition as one remedy for the excesses of cooperative federalism.

Although both fiscal federalism and competitive federalism are based primarily on economic principles, the two approaches are different. Whereas fiscal federalism focuses on the benefit and cost characteristics of public goods provision, competitive federalism focuses on competition among governments as a constraint on government behavior. In a sense, competitive federalism is a response to one criticism of fiscal federalism, that it does not explicitly take into account the potential for government failure.

Analogy of the Competitive Market

The most important economic model of competition among states and local governments is the Tiebout (1956) model, published 35 years ago. The core of Tiebout's theory is that citizen mobility combined with interjurisdictional competition can result in an efficient allocation of resources to the public sector. Tiebout's primary concern was not to analyze the effects of interjurisdictional competition but to find a marketlike mechanism that would achieve an efficient allocation of resources to the public sector. As it turned out, though, interjurisdictional competition was a key component of the mechanism discovered by Tiebout.

The actors in Tiebout's model are individuals (whom he calls consumer-voters) and governments. Business firms are not an explicit part of the model. Tiebout's model was meant to apply to local governments and, to a lesser degree, to state governments. Some of his assumptions parallel those typically made in the economic theory of perfect competition. For example, Tiebout assumed that consumer-voters have full knowledge of government revenue and expenditure packages, that there are a large number of communities among which individuals can choose to live, and that people will choose the community that best satisfies their preferences. He also assumed that government services exhibit no spillover effects. (An example of a beneficial spillover is the effect that one town's mosquito spraying program has on an adjoining town.)

Tiebout made three additional assumptions: (1) that jobs impose no locational constraint on individuals; (2) that a community's optimal size, meaning the size for which the average cost of producing a particular package of public services is minimized, can be determined; and (3) that each community seeks to attain its optimal size. Tiebout envisioned consumer-voters sorting themselves out among available communities so that demands for government services within any particular community would become homogeneous.

Tiebout concluded that to the extent these rather restrictive assumptions are met, goods and services provided by the local public sector will exhibit both allocative efficiency (the right amounts of the various goods and services are produced) and productive efficiency (they are produced at least cost). In Tiebout's model, community taxes would be benefit taxes, or proportional to the benefits consumer-voters receive from public services, rather than taxes based on ability to pay. Tiebout's model implies that any redistribution of income is taken care of by the federal government.[14]

Since 1956, a voluminous literature has arisen that elaborates on, extends, and tests aspects of the Tiebout model.[15] Chapter 7 in this volume, by Wallace E. Oates and Robert M. Schwab, describes a model of local fiscal competition clearly in the spirit of the Tiebout model. A major difference in the Oates-Schwab model is that business firms instead of individuals are the mobile entity.

EVALUATING THE EFFECTS OF INTERJURISDICTIONAL COMPETITION

To provide an acceptable answer to the question of whether interjurisdictional competition is good or bad for the federal system, one must propose criteria for evaluation. Just as political scientists and economists rely on different models to analyze interjurisdictional competition, they tend to emphasize different criteria in evaluating its effects. Even when they agree on basically the same criterion, they often describe it in different terms.

Economists usually evaluate public policies according to the criteria of efficiency and equity. Two major components of efficiency, allocative and productive efficiency, were introduced earlier. Ideas of equity are usually based on an ability-to-pay or a benefit-principle framework. Policies aimed at redistributing income from rich to poor are implicitly based on the ability-to-pay principle. Policies intended to tax individuals in proportion to the benefits they receive from public services are based on the benefit principle.

The political science literature adopts broader criteria for evaluating public policies. In evaluating interjurisdictional competition, political scientists are likely to mention its beneficial effects on individual liberty or on the rate of policy innovations adopted by state and local governments, and its constraining effects on political elites, in addition to its effects on equity and efficiency. Although concerned with efficiency, political scientists are likely to discuss the value differently than economists. Policy responsiveness as discussed by political scientists amounts to much the same thing as allocative efficiency as defined by an economist. Both concepts examine whether a government produces goods and services (or policies) that match the preferences of its citizens.

Because most of the papers in this volume were contributed by economists, equity and efficiency are the two primary criteria by which interjurisdictional competition is evaluated throughout most of this book.

SUMMARY OF CHAPTERS

This book is organized into four major parts, plus a summary, as follows. Parts One and Two (chapters 2 through 10) address basic issues regarding interjurisdictional competition and its effects. The two chapters in Part Three explore more specific aspects of interjurisdictional competition, including the effects of the Tax Reform Act of 1986 (TRA) on interstate tax competition (chapter 11), and the effects of interstate competition on state income-tax policies (chapter 12). Part Four (chapters 13 through 15) examines interjurisdictional competition for economic development. The concluding chapter 16 summarizes themes addressed in the rest of the volume and suggests paths for future research.

Part One: General Theories and Models

Albert Breton's paper is an appropriate starting point for this volume because it represents part of the continuing effort to develop a general theory of federalism based on competition among governments. Breton addresses two basic questions generally overlooked in the literature: (1) What evidence do we have that interjurisdictional relationships are competitive? and (2) Is competition among states and local governments likely to be stable or unstable?

Breton gathers three types of evidence suggesting that interjurisdictional relationships are competitive. First he argues that the diffusion of innovations among states and local governments arises in part because of the potential threat that individuals and businesses might leave unresponsive jurisdictions to move into innovative jurisdictions. He also reviews tax and public-service capitalization studies inspired by the Tiebout model, which he claims provide additional evidence of interjurisdictional competition. Finally, he argues that widespread state and local use of special tax incentives and financial subsidies to attract labor, capital, and technology is direct evidence of interjurisdictional competition.

Breton then examines whether such competition is stable. It is standard in economic theory to determine whether a market is stable or unstable before analyzing whether the market equilibrium is efficient. Breton does not find definitive evidence of unstable interjurisdictional competition, but he provides several types of suggestive evidence. One of these is the migration of high-income residents to suburban jurisdictions to escape a central city's high taxes and poor public services. The loss of high-income taxpayers forces the central city to raise tax rates again, thereby inducing further migration, and so forth. Breton concludes his chapter by examining federal policies that might ensure stable interjurisdictional competition, including provision of grants-in-aid to poorer jurisdictions, prohibition of tax exporting, and imposition of maximum or minimum national standards.

John E. Chubb, in chapter 3, provides a thought-provoking challenge to several of Breton's arguments. Most important, Chubb finds the evidence that interjurisdictional relations are competitive or that interjurisdictional competition can be unstable less convincing than does Breton. Chubb argues that state and local government efforts to lure businesses through tax breaks and other inducements constitute stronger evidence for the existence of interjurisdictional competition than does the diffusion of innovations or the public finance literature inspired by the Tiebout model.

Maintaining that a general theory of federalism should be crafted somewhat differently than that suggested by Breton, Chubb contends that such a theory should begin with a well-developed model of the internal politics of government decision making and should include the phenomenon of interjurisdictional competition as a constraint on government behavior. In other words, Chubb's model of federalism would assign a much smaller role to interjurisdictional competition than would Breton's.

Daniel J. Elazar's review of the history and theory of cooperative federalism, in chapter 4, provides a counterbalance to Breton's efforts to launch a general theory of competitive federalism. Breton emphasizes competitive relations among governments of the same type (i.e., between states or provinces and between localities), whereas

Elazar emphasizes cooperative relations between the federal government and state and local governments. Indeed, he notes that federalism derives from the Latin *foedus* (covenant).

Elazar describes the historical transition from a theory of dual federalism, under which the national and state governments were viewed as controlling separate spheres of authority, to a theory of cooperative federalism, under which the national and state governments shared authority, to the recent practice of coercive federalism, under which the national government, he argues, has preempted substantial portions of the legitimate authority of state governments.[16]

Most of Elazar's chapter is devoted to describing a theory of cooperative federalism. At the outset, he distinguishes between operational theories, or empirical descriptions of reality, and normative theories. According to Elazar, cooperative federalism is both an operational and a normative theory of intergovernmental relations. He maintains that cooperative federalism has been the dominant operational theory of American federalism since at least the New Deal, and the dominant normative theory of federalism since the Kennedy-Johnson administration.

An important component of Elazar's theory is his rejection of a hierarchical model, in which state governments are subordinate to the federal government, and his adoption of a "matrix model" of the intergovernmental system, in which none of the governments ("cells") is intrinsically higher or lower in importance than any other. Because Elazar rejects the hierarchical model, he does not characterize federal-state relations in a manner substantially different from interstate relations. Other important components of his theory include partnership between federal, state, and local governments and private entities; sharing of responsibilities and powers; and bargaining as the proper means for determining the appropriate patterns of sharing.

Although other scholars, including Breton, have presented competitive federalism as an alternative to cooperative federalism, Elazar rejects this notion on the grounds that all governments must ultimately cooperate. Instead, he portrays competitive federalism as an "economic extension or variant of cooperative federalist theory." Because Elazar defines cooperation as sharing or interdependence, he subsumes competitive relations under the heading of cooperative relations by labeling competitive relationships as "antagonistic cooperation." However, to the extent that competitive federalism operates as a normative, rather than merely a descriptive, model of intergovernmental and interjurisdictional relations, it can be said to be an alternative to cooperative federalism.

John Kincaid, writing in chapter 5 from a political science perspective, bridges the competitive and cooperative models. He argues that federalism requires cooperation to have competition, and competition to have cooperation. Kincaid also ties interjurisdictional and intergovernmental competition into a single model.

According to Kincaid's model, the constituent governments (e.g., states) of a federal union must voluntarily consent to a fundamental covenant or constitution in which they agree not to engage in unbridled competition, but rather to compete and cooperate within the bounds of the civil order established by the constitution and within the agreed-upon rules enforced by an overarching government (i.e., the federal government). At the same time, to prevent the overarching government from acquiring monopoly power (the antithesis of federalism) or losing all of its powers to the constituent governments (the apotheosis of confederalism) a federal system must provide for competition between the overarching and constituent governments. In turn, this very competition creates incentives for intergovernmental cooperation because, if one or another government possessed monopoly power, it would have little incentive to cooperate. In sum, intergovernmental competition constrains the monopolistic tendencies of the overarching government, and interjurisdictional competition constrains constituent governments with respect to each other, while the overarching government is sufficiently empowered to prevent interjurisdictional competition from degenerating into anarchy.

Kincaid further develops a distinction between what he calls "mediated" and "unmediated" competition. Mediated competition occurs through government institutions that ultimately decide the winners, such as interstate competition for federal dollars in the U.S. Congress. Unmediated competition occurs in the open market, so to speak, such as when states compete directly for business firms—the type of interjurisdictional competition examined in this volume. Kincaid argues that an exclusive focus on unmediated competition, and especially on its costs, is misleading because there is often an inverse relationship between unmediated and mediated competition. That is, as unmediated competition is depressed, mediated competition is likely to increase as states, for example, transfer their competition to government institutions, mainly Congress. Thus while certain forms of unmediated competition, such as tax giveaways, are wasteful from an economic perspective, attempts to prevent this type of competition may not be helpful if states turn to competition through congressional mediation, which may be equally wasteful.

Kincaid examines government competition in the context of democratic theory and the principles expressed by such founding Federalists as James Madison and Alexander Hamilton. He looks at evidence of competitive federalism in the 19th century, then at factors that gave rise to cooperative federalism in the 20th century, and finally to the recent revival of interest in competitive federalism. Kincaid argues that the development of cooperative federalism increasingly transformed unmediated government competition into mediated competition in which the federal government gained the upper hand in the balance of power in the federal system. As the federal government moved toward a monopoly position, intergovernmental competition declined, thus reducing the federal government's incentives to cooperate with state and local governments. Consequently, there has been a dramatic increase in federal preemption of state and local authority and in the federal government's ability to mandate or dictate policy for state and local governments. In essence, this has transformed cooperative federalism into coercive federalism.

Part Two: Effects of Interjurisdictional Competition

The first chapter in Part Two, by John Shannon, focuses primarily on the effects of interjurisdictional competition. Unlike many past analyses, Shannon considers interjurisdictional expenditure (or public-service) competition as well as tax competition.

Shannon describes two avenues through which competition can pressure state and local governments to increase spending on services. By a process he calls the "pacesetter phenomenon," the adoption of innovative public services by liberal, high-spending governments pressures other governments to follow suit. The other side of his expenditure-competition coin is the "catch-up" imperative, in which poor jurisdictions cannot afford to lag too far behind other jurisdictions in providing basic services such as education and physical infrastructure, because they will lose out in the competition for economic development.

Shannon details how tax competition pressures state and local governments to hold down taxes, at the same time that expenditure competition encourages them to offer attractive services. Shannon uses the metaphor of a naval convoy to describe how the dual forces of tax and expenditure competition regulate state and local government fiscal behavior: "Interstate tax *and* expenditure competition serve jointly as the two 'unseen hands' that set the outer limits on how far any state can push ahead of the other states on the tax front or lag behind them in the public service area." In other words, interjurisdictional competition sets the outer limits on interjurisdictional fiscal diversity. Shannon cites New York as an example of a state forced by tax competition to moderate its progressive income-tax policies, and Mississippi as an example of a state forced by expenditure competition to improve its education system.

Shannon also considers the aggregate effects of tax and expenditure competition. He asks whether, on net, the stimulating effects of expenditure competition are stronger or weaker than the restraining effects of tax competition. Shannon notes that U.S. state and local own-source general revenue has more than doubled since World War II. Although factors other than interjurisdictional competition must be considered, so that one cannot yet conclude that expenditure competition has outweighed tax competition during the postwar period, Shannon argues that this growth in state-local revenue "has . . . knocked into a cocked hat the old conventional wisdom that states and localities were destined to have anemic revenue systems because they were 'crippled by fears' of [interjurisdictional] tax competition."

Wallace E. Oates and Robert M. Schwab, in chapter 7, offer another evaluation of the results of interjurisdictional competition, this time within the context of an explicit model. In their model, jurisdictions compete for a mobile capital stock (i.e., businesses and jobs) by lowering taxes and providing services needed by businesses, such as highways and police and fire protection. Oates and Schwab assume that there are no important beneficial or negative spillovers, and that a sufficient number of local governments exist to approximate a competitive market. Both their model and the Tiebout model exhibit strong parallels with the perfectly competitive model of market competition.

Oates and Schwab conclude that under interjurisdictional competition, all taxes become benefit taxes. In other words, in equilibrium, business taxes will equal the value that businesses place on the government services they receive, while taxes on individuals will equal the value that individuals place on the government services provided them. A corollary is that competition will prevent local governments from redistributing income from businesses to individuals. A local government will not be able to tax businesses in excess of the benefits the government provides to those businesses, without causing businesses to flee its jurisdiction and ultimately making its citizens worse off. Finally, Oates and Schwab assert that, given their simplifying assumptions, interjurisdictional competition is efficient, providing the best package of government services for individuals and firms, and at the lowest cost.

Oates and Schwab admit, however, that their overall evaluation of the effects of interjurisdictional competition depends crucially on whether the federal government redistributes income to the appropriate degree. If the federal government is adequately performing the redistributive function, the authors applaud the efficiency results of competition. However, if the federal government is not adequately performing its redistributive role, then the authors contend that some limits on interjurisdictional competition may be required so that state and local governments can also play a role in redistributing income.

In his examination of the Oates-Schwab model, Andrew Reschovsky, in chapter 8, raises an important question: How applicable is their perfectly competitive model to real-world state and local government behavior? For example, Reschovsky questions the ability of local governments to link the taxation of business to the benefits those businesses receive from government. He notes that the collective provision of government services frustrates the linkage between a tax price and a public-service benefit. Reschovsky also argues that businesses may not act as perfect competitors, either because of government officials' fear of the political damage resulting from a firm's decision to move out of their jurisdiction or the influence that business firms can exert on the political process through lobbying.

Reschovsky concludes his critique by reviewing some of the scant and inconclusive evidence on whether state and local taxes tend to be benefit taxes or ability-to-pay taxes. For example, he refers to a study that concludes that state and local taxes in Massachusetts are fairly regressive. This tends to support the benefit-tax view. However, he cites another study that concludes that almost one-third of state spending in Massachusetts is targeted to low-income individuals. This latter evidence would tend to support the ability-to-pay view.

Chapter 9, by Therese J. McGuire, takes on two tasks. First, McGuire compares a general version of the Tiebout model to a second model of what she calls "destructive competition." Using these alternative models, she then asks whether interjurisdictional competition provides a new rationale for federal aid to state and local governments, in addition to the traditional rationales of correcting for benefit spillovers and for disparities in fiscal capacity. The effects of interjurisdictional competition that follow from McGuire's version of the

Tiebout model are the same as those derived by Oates and Schwab from their model of fiscal competition. Interjurisdictional competition is to be applauded because it produces efficiency: the best mix of public goods and services is produced at the lowest cost.

In McGuire's destructive competition model, voters within jurisdictions want to redistribute income from high-income to low-income individuals, and they levy ability-to-pay taxes to accomplish this. However, because high-income citizens have an incentive to relocate from jurisdictions levying comparatively progressive taxes, governments are frustrated in their ability to redistribute income. In equilibrium, a smaller amount of income redistribution is accomplished than citizens collectively desire. In other words, in destructive competition, the optimal mix of government goods and services is not provided; interjurisdictional competition does not result in an efficient provision of public goods and services.

McGuire offers several reasons why her model of destructive competition is more applicable to interstate competition, whereas a model of Tiebout competition is more applicable to interlocal competition. She argues that the taxes levied by states are more nearly based on ability to pay than are the property taxes that are the mainstay of local governments. She further cites the redistributive nature of a significant proportion of state government services. In addition, she argues that residents of a state are more likely to be heterogeneous in tastes, income, and mobility than citizens of a local government. (Oates and Schwab, in chapter 7, support McGuire's reasoning when they note that their model of fiscal competition may be more applicable to competition among local governments than among states.)

McGuire's two models lead her to two different conclusions about the role of federal grants-in-aid to state and local governments. According to the Tiebout model, there is no additional rationale for federal grants in response to interjurisdictional competition, because such competition is efficient. Within the framework of the destructive competition model, however, one can argue in favor of federal grants as a means to moderate competitive tendencies, thus moving state and local spending toward the desired higher level. McGuire argues, however, that federal grants alone are unlikely to dampen interjurisdictional competition sufficiently, and that measures such as federal restrictions on state and local tax policies may also be necessary. An example of such a restriction is a requirement that states adopt the federal tax base for personal and corporate income taxes.

In the final chapter in Part Two, Robert W. Rafuse, Jr., comments on the nature of interjurisdictional competition and on obstacles to improving the equity and efficiency of federal grant policies. Assessing obstacles to federal grant reform is important because both Breton (chapter 2) and McGuire (chapter 9) recommend federal grants to states and localities in response to potential problems with interjurisdictional competition.

Rafuse believes that "competition among state and local governments is healthier, on balance, than it is, in any sense, destructive." He acknowledges that state and local redistribution of income is frustrated by interjurisdictional competition. However, this does not prompt him to suggest policies to moderate such competition, because he believes that redistribution is the responsibility of the federal government.

Rafuse describes four potential obstacles to grant reform. First, not enough is known to determine the proper matching requirements for grants intended to improve the allocation of resources in response to the presence of externalities. Second, to the extent that taxes and public services are capitalized into property values, the need for equalization grants is lessened. Third, the existence of a flypaper effect presents the following difficulty. The flypaper effect is the empirical finding that grant money "sticks where it hits," or that grant funding has a greater stimulative effect on state and local spending than do equivalent increases in income. Because public finance experts have not been able to agree on the reasons for a flypaper effect, its existence raises questions about our understanding of state and local fiscal behavior.[17] Without sufficient knowledge of state and local government behavior—in particular, of how these governments are likely to respond to federal grants—it is difficult to design an effective federal grant program. Finally, alternative models of state and local government behavior, such as the models of Leviathan and budget-maximizing bureaucracies, also raise questions about our understanding of state and local fiscal behavior. Of these four potential obstacles, Rafuse considers the lack of knowledge about appropriate grant-matching ratios the most important, and argues that academics could greatly help policymakers by conducting empirical analyses in this area.

Part Three: Interstate Competition and Tax Policy

In the two chapters comprising Part Three, Robert Tannenwald (chapter 11) and Steven D. Gold (chapter 12) examine the relationship between interstate competition and state tax policy. Tannenwald analyzes the likely effects on the relative competitive standing of the 50 state-tax systems of the Tax Reform Act of 1986 (TRA), probably the most important U.S. tax law enacted since ratification of the federal income tax amendment in 1913.

Tannenwald argues that there are two plausible measures of the attractiveness of a state's tax system: (1) the marginal personal income-tax rate levied on the highest-income families, net of the federal offset (or the net burden of a state's top marginal income-tax rate) and (2) the ratio of total state and local taxes, fees, and charges, net of the federal offset, to statewide personal income (or the net burden of a state's own-source revenues). (The federal offset is the reduction in effective state and local tax liability that arises when certain state and local taxes are deducted on a federal income-tax return. The federal offset reduces the burden of each dollar of state and local taxes by one dollar times the taxpayer's marginal federal income-tax rate.)

The effect of the TRA on Tannenwald's first measure of a state's competitive standing can be described as follows. Because the TRA lowered the marginal federal income-tax rate faced by the highest income households from 50 percent to 28 percent, the net burden of each state's top marginal income-tax rate rose. Before the TRA, the net burden was $(1m - .5m)$, or $.5m$, where m is the nominal tax rate levied on the highest-income families. After the TRA, the net burden became $(1m - .28m)$, or $.72m$. According to Tannenwald's calculations, the TRA increased the dispersion among the states of the net burden of top marginal income-tax rates. This made high-tax states more "out of line" with other states. Tannenwald argues that the reduction in relative competitive standing felt by high-tax states may have prompted their cuts in top income-tax rates in 1987 and 1988.

The effect of the Tax Reform Act of 1986 on the net burden of own-source revenues, Tannenwald's second measure of the relative attractiveness of a state's tax system, is more complicated to describe and to estimate. In computing his state-by-state estimates, Tannenwald takes into account a number of factors, including the reduction in the percentage of taxpayers itemizing deductions, elimination of the deductibility of state and local sales taxes, and reductions in the average marginal tax rates of individuals and corporations. After accounting for these factors, Tannenwald finds that the TRA had only a small impact on interstate variation in the net burden of own-source revenues. In other words, according to Tannenwald's second measure of the relative attractiveness of a state's tax system, the TRA had little effect on the relative competitive standing of the states, and thus should have had little effect on interstate tax competition.

Although Gold, in chapter 12, is also concerned with the effect of the Tax Reform Act of 1986 on interstate tax competition, he maintains that interstate competition has been increasing since at least 1980, and he examines its effects on state personal income-tax policy since then. Specifically, Gold examines a three-part hypothesis that increased interstate competition: (1) causes states to reduce their reliance on income taxes relative to other taxes, (2) leads to reductions in top marginal income-tax rates in high-tax-rate states; and (3) causes states to reduce the progressivity of their income taxes.

Gold contends that only one of the three hypotheses is supported by the evidence. He concludes that during the 1980s, high-rate states tended to reduce their top marginal personal income-tax rates, a reduction that he attributes, in part, to interstate competition. Among states with the highest marginal tax rates in 1981 were California, Delaware, Hawaii, Minnesota, New York, Oregon, and Wisconsin; all significantly lowered their tax rates by 1990. (Over the same period, tax-rate increases occurred in states like Arizona, Indiana, and New Jersey, which began the decade with relatively low marginal income-tax rates.)

Gold finds that, contrary to his hypothesis, states increased their reliance on personal income taxes relative to other taxes. In 1980, income-tax revenue was 27.1 percent of state tax collections; by 1989, it equaled 31.3 percent. Finally, Gold finds that states have increased, not decreased, the progressivity of their personal income taxes. States accomplished this after the TRA by taxing capital gains in full and eliminating certain tax shelters (which increased tax burdens on high-income individuals) and by increasing standard deductions and personal exemptions (which provided tax relief to the poor).

Part Four: Competition for Economic Development

The chapters in Part Four of this volume examine competition among state and local governments for economic development. Dick Netzer, in chapter 13, discusses a wide array of devices used by state and local governments to influence the location of economic activity, including, but not limited to, subsidized credit, tax preferences, grants, and tax-exempt bonds. In a perfectly competitive world, Netzer argues, competition for economic development would be a negative-sum game, in terms of the consequences for efficiency of resource allocation, until all governments had adopted the same economic development package, at which time such competition would become a zero-sum game. (In a negative-sum game, we all lose; in a zero-sum game, if I win, you lose, or vice versa.)

Netzer then expands his discussion to incorporate the facts that the United States does not have a closed economy, spillover effects exist, inefficient taxes are levied by state and local governments, and other market imperfections affect the system. After reviewing the empirical evidence regarding the effectiveness of various economic development mechanisms, Netzer concludes:

> Economic development incentives are, for the most part, neither very good nor very bad from the standpoint of efficient resource allocation in the economy. With all the imperfections, the offering of incentives does not represent a fall from grace, but neither does competition in this form operate in ways that truly parallel the efficiency-creating operations of private competitive markets. Given the low cost-effectiveness of most instruments, there is little national impact, only a waste of local resources in most instances.

Netzer offers advice to federal, state, and local policymakers regarding which economic development incentives are the most and least effective. He argues that capital subsidies, other than the federal subsidy provided through tax-exempt bonds, are not cost-effective from a state-local perspective, and that tax-exempt bonds are not cost-effective from a national perspective. He supports certain public programs that reduce information costs, such as technology transfer and new product development efforts. He also argues that certain state and local tax reforms can achieve the dual purpose of improving the tax system and promoting economic development.

Whereas Netzer looks at state and local economic development efforts as a "glass half empty," R. Scott Fosler, in chapter 14, looks at those efforts as a "glass half full." Fosler also considers a broader range of state and local government activity than does Netzer. Fosler would have us include most state and local spending (now equaling approximately 14 percent of gross national product) as relevant to economic development, whereas Netzer would have us focus solely on programs specifically enacted to foster economic development (which he claims would equal only a fraction of 1 percent of gross national product if converted to expenditure-equivalent terms).

Fosler applauds states' efforts to move beyond the economic development programs that are most likely to have zero- or negative-sum results, such as blatant efforts to recruit business firms from other jurisdictions. He also praises state and local governments' recent emphasis on internal economic development, and notes favorably the return to a concern with basics, such as education and physical infrastructure. Fosler's charge to economists and other analysts is to broaden their conception of economic development to reflect both the changing economic development programs of state and local governments and the recognition that the public and private sectors are highly interdependent.

In chapter 15, Nonna A. Noto begins her comment on Netzer's paper with the question: If research fails to support the efficacy of most specific economic development incentives, why do state and local officials still use them? Noto presents three partial answers. First, an "early bird" can gain clear, though temporary, benefits from adopting a particular economic development program before other states and localities adopt the same program and thereby cancel out its effectiveness. Second, in light of the boom-and-bust cycles for local economies as well as personal attachments to communities, it may be sensible to provide business subsidies in the hopes of saving jobs or helping to reverse the bust part of the cycle. Third, there is the political accountability of the economic development official. Noto argues that it behooves that official to err on the side of granting too many tax breaks or subsidies to business firms, rather than to risk the politically visible exit of a major local job provider.

Noto closes her chapter with suggestions for changing the rules of the game facing economic development officials and for improving the usefulness to policymakers of research on economic development. Her objective is to improve the cost-effectiveness of state and local economic development efforts. For example, to improve accountability, the rules of the economic development game could be changed, she says, to require the costs of economic development programs to be included in a public tax-expenditure budget. Public finance researchers could also shift their emphasis from econometric studies to methodologies, such as break-even analysis, that are easier to communicate to policymakers.

Summary View

The final chapter, by Ronald C. Fisher, presents new perspectives on selected issues regarding interjurisdictional competition, ties together certain themes addressed in the volume, and suggests directions for research. Among his other contributions, Fisher makes use of Shannon's (chapter 6) convoy metaphor to test the hypothesis that interstate competition has increased in recent years. Shannon maintains that interjurisdictional competition sets the outer limits on interjurisdictional fiscal diversity. One might argue that the more heated the interjurisdictional competition, the more constraining the limits, and thus the less fiscal diversity—or, to use Shannon's metaphor, the shorter the length of the convoy.

Fisher computes the coefficient of variation for various state-local fiscal variables as alternative measures of the extent of fiscal diversity among the 50 states. He finds that the coefficient of variation among the states for per-capita state-local expenditures, own-source revenues, and taxes has not changed appreciably over the last 15 years. These data would seem to indicate that interstate fiscal competition has neither increased nor decreased appreciably. Fisher is cautious in interpreting these data, but concludes that fears that competition is greatly reducing interstate fiscal diversity appear to be unfounded.[18]

Fisher's agenda for future research includes: (1) development of a general model of interjurisdictional interaction, (2) empirical testing of the model's assumptions and predicted results, and (3) examination of the manner in which state and local governments make decisions about interjurisdictional relations. He is noncommittal as to whether a general model of interjurisdictional competition can be based on the economic model of perfect competition. He does maintain that the assumptions and predictions of a perfect competition model of interjurisdictional interaction should be tested empirically. Because the perfect competition model assumes easy interjurisdictional mobility and minimal spillovers of public-service benefits between jurisdictions, he argues that there should be more research on the empirical validity of these assumptions. Fisher also notes that because the competitive models of both Tiebout and Oates and Schwab (the latter, chapter 7, this volume) predict that local taxes will be benefit taxes, it would be useful to subject this prediction to empirical testing. Finally, Fisher argues that future research should investigate the manner in which state and local governments make fiscal decisions in a competitive environment. For example, how do governments decide to adopt tax or economic development incentives? The bulk of previous research has investigated the other side of the coin: individual and business-firm responses to state and local fiscal policies.

CONCLUSION

A major issue addressed by this volume's authors is the effects of interjurisdictional competition. Is interjurisdictional competition a beneficial regulator of state and local government behavior, or does it induce governments to adopt "beggar-thy-neighbor" strategies?

By and large, this volume's authors suggest that interjurisdictional competition can serve as a regulator of state and local fiscal behavior. As Shannon argues, such competition pressures state and local governments to hold down taxes at the same time that it encourages them to offer attractive public services. Most of the other authors would generally agree that interjurisdictional competition can be an important constraint on state and local government behavior. Whether such competition has predominantly benign effects is less clear.

In the perfect competition model of Oates and Schwab (chapter 7), competition spurs efficiency in the public sector; the optimal mix of public goods and services is produced at minimum cost. The resulting pattern of taxes and public services can be considered equitable from a benefit-principle perspective. The resulting pattern can also be considered equitable if one assumes that the federal government should, and does, adequately redistribute income.

McGuire's (chapter 9) analysis of the effects of interjurisdictional competition, which explictly considers both interstate and interlocal competition, is less sanguine. She argues that interstate competition is best characterized as "destructive competition" in which governments achieve productive, but not allocative, efficiency. In her model, the failure to achieve allocative efficiency is the same as state governments' inability to redistribute income to the desired degree. She further argues that destructive competition is likely to be inequitable because less-mobile, less-wealthy citizens are likely to bear a disproportionate share of the tax burden. McGuire concludes that even in the case of interlocal competition, real-world competition is likely to produce results that fall short of the perfect competition theory.

However, Gold's (chapter 12) review of data on state tax policy during the 1980s cautions analysts about the limits of theoretical analyses. Gold finds that interstate competition during the 1980s did not produce reduced reliance on ability-to-pay taxes or a decrease in the progressivity of income taxes. Instead, both the reliance on and the progressivity of state income taxes generally increased.

Netzer's (chapter 13) analysis of interjurisdictional competition for economic development presents the most critical view. According to Netzer's interpretation of economic theory, interjurisdictional competition for economic development through the use of specific incentives is likely to be a zero-sum or negative-sum game. When Netzer expands his analysis to account for a number of real-world departures from his model, he concludes that even though incentive-based competition for economic development is unlikely to be very harmful from the national perspective, it usually wastes the resources of the governments offering the incentives.

Fosler's (chapter 14) approach to this issue, however, parallels that of Shannon. Insofar as state and local governments compete for economic development by behaving in more innovative and efficient ways and by improving education systems and infrastructure, then interjurisdictional competition can have generally beneficial effects, both for particular jurisdictions and the nation as a whole.

How do this volume's assessments of interjurisdictional competition compare to the old consensus? The traditional critique held that interjurisdictional competition leads to inadequate state and local spending, reduced reliance on ability-to-pay taxes, lowered reliance on taxes borne by business, and wasted resources, as efforts to attract industry from other jurisdictions result in a zero-sum game.

The authors in this volume suggest that interjurisdictional competition can have either beneficial or harmful effects, depending on the circumstances surrounding such competition. Interjurisdictional competition will not always lead to inadequate state and local spending, and may even encourage higher spending. Furthermore, competition may improve public-service efficiency and, thereby, government responsiveness to citizen preferences. Oates and Schwab (chapter 7), the only authors who directly address the business tax issue, conclude that interjurisdictional competition will cause business taxes to equal the public service benefits received by business. They are not critical of this result.

This volume's authors do partially reaffirm the traditional conclusion that interjurisdictional competition will reduce state and local reliance on ability-to-pay taxes. However, their assessment of this result varies, depending largely on their view of the federal role in redistributing income. To the extent that they view redistribution as a federal responsibility, the authors are not critical of this result. Finally, the volume reaffirms the traditionally negative view of state and local uses of special tax incentives and subsidies to recruit businesses from other jurisdictions; however, common-good policies—such as innovation and infrastructure investment—motivated by competitive pressures are likely to have generally beneficial effects.

In addition to the general policy implications discussed earlier, several authors offer specific policy recommendations arising from their assessments of interjurisdictional competition. Breton (chapter 2) is concerned with the potential instability of interjurisdictional competition, which he claims has led to an exodus of middle- and upper-income households from some central cities, among other difficulties. Breton argues that intergovernmental grants to low-income jurisdictions are one of the most effective instruments to alleviate unstable competition. He also mentions other federal policies toward state and local governments that can be used to prevent unstable competition, including imposition of minimum or maximum standards of service provision, federal assumption of particular responsibilities, and prevention of state and local tax exporting.

McGuire (chapter 9) also suggests a program of federal grants, but as a response to another difficulty—the potential for destructive competition. She recommends a general revenue-sharing program for state governments, with poorer states receiving comparatively greater funding, together with federal restrictions on allowable state tax bases. Through these policies, she hopes to alleviate insufficient spending by state governments and reduce the desirability of tax competition.

Netzer (chapter 13) suggests changes in both federal and state policies to reduce the negative consequences of incentive-based competition for economic development. He urges the federal government to (1) eliminate its subsidy to competition for economic development that is provided through tax-exempt financing, (2) prevent state tax exporting, and (3) provide a more adequate safety net for the poor. To channel state and local competition toward more beneficial efforts, Netzer suggests that state and local governments should not subsidize capital and credit, but should concentrate on training programs, technology transfer, new product development, and business tax incentives that help reform the tax system.

A number of issues regarding interjurisdictional competition are left unresolved in this volume. In addition, there are areas in which the authors disagree. One unresolved issue is the proper way to measure interjurisdictional competition. Fisher (chapter 16) suggests one method, but there may be others. A related question is whether it is possible to determine whether interjurisdictional competition is increasing or decreasing. In addition, there are disagreements on how to measure the competitiveness of a state tax system. Gold (chapter 12) implies that policymakers judge their state's competitiveness by the nominal income-tax rate applicable to the highest-income households. Tannenwald (chapter 11) argues that either the net burden of a state's top marginal income-tax rate or the net burden of a state's own-source revenues is likely to be a better measure.

But perhaps the most important unresolved issue is that of which model or view of interjurisdictional competition is most applicable in the real world, and to what kinds of competition. Does interjurisdictional competition tend to be unstable in the absence of countervailing federal interventions, as Breton (chapter 2) argues? Does interlocal competition produce a benefit-tax equilibrium, as Oates and Schwab (chapter 7) would have us believe? Or do states' attempts to fund spending on the poor with ability-to-pay taxes lead to destructive competition, as McGuire (chapter 9) describes in one of her models?

As an example of conflicting views, consider chapters 7 and 13 by Oates and Schwab and Netzer respectively, both of which examine interjurisdictional competition for business. According to the Oates-Schwab model, in equilibrium, jurisdictions will neither tax business in excess of the benefits they receive from governments nor provide them with net subsidies. Oates and Schwab take the most positive view of the results of interjurisdictional competition. Netzer, however, begins with the fact that economic development subsidies do exist. His evaluation of the results of interjurisdictional competition is predominantly negative. How does one reconcile these two views?

One possibility is that the business tax incentives that jurisdictions offer tend to make up for what Oates and Schwab would view as "excess" business taxes. In that case, Netzer's concern about the national inefficiency of fiscal incentives for business is misplaced. Another possibility is that the Oates-Schwab analysis is most applicable to interlocal competition, whereas the Netzer analysis is most applicable to interstate competition. In that case, interlocal competition would appear to have predominantly benign results, and interstate competition, predominantly negative results. A third possibility might be that a key assumption of the Oates-Schwab perfect competition model, such as the availability of information regarding tax and benefit levels, may be inapplicable to interjurisdictional competition for economic development. This would tend to reduce the applicability of the Oates-Schwab analysis and increase the usefulness of Netzer's discussion. As Fisher argues in his summary (chapter 16), more empirical work needs to be done to test alternative assumptions and predictions in order to determine the extent to which a perfect competition model, or some other model, is the most helpful guide to understanding competition among states and local governments.

Clearly, much more conceptual and empirical research needs to be done on interjurisdictional competition and the concept of competitive federalism. In addition to the issues already noted, it would be desirable to develop a general theory of interjurisdictional competition that is applicable to federal systems other than our own. A particular challenge will be to extend the analysis to other federal systems—such as those in Yugoslavia, Nigeria, and potentially the Soviet Union. In many federations, national unity is weak and strong ethnic, religious, and linguistic ties inhibit mobility among jurisdictions. In addition, interjurisdictional and intergovernmental competition may become truly destructive, degenerating into civil strife. As Kincaid (chapter 5) suggests, peaceful competition in a federation seems to require an underlying covenant of cooperation.

This volume can hardly do more than scratch the surface of the topic, but, it is hoped, in ways that advance our understanding of the competitive aspects of federalism and also point to areas for further research. Most important, in this era of fiscal stress, global competition, and worldwide trends toward democratization, this volume contributes to another view of relations among federal, state and local governments and, thereby, of new ways of thinking about public policies to improve the operation of our federal system, and perhaps of others as well.

Notes

1. This concept of interjurisdictional competition can be labeled "active rivalry." An alternative, which can be called "implicit competition," is the manner in which the free movement of goods, services, people, and capital constrains the actions of independent governments in a federal system. See U.S. Advisory Commission on Intergovernmental Relations (1991).

2. But see, for example, Shannon and Kee (1989: 5–20) and Kincaid (1988: 37–41).

3. Some analysts are comfortable defining vertical competition as competition among governments at different levels, and horizontal competition as competition among governments at the same level. We have avoided this terminology because other scholars object to the concept of levels of government in the federal system. For example, Daniel Elazar in chapter 4 of this volume states that, "to the extent that those involved in governance now conceive of the American federal system as a pyramid with federal, state, and local 'levels,' they have opened the door to the

transformation of cooperative federalism into coercive federalism. In a hierarchy, the top is expected to have more authority and power than the middle or bottom. Such an arrangement contradicts the basic principles of federalism."

4. See, for example, U.S. Advisory Commission on Intergovernmental Relations (1981b: 9–12).

5. For a general discussion, see U.S. Advisory Commission on Intergovernmental Relations (1991).

6. See, also, Fix and Kenyon (1990).

7. See, also, U.S. Advisory Commission on Intergovernmental Relations (1987).

8. See, for example, Strauss (1990: 13). As one example, the United States is the only modern country not to allow national banking. See Brady (1990: 5) and U.S. Advisory Commission on Intergovernmental Relations (1988).

9. Economists have tended to define a federal system of government differently than political scientists. Wallace Oates's definition of a federal government is "a public sector with both centralized and decentralized levels of decision-making in which choices made at each level concerning the provision of public services are determined largely by the demands for these services of the residents of . . . the respective juris-diction." As Oates has noted, virtually all governments have federal systems of government according to the economist's definition, whereas fewer than two dozen countries may have a federal system according to the political scientist's definition (see Oates 1972: 15–18).

10. See chapter 4, by Daniel J. Elazar, in this volume as well as U.S. Advisory Commission on Intergovernmental Relations (1981a: 3–5).

Although this introduction focuses on only three theories of federalism, there appear to be almost as many theories of federalism as there are authors who have written about the topic. For example, Thomas Dye's review of federalism theories includes dual federalism, cooperative federalism, centralized federalism, representational fed eralism, fiscal federalism, and new federalism (1990: 6–13). Alternatively, Shannon and Kee (1989) divide U.S. history into three periods of federalism: constitutional federalism, centralizing federalism, and competitive federalism.

11. The report found that "tax competition between neighboring states has not yet become a serious problem for our federal system," and that "short of highly coercive or discriminatory legislation, Congress appears to have no ready means to prohibit states from using tax and fiscal measures to try to advance their individual devel-opment prospects" (U.S. Advisory Commission on Intergovernmental Relations 1981b: 1, 4, 8).

12. Probably the most important statement of the theory is contained in Oates (1972). Most public finance texts contain some variant of fiscal federalism theory. See, for example, Fisher (1988: 82–97). For a critique of fiscal federalism from the political science perspective, see U.S. Advisory Commission on Intergovernmental Relations (1981a: 11–16).

13. See, for example, Breton, (1985: 486–526), Dye (1990), and Kincaid (1988).

14. For lengthier summaries of the Tiebout model, including certain important ex-tensions and qualifications, see Fisher (1988: 66–80) and Mueller (1989: 154–63, 168–70).

15. See, for example Zodrow (1983) and Wildasin (1986).

16. See, also, Kincaid (1990: 139–52).

17. For reviews of evidence of the flypaper effect, see Fisher (1982: 324–45) and Inman (1979: 270–321).

18. Other factors affecting fiscal diversity among state and local governments that

would have to be taken into account in a more definitive test of Shannon's convoy hypothesis include federal grants and mandates on state and local governments. Grants can have the effect of stimulating state and local taxing and spending, whereas mandates may require increases in the same. Changes in either grants or mandates would affect Fisher's statistics but would not necessarily reflect changes in the degree of interjurisdictional competition.

References

Brady, Nicholas F. 1990. "Remarks before the Annual Convention of the Securities Industry Association, November 30, 1990." *Treasury News* (Press Release) (U.S. Department of the Treasury, Washington, D.C.).

Breton, Albert. 1985. "Supplementary Statement." Vol. 3, p. 486–526. In *Report of the Royal Commission on the Economic Union and Development Prospects for Canada*. Ottawa: Minister of Supply and Services. Reprinted, 1987, as "Towards a Theory of Competitive Federalism." *European Journal of Political Economy* 3: 263–329.

Dye, Thomas R. 1990. *American Federalism: Competition among Governments*. Lexington, Mass.: D. C. Heath.

Fiordalisi, Georgina. 1989. "Did Kentucky Pay Too Much for Toyota Plant?" *City & State*, June 19: 13.

Fisher, Ronald C. 1982. "Income and Grant Effects on Local Expenditure: The Flypaper Effect and Other Difficulties." *Journal of Urban Economics* 12 (November): 324–45.

————. 1988. *State and Local Public Finance*. Glenview, Ill.: Scott, Foresman.

Fix, Michael, and Daphne A. Kenyon, eds. 1990. *Coping with Mandates: What Are the Alternatives?* Washington, D.C.: Urban Institute Press.

Inman, Robert P. 1979. "The Fiscal Performance of Local Governments: An Interpretative Review." In *Current Issues in Urban Economics*, edited by Peter Mieszkowski and Mahlon Straszheim. Baltimore: Johns Hopkins University Press.

Kincaid, John. 1988. "Assessing Competitive Federalism in Light of Excessive Cooperative Federalism." In *Proceedings of the Eighty-first Annual Conference, 1988*, National Tax Association–Tax Institute of America. Columbus, Ohio: National Tax Association–Tax Institute of America.

————. 1990. "From Cooperative to Coercive Federalism." *Annals of the American Academy of Political and Social Science* 509 (May): 139–52.

Mueller, Dennis C. 1989. *Public Choice II*. Cambridge, England: Cambridge University Press.

National Association of State Development Agencies. 1991. *Directory of*

Incentives for Business Investment and Development in the United States, 3rd ed. Washington, D.C.: Urban Institute Press.

Oates, Wallace E. 1972. Fiscal Federalism. New York: Harcourt Brace Jovanovich.

Public Law 86-380. 1959. An Act to Establish an Advisory Commission on Intergovernmental Relations. U.S. Congress. 86th Cong. 1st Sess.

Shannon, John, and James Edwin Kee. 1989. "The Rise of Competitive Federalism." Public Budgeting and Finance 9 (Winter): 5–20.

Strauss, Robert P. 1990. "The EC Challenge to State and Local Government." Intergovernmental Perspective 16 (Winter): 13–14.

Tiebout, Charles M. 1956. "A Pure Theory of Local Expenditures." Journal of Political Economy 64 (5, October): 416–24.

U.S. Advisory Commission on Intergovernmental Relations. 1981a. The Condition of Contemporary Federalism: Conflicting Theories and Collapsing Constraints. Washington, D.C.: Author.

_____. 1981b. Interstate Tax Competition. Washington, D.C.: Author.

_____. 1987. The Organization of Local Public Economies. Washington, D.C.: Author.

_____. 1988. State Regulation of Banks in an Era of Deregulation. Washington, D.C.: Author.

_____. 1991. Interjurisdictional Tax and Policy Competition: Good or Bad for the Federal System? Washington, D.C.: Author.

Wildasin, David E. 1986. Urban Public Finance. New York: Harwood.

Zodrow, George R., ed. 1983. Local Provision of Public Services: The Tiebout Model after Twenty-five Years. New York: Academic Press.

Part One

GENERAL THEORIES AND MODELS

Chapter Two

THE EXISTENCE AND STABILITY OF INTERJURISDICTIONAL COMPETITION

Albert Breton

Students of federalism still disagree on the fundamental matter of what constitutes the most appropriate framework for analyzing basic federalist issues such as intergovernmental relations and the division of constitutional powers between jurisdictions. The disagreement would extend even farther if one were to acknowledge that much of the accepted doctrines on an issue as important as intergovernmental grants cannot be derived from the dominant models of federalism. Some scholars (e.g., Friedrich 1968) believe that the disagreement is inherent because, in their view, there can be no theory of federalism. To be a student of federalism, according to that view, is to be an expert on the structure, history, performance, problems, and processes at work in particular federations. In the practice of this expertise, use is made of concepts that seem apposite to the matters at hand—conflict, cooperation, centralization, autonomy, stability, and so on—but these concepts are not integrated in a structured model.

I do not wish to belittle this expertise, but experts would be even better experts if they could make use of a unified and consistent theory. Such a theory is still in the making, but what is emerging under the new title of competitive federalism is promising.[1] As the expression suggests, the "new" theory is erected on the assumption that intergovernmental relations are competitive. There is often resistance and even opposition to such an assumption. My purpose in this chapter is to confront this resistance. To that effect, I first present evidence suggesting that intergovernmental relations are, in fact, competitive. The term *intergovernmental relations* is commonly used in the literature to identify both federal-provincial, or federal-state, relations and province-to-province, or state-to-state, relations, or what might be called vertical and horizontal relations. The evidence examined here pertains only to horizontal relations. Based on economic theory and established findings, I argue that intergovernmental competition, or more precisely the equilibria generated by this competition, may be unstable. I conclude by pointing to some of the institutions that serve to guarantee stability.

SOME EMPIRICAL EVIDENCE ON
INTERGOVERNMENTAL COMPETITION

One cannot be exhaustive in presenting evidence to support the view that intergovernmental relations are competitive. I refer here to three bodies of "data" whose most obvious interpretation provides evidence of competitive behavior. Further research will no doubt bring additional "data" to light. Accordingly, I resist providing here a formal definition of *intergovernmental competition*, but, instead, contend that competition is defined by the behaviors to which it gives rise. The definition will, therefore, become broader as more evidence and behaviors are discovered. The three bodies of data are: (1) studies of the rate of diffusion among jurisdictions of legislative and other public policies; (2) estimates of the elasticity of population migration resulting from fiscal and other policy changes; and (3) observations of "price" adjustments by governments to secure particular objectives.

Diffusion Indices

The literature on the diffusion of legislative and other public policy measures is enormous and goes back at least to Ada Davis's (1930) analysis of the diffusion of "mothers' pensions" or more exactly of widows' allowances designed to enable dependent children "to remain in their own home" (575). The number of legislative enactments studied is also large, running in the hundreds.[2] The cumulative distributions over time—from the moment of first adoption—of the number of jurisdictions enacting particular measures, all graph as S-curves. This indicates that the proportion of jurisdictions adopting a particular measure—for example, fluoridation—increases with the passage of time, first at a "slow" rate, then at an accelerated pace, and finally, once more, at a "slow" rate, thus describing a stylized S. There appears to be no exception to this proposition. One should mention, however, that some classes of legislative enactments have not been studied. In particular, measures that have not diffused among jurisdictions, or whose diffusion is very limited, do not appear to have gained much scholarly attention. That is regrettable, because analyses of these cases would help us to better understand the reasons for diffusion and the characteristic S-shape. Finally, the density of the cumulative distributions—the rate of diffusion or the "process of diffusion," to use James Coleman, Herbert Menzel, and Elihu Katz's (1959) expression—and the extent of diffusion vary considerably between legislative measures.

Explanations for the S-shape of the distributions abound. Hypotheses have been centered, for example, on the way information propagates (Coleman et al. 1959), on the presence of internal adjustment costs (Reinganum 1981), on regulatory barriers (Oster and Quigley 1977), on the mode of operation of pressure groups and "propaganda" (Davis 1930), on the size of units (Mansfield 1963), and on the "bounded rationality" of decision-making units (Walker 1969). Why policies and programs diffuse in the first place has received less attention. True, some of the factors just listed provide part of an explanation, but these are not articulated as a consistent hypothesis. Jack Walker (1969) was the first, I believe, to suggest that competition was the driving force behind the diffusion indices he was trying to explain.[3] The idea, in a game-theoretic framework, was also important in Jennifer Reinganum's (1983) work. Roberta Romano (1985) used measures of diffusion as indicators of competition in an explicit way.

It may not be possible in the near term to produce a general model capable of explaining how all innovations diffuse in response to competitive forces, but simple models can readily be formulated. Consider the case of a policy or program that has been implemented in some jurisdictions, but not in others. What could move public officials to implement a new policy that has been implemented elsewhere? One answer, no doubt still acceptable in some quarters and for which supportive evidence will likely always be available, is that officials wish to benefit their constituents. Still, one must acknowledge that officials sometimes appear to be doing less good than they could or to be doing more good in some circumstances than in others. If, perchance, officials were doing more good when the net advantage to them of doing so was greater, then it would not only be legitimate to conclude that they are governed by self-interest, but, more significantly, it would be important to look at the forces that cause their net advantage to change.

It is easy to identify some of these forces. For example, the threat of exit by people and/or capital could change the net advantage of public officials. (Note, in this context, that the operative force is not actual exit or actual mobility, but potential exit.) Actual (political) exit, again in this context, is only a measure of the unwillingness or incapacity of a jurisdiction to compete effectively. Potential exit is the exact counterpart of potential entry in the theory of monopoly and oligopoly. If the threat of entry is effective, potential entrants will not enter, but the incumbent(s) will set the price of their output nearer the competitive price. Actual entry, in this case also, is a measure of the unwillingness or the incapacity to provide a competitive response.

Potential exit is sufficient, but it is not necessary to cause changes in the net advantage facing governing politicians. In two recent papers, Pierre Salmon (1987a, b) has shown that if the citizens of a jurisdiction use information about the policies implemented in other jurisdictions to gauge and evaluate the performance of their own government, that process will increase electoral competition at home and thus incite the governing politicians to act in their benefit more than they would otherwise. The mechanism described by Salmon would, incidentally, seem to imply that diffusion curves would not only be S-shaped but would look like a logistic curve, according to which the rate of diffusion is proportional to the number of jurisdictions that have already implemented the policy *and* to the number that will eventually implement it. Inspection of diffusion curves would appear consistent with the view that the mechanism discovered by Salmon is in full force.

Political Mobility

In 1956, Charles Tiebout proposed a preference revelation mechanism for local public goods, based on political mobility. At its simplest, the mechanism assumes that people choose bundles of local public goods and the tax prices at which they are provided by choosing communities in which to reside. Because the decision to migrate is dichotomous—citizens move or stay put—the choice of communities is based not on marginal net benefits but on total net benefits from private and public provisions. If the communities are governed (or administered) by "entrepreneurs," such as elected officials or community managers, who maximize an index defined over the earlier-mentioned bundles such that, in the words of George Meadows (1976: 870), they seek to "make [the] community a more desirable place to live," mobility between communities becomes a measure of the competitiveness of community entrepreneurs and of the extent of intergovernmental competition.

In a pathbreaking article, Wallace Oates (1969) inverted the Tiebout mechanism by assuming that differences in property taxes and in local public goods provisions would be reflected in property values. According to his view, if taxes were lower in Community *A* than in Community *B*, but the supply of local public goods was the same in both, migration from Community *B* into Community *A* would cause the price (rental value) of real property (assumed to be a fixed supply) to rise in Community *A* and fall in Community *B*. Tax and expenditure levels would be capitalized in property values. The degree of capitalization would be both a measure of the extent to which citizens take tax and expenditure levels into account in deciding where to locate and a measure of the differential attractiveness of communities.

Critics of the Oates model, among them Matthew Edel and Elliott Sclar (1974) and Bruce Hamilton (1976), have correctly argued that capitalization is an indication of the absence, not of the presence, of a Tiebout equilibrium, because in such an equilibrium, property taxes are benefit taxes: they are the real efficiency prices of the local public goods provided. As a consequence, neither taxes nor expenditure levels are capitalized in property values. If a steady-state Tiebout equilibrium can be presumed to exist,[4] estimates of capitalization point to a disequilibrium—in Hamilton's words, to a situation "in which there is a temporary shortage of fiscal havens" (648).[5] To put it differently, because some scholars assumed, explicitly or implicitly, the existence of a Tiebout *equilibrium*, they (for example, Epple and Zelenitz 1981 and Gramlich and Rubinfeld 1982) have been able to interpret statistically significant estimates of capitalization as evidence of the presence of a Tiebout mechanism. However, as Mark Pauly (1976) as well as Dennis Epple, Allan Zelenitz, and Michael Visscher (1978) have noted, nothing can be surmised about the existence and properties of an equilibrium from an empirical analysis of disequilibrium states.

Suppose, however, that a Tiebout equilibrium is assumed, as well as the presence of natural and economic "scarcities"—the latter being the product of Schumpeterian ([1942] 1975) entrepreneurship, innovation, and investment. In that equilibrium, some communities will be "more desirable places to live" because the environment and the scale as well as the mix (Meadows 1976) of public policies provided will make them so. These scarcities (or specific qualities) will command higher prices and will, thus, generate rents that will be capitalized in property values. If one reads the empirical studies of

Oates (1969), Meadows (1976), Andrew Reschovsky (1979), Kenneth Rosen (1982), and other students of local public finance in that spirit, they indicate that intergovernmental relationships are competitive.

Price Rivalry

The widespread use of direct subsidies, tax holidays, purchase agreements, land grants, and wage subsidies, to name but a few of the "price" instruments that governments use to attract labor, capital, and technology, is a vibrant testimony to the fact that intergovernmental relations are competitive. At the risk of overstretching the notion of "price," one should add to the instruments just listed such policies as the subsidization or outright provision of concert halls, museums, sports arenas, conference centers, and the host of other projects intended to make a jurisdiction more attractive. In the international arena, it is also easy to document the competitiveness of governments. Instruments that cannot be used in the home economy, such as tariffs, exchange rate devaluations, and quotas—voluntary or not—as well as innumerable nontariff barriers, have been and continue to be widely used. Price competition between governments is direct evidence that intergovernmental relations are competitive relations.

STABILITY OF COMPETITIVE OUTCOMES

If a mechanism or a configuration of forces moves an institutional structure from *any* position of disequilibrium to one of equilibrium, that equilbrium is said to be globally stable. The equilibrium is locally stable (stable in the small) when the mechanism or the configuration of forces can move the institutional structure to equilibrium only from states or positions already close to it (see Samuelson 1953: chapter 9). Intergovernmental competition, conceived as a configuration of forces, can, therefore, be globally or locally stable, and it can obviously also be globally or locally unstable. One must avoid identifying instability with collapse; sometimes instability will mean collapse, but at other times "restoring forces" (Lancaster 1974: 287) are set in motion that prevent collapse from happening. Following upon Kelvin Lancaster, one could say that when this happens, instability is "bounded." (Lancaster wrote that "perhaps the unemployment levels in the thirties represented the boundary of disequilibrium" (287) for that phenomenon.

At times instability is easily observable, whereas at other times it is difficult, if not impossible, to detect because it prevents institutions from emerging. For example, there are risks against which it is impossible to buy insurance because insurance markets do not emerge for these risks. The reason is that those who would want to purchase insurance against these risks can also affect the probability of occurrence of the events against which insurance is sought, without being easily detected. An insurer cannot, under these circumstances, estimate what his or her payments would be. Nonemergence of markets, in such cases, is said to be caused by moral hazard. But sometimes instability is readily observable. Price wars are an example, as are downward matching adjustments in product quality to reduce production costs. Other examples will emerge as this discussion proceeds.

Stability and efficiency are closely related phenomena, but they are distinct and must be analyzed separately. This is especially true when considering global, as distinguished from local, stability. For example, intergovernmental price competition may be shown to be efficient or inefficient, but that matter is clearly different from the question of whether intergovernmental price competition degenerates into unstable price wars. The point can be illustrated by reference to standard discussions of externalities. As is well known, externalities cause inefficiencies in the allocation of resources. In general, however, the analysis of externalities and of the remedies to deal with them is conducted within a framework of assumptions that guarantee that the institutional structure is stable.[6]

The remainder of this section is concerned with institutional instability. I am, furthermore, setting efficiency questions aside, if only because stability must generally be assumed when addressing questions of efficiency. In a way, matters pertaining to efficiency can be addressed within a given institutional framework, whereas problems of stability require changes in that framework, so that the latter has some priority over the former. This section first discusses issues related to stability as they pertain to the diffusion of public policies, and then moves on to political mobility and to price competition.

Although Walker (1969: 890) had already recognized that a problem of institutional stability could exist, it seems that the first systematic discussion of the problem of stability as it pertains to the diffusion of legislation was that of William Carey, in 1974. He argued that competition for the revenues produced by the supply of corporate charters has led state governments to make corporate statutes increasingly more appealing to managers—namely, to those who "buy" the incorporation or reincorporation charters—by increasing their freedom vis-à-vis stockholders. As a consequence, both the stockholders and the general public receive inadequate legal protection. Carey described the process as a "movement toward the least common denominator" (663), and as a "race for the bottom" (666). Phrases like these could imply either global or local instability. His argument would, however, appear to be more consistent with a notion of local instability.

Carey's methodology of proof was one common in legal writings and standard in legal and jurisprudential proceedings. By marshaling and analyzing cases deemed to be relevant, Carey sought to establish that in matters pertaining to "fiduciary responsibility and fairness" and to "shareholder's rights," corporate law in the state of Delaware had been "shrinking" and had been "water[ed] down" (696). The "race for the bottom" language and the regular use of the word "competition" leads one to believe that what was happening in Delaware was a response to competitive pressures from the outside, although Carey did not offer any analysis of what other states were doing in the area.

Furthermore, because the evidence brought forward to document what could be called collusion between the courts and the Delaware legislature to explain the "watering down" of legislation can be interpreted as a response to competitive pressures from the outside, I assume that the "collusive" arrangements and other behaviors noted by Carey were the result of competitive pressures.

Carey's paper was not long without a response. In particular, his policy prescription that to deal with competitive instability, the responsibility for corporation-shareholder relationships should be transferred extensively to the national government, provoked a number of rejoinders, among which one can mention Ralph Winter (1977) and Daniel Fischel (1982). Carey's ideal solution would have been "federal incorporation"; however, because that solution was, in his view, "politically unrealistic," he proposed the adoption of federal "minimum standards" of regulation. There can be little doubt that in Carey's mind instability is removed by eliminating horizontal intergovernmental competition itself. He wrote: "The third [principle on which we should proceed] is to emphasize the need for uniformity, so that states shall not compete with each other by lowering standards for competitive reasons or for the purpose of generating revenue." To a Canadian at least, that solution has a familiar ring to it: it was also the solution proposed to perceived problems of competitive instability by the famed, though seldom read, 1940 report

of the Rowell-Sirois Royal Commission on Dominion-Provincial Relations in Canada.

The corporate charter debate is not an easy one to enter. It is
constantly menaced by strong philosophical positions and is obviously influenced by current American policy discussions. I will
therefore tread lightly and remain close to my own special concerns.
Carey's major point has not been addressed by his critics. The notion
that any stockholder who does not like the activities of the corporation in which he or she owns stock has only to sell and buy elsewhere would appear to conflict with the fact, central to Carey's analysis,
that shareholders sometimes litigate. Carey's main point is that because of competitive adjustments in corporate law, the chances of
successful litigation by shareholders in Delaware have eroded over
time. That is where the instability lies.

That Carey limited his analysis to Delaware weakened his argument. Is it only in Delaware that "shareholders' rights" are being
"water[ed] down," or is one witnessing a genuine "race for the bottom"? If competition is producing what Carey alleged, then one has
to look at what is happening elsewhere also, because Delaware is
either responding to, or acting in anticipation of, actions in other
jurisdictions. If what is happening in Delaware is not governed by
competitive pressures, then the argument of Carey's critics—that
shareholders in Delaware corporations should rearrange their port-
folios by substituting non-Delaware for Delaware shares—could be
adapted to imply that would-be litigators should buy into non-Delaware, instead of Delaware, corporations, although the management
of an asset portfolio governed by expected returns is surely very
different than that governed by expected litigations.

Peter Dodd and Richard Leftwich (1980) and, more unequivocally,
Romano (1985) have shown that the earnings of corporations chang
ing their charter domicile to Delaware do not fall. In other words, if
Delaware is promanagement, it is so in a way that allows management
to maintain and even increase the present value of the firm. These
results, both based on econometric "event analysis," appear incon-
trovertible, at least to the extent that "news" is still, after October
19, 1987, considered the prime factor in explaining changes in share
prices. However, it is not clear that the kind of instability Carey had
in mind could not happen in the presence of the price stability
revealed by these apparently robust results. After all, price stability
can exist in markets characterized by quality deterioration or by what
one could call quality instability.

Romano (1985) noted that respondents in her survey "consistently alluded . . . [to] Delaware's well-developed case law, which provides a pool of handy precedents, and the basis of obtaining almost instantaneously a legal opinion on any issue of Delaware law" (274) as an important reason for Delaware's dominance in the reincorporation "market." Delaware, in other words, has specialized in corporate law; hence, what one observes is not instability, but a division of labor and its consequences. The argument is appealing, but it is also difficult to reconcile with the fact that 66 of the 140 reincorporations of New York Stock Exchange firms that took place between 1928 and 1977 occurred between 1966 and 1970, after a "major revision" of the Delaware corporate code (Dodd and Leftwich 1980: 267–68).

The question is still open. It would be unwise on the basis of this one case to conclude that the competitive forces underlying interjurisdictional diffusion processes cannot be unstable. However, if they are unstable, it does not follow, as suggested by Carey and others, that intergovernmental competition should be suppressed by reassigning the power to a higher level of government. That solution would be "optimal" only if other means of stabilizing competition did not exist or were shown to be less efficient.

The analysis of stability as it pertains to the other two manifestations of competitive behavior identified earlier—namely, political mobility and price rivalry—has received considerable attention in the literature; therefore, these questions can be dealt with here much more rapidly.

A pure Tiebout equilibrium is stable because the adjustment mechanism that describes behavior when the system is in disequilibrium is one based on U-shaped average (per-capita) cost curves for local public services. This is an acceptable assumption when the number of communities is postulated to be large enough to allow a partition of the entire population according to preferences (total utility) into strictly homogeneous groups. If the number of communities is smaller than needed to achieve this degree of homogeneity because there is, say, "a scarcity of community sites" (Westhoff 1979: 537), then equilibrium can be unstable, as has been demonstrated by Frank Westhoff (1979) and Susan Rose-Ackerman (1979). Other causes of instability have been analyzed (see, for example, Stiglitz 1977). There is no need to review that literature here, although the logic of instability that it describes is always fairly simple: a movement from *A* to *B* worsens the situation in *A* and improves it in *B*, so that it induces further movement in the same direction.

A body of empirical evidence bearing on the stability of political mobility relates to the "urban crisis" in the United States. The "urban crisis" can be described as the presence in the central city of "undernourished and poorly educated children, dilapidated housing and abandoned neighborhoods, or rising unemployment and high rates of crime" (Bateman and Hochman 1976: 283). The causes of this crisis can be attributed to a "fiscal imbalance," which, in turn, is a consequence of migration to the suburbs. To the extent that the "urban crisis" is real, it can be interpreted as a manifestation of unstable intergovernmental competition.

As indicated, the literature on the subject is enormous and so specialized that I cannot do it justice. It comprises at least three strands: one that is preoccupied with the forces that have caused the "crisis," a second that is concerned with the morphology of the phenomenon, and a third that is prescriptive, in search of remedies to deal with the problem. I am concerned here exclusively with the first strand, and refer to such writers as Worth Bateman and Harold Hochman (1976), Edwin Mills (1980), and Harvey Rosen (1985), who, addressing the question in the framework of the Tiebout model, viewed the "crisis" as being caused by migratory adjustments. None of these authors, nor any other, to my knowledge, has interpreted the "crisis" as a sign of competitive instability, but that is surely what it is.

Richard Bird and Enid Slack (1983), in *Urban Public Finance in Canada*, provided enlightenment on the matter. They disavowed any "urban crisis" in Canada, and said that one is not "likely to emerge . . . with anything like the same force" as in the United States. They gave three reasons for this: (1) the relative youth of Canadian cities and the consequent continued significant growth in property tax bases; (2) a more centralized division of powers between provincial and local governments in Canada than between state and local governments in the United States; and (3) a much tighter control of local finance by provincial governments in Canada than by state government in the United States (13). The second and especially the third of these three reasons imply that there is less intergovernmental competition among local governments in Canada than in the United States. That, by itself, would mute competitive instability in Canada. But, as Bird and Slack also noted, "provincial support of municipal finance . . . is much greater in Canada" (13). This means that interjurisdictional mobility will not erode tax bases as much as occurs in the United States; consequently, a process of migration that would otherwise have been unstable can operate in a stable manner. I return to the role of interjurisdictional grants in promoting stability in the next section.

I turn now briefly to price rivalry. There is an extensive empirical literature on the activities of governments bidding against each other for labor (jobs, skills), capital (businesses, research laboratories), and technology. That literature leaves no doubt about the existence of competitive relations. Phenomena such as tariff "wars" and competitive exchange devaluation in the international arena have also been documented. This type of competition may not always be unstable, but there can be no doubt that when it was allowed to develop unchecked during the interwar years (1919–39), it was unstable (see Nurkse 1944[7] and Kindleberger 1986). I mention these events, even though they are far removed from a federalist context, only because a dominant explanation for their occurrence is particularly revealing in a search for competitive stability in federations.

SECURING STABILITY

At the level of institutional structures, stability requires the existence of a "third party," which I will call the central or the federal government. The point is that stability cannot, in general, be achieved through cooperation. Before addressing this matter, let me insist that this is not an indictment or, at least, not a complete indictment, of the notion of cooperative federalism. Recall the distinction between horizontal and vertical intergovernmental relations introduced earlier. Models of cooperative federalism are mostly concerned with vertical relationships: they are largely tacit on the question of horizontal competition. The point is that horizontal cooperative federalism is not a solution to horizontal competitive instability.

Cooperation is one way to suppress competition, but it is not the only way. It is easy to generate a division of powers between jurisdictions that will also extinguish competition by simply "overcentralizing" the federation. The argument, then, is not that cooperation is inefficient because it suppresses competition, but because it cannot deliver stability. Let me illustrate by referring to market calisthenics. If each oligopolist in a particular market assumes that the others will keep their current prices unchanged, and if each has sufficient capacity to supply the entire demand, the stage is set, as is well known, for the instability sometimes called "cutthroat competition." The formation of a collusive (cooperative) cartel is not a solution to this problem of instability, because cartels are also, generally, unstable (see Stigler 1964).

Why is horizontal cooperation incapable of "solving" the stability problem? Among the many reasons, a few of the more important are as follows. First, a cooperative agreement cannot be, in the language of Lester Telser (1980), a self-enforcing agreement. This is because agreements of that kind are possible when the expected net gains from a cooperative relationship exceed those from cheating on the agreement. The problems of self-enforcement are, therefore, most acute when the time horizon of the agreement is finite and more or less certain. In other words, if A knows that two years hence, B cannot be assumed to be a party to the agreement, then A must assume that B will violate the agreement before the two years are over. That expectation on A's part is sufficient, by itself, to prevent the emergence of an agreement. Is that not the kind of expectation fostered by electoral politics? Which provincial premier or state governor can assume that other premiers or governors will be reelected in the next electoral contest?

When self-enforcement is not possible, another way of ensuring cooperation is to have all the parties to the agreement post a bond (Becker and Stigler 1974). Violation causes loss of the bond. As Telser noted (1980), it is not obvious that bond posting does not require a third party. Who decides whether there has been a violation? In any case, premiers and governors do not post bonds.

Trust, as defined by Breton and Wintrobe (1982: chapter 4), and by Coleman (1983), can also lead to relationships that do not require the presence of a third party. But trust requires repeated interaction, which periodic electoral competition makes difficult, if not impossible. Much of the stress in the literature on cooperative federalism, to the extent that this literature can be brought to bear on the question of horizontal cooperation, is largely concerned with cooperation at the bureaucratic level, where relationships are often more permanent and where trust is, as a result, more likely to accumulate.

The existence of a central government is, however, insufficient for stability. Certain conditions must be satisfied if that government is to guarantee the stability of horizontal intergovernmental competitive relationships. In trying to define some of these conditions, I will disregard measures designed to suppress competition, because these, if generalized, would suppress federalism. A wholesale transfer of powers to the federal government, as has sometimes been advocated, as a way of dealing with instability is, therefore, ruled out. To address the question of the "optimal" assignment of powers—an issue intimately related to the nature and properties of vertical competition—would be too lengthy an undertaking here. Still, the assignment of powers must be assumed to be consistent with horizontal competitive stability.

The Role of Federal Governments

Federal governments have dealt with competitive instability in the diffusion process in a number of ways. They have, for example, introduced minimum[8] and even maximum[9] standards of provision. This is not to say that in all instances standards were introduced to deal with instability. Surely the instrument has been abused, but there is no doubt that it has also been used efficiently. Neither minimum nor maximum standards are easy to devise: the minimum can be set too high and the maximum too low.[10] When that happens, it is like a reassignment of the power or powers to the central government. This notwithstanding, the best way to begin analyzing existing standards is to regard them as stabilization devices.

Instability in the diffusion process may come about because some jurisdictions do not have the resources required to adopt whatever policy they should to compete with wealthier jurisdictions. There are many ways to deal with this problem. One of them is federal provision, with or without a formal reassignment of powers. One would expect that when the motive for federal assumption of a power is lack of means, there should be retrenchment whenever the means become available. An alternative to federal provision is subsidies combined with minimum standards.

Subsidies, typically in the form of interjurisdictional grants, can do more than help stabilize a competitive diffusion process; they can also help stabilize the competition associated with political mobility. The point has already been made by Bird and Slack (1983), who argued that there is no "urban crisis" in Canada because provincial (and federal) grants to local governments have led to the kind of urban development that has prevented an exodus of middle- and upper-income residents from central cities to the suburbs.

Well-designed intergovernmental grants programs are among the most effective instruments available to deal with competitive instability. In federations like Canada, where differences in size, wealth, and capacity of jurisdictions are large, this has been the primary and most significant role of intergovernmental grants. Of course, the grants have served to redistribute incomes—virtually all policies have substitution and income effects—but they have been, above all, allocational devices. That is why they have consistently been accepted by "payer" provinces.

Regarding price rivalry, the problem has two dimensions: first, competition requires that all jurisdictional units have the "ability" to compete; and second, the process of bidding and counterbidding should converge to a stable equilibrium. Neither of these objectives is easy to achieve.

To achieve competitive viability, central governments have often, in addition to using intergovernmental grants, pursued "regional" development policies. These are policies aimed at ensuring that a province or a state will not always lose in competitive struggles with other jurisdictions because of an inability to make attractive offers. Although much of what occurs under the rubric of regional policy is unrelated to competitive stability, many policies related to the organizational infrastructure of jurisdictions should be construed that way. Programs related to the building of transportation networks (roads, canals, railways, air routes, etc.), to the development of communication systems (telegraph, telephone, etc.), to research facilities, and to other similar "basic" policies are, in many instances, of that kind. One of the difficulties in analyzing regional policies is that, often, they are conducted under a different label: for example, what proportion of the U.S. defense budget is implicit regional policy, and what fraction of Canada's unemployment insurance program is implicit regional policy?

To guarantee that competitive bidding is not unstable in one direction or the other, the central government must, first and above all, ensure that the costs of any action by the government of a jurisdiction are borne by that government and its citizens. It is important, for example, that a jurisdiction not be able to "export" its tax burden or to tax out-of-jurisdiction bases.[11] Yet, even if all the effects of "price" policies are fully internalized, provincial or state governments may still resort to beggar-thy-neighbor policies. There is no alternative, if that happens, to direct intervention by the central government. In one instance of what was threatening to become very unstable bidding for a particular asset, the Canadian government put an end to the process by effectively bribing both parties. The federal government, in a word, decided who would "win" and bought the consent of the rival with a bribe (a subsidy). An unstable process was "artificially" brought to a stop. The media and many observers saw this as a triumph of cooperative federalism.

I conclude by noting that in the area of international competition, it would be impossible to prevent an unstable competitive process from degenerating, unless, in the language of international relations "realists," a hegemonic power undertook to prevent the debacle. I agree with Robert Keohane (1984), Charles Kindleberger (1986), and others that the instability of the interwar years could have been checked by an active hegemon. The inability of the United Kingdom and the unwillingness of the United States to assume that role is not an unimportant factor in explaining the economic collapse of the period.

CONCLUSION

The premise of this chapter has been that the most promising approach to a theory of federalism is one that assumes that intergovernmental relations are competitive in nature. Three bodies of "data" were shown to be consistent with this assumption. It was also argued that both theory and evidence indicate that intergovernmental competition or, more exactly, the equilibrium positions that result from competition are often unstable. The discussion then asserted that stability can be achieved by certain policies of federal or central governments. Stated another way, federal governments, in addition to being suppliers of goods and services, must "arbitrate" competition if intergovernmental relations are to be stable.

Notes

1. It would take me too far afield to sketch the main contours of what is emerging. The reader is referred to Breton (1985, 1989) and to the literature cited there.

2. Walker (1969) examined 88 programs. In addition to this important piece of research and to Davis's study, one can note McVoy (1940), Sutherland (1950), Crain (1966), Hofferbert (1966), Scott (1968), Sharkansky (1968), Gray (1973), and Savage (1985).

3. Walker (1969) also distinguished between vertical and horizontal relationships in federal states and, in addition, briefly addressed the question of the stability of horizontal competition (890).

4. "An equilibrium may *exist* in the sense that an equilibrium configuration is *possible*, but it may not automatically be either *attained* or *maintained*" (Lancaster 1974: 285, emphasis in original).

5. The word "temporary" is surely an indication that an equilibrium is postulated.

6. If negative externalities are strong enough, they may, as Baumol (1964) and Baumol and Bradford (1972) have shown, lead to a reversal in the sign of the second-order, or stability, condition and thus cause instability.

7. Friedman's (1953: 176) strictures on Nurkse's work, even if one were to accept them, do not apply to Nurkse's analysis of intergovernmental competition, but to his discussion of the tendency of flexible exchange rates to display large unstable movements.

8. The use of instruments, such as minimum standards, to stabilize competition in the face of moral hazard resulting from asymmetric information in markets is recognized by Leland (1979).

9. The province of Ontario imposes a ceiling on tuition fees that "private" institutions can charge students.

10. I cannot judge whether William Carey's seven minimum standards are excessive. I only note that he, himself, suggested that they be part of a Federal Corporate Uniformity Act (1974: 701).

11. Here, again, one must avoid identifying instability with collapse. Not all transfers of tax burdens need degenerate into "tax wars." At the same time, it is well to keep in mind that unless one knows why tax wars do not happen, one cannot presume that the system is stable.

References

Bateman, W., and H. M. Hochman. 1976. "Social Problems and the Urban Crisis: Can Public Policy Make a Difference?" In *The Urban Economy*, edited by H. M. Hochman, 283–93. New York: W. W. Norton.

Baumol, W. J., 1964. "External Economies and Second-Order Optimality Conditions." *American Economic Review* 54 (4, pt. 1, June): 358–72.

Baumol, W. J. and D. F. Bradford. 1972. "Detrimental Externalities and Non-Convexity of the Production Set." *Economica* 39 (154, May): 160–76.

Becker, G. S., and G. J. Stigler. 1974. "Law Enforcement, Malfeasance, and Compensation of Enforcers." *Journal of Legal Studies* 3 (1, January): 1–18.

Bird, R. M. and N. E. Slack. 1983. *Urban Public Finance in Canada*. Toronto: Butterworths.

Breton, A. 1985. "Supplementary Statement." In *Report of the Royal Commission on the Economic Union and Development Prospects for Canada*. Ottawa: Minister of Supply and Services. Reprinted, 1987, as "Towards a Theory of Competitive Federalism." *European Journal of Political Economy* 3: 263–329.

————. 1989. "The Organization of Governmental Systems." Photocopy.

Breton, A. and R. Wintrobe. 1982. *The Logic of Bureaucratic Conduct*. New York: Cambridge University Press.

Carey, W. L. 1974. "Federalism and Corporate Law: Reflections upon Delaware." *Yale Law Journal* 83, (4, March): 663–705.

Coleman, J.S. 1983. "Recontracting, Trustworthiness, and the Stability of Vote Exchanges." *Public Choice* 40 (1): 89–94.

Coleman, J. S., H. Menzel, and E. Katz. 1959. "Social Processes in Physician's Adoption of a New Drug." *Journal of Chronic Diseases* 9 (1, January): 1–19.

Crain, R. L. 1966. "Fluoridation: The Diffusion of an Innovation among Cities." *Social Forces* 44 (4, June): 467–76.

Davis, A. J. 1930. "The Evolution of the Institution of Mothers' Pensions in the United States." *American Journal of Sociology* 35 (4, January): 573–87.

Dodd, P., and R. Leftwich. 1980. "The Market for Corporate Charters: 'Unhealthy Competition' versus Federal Regulation." *Journal of Business* 53 (3, July): 259–83.

Edel, M., and E. Sclar. 1974. "Taxes, Spending, and Property Values: Supply Adjustment in a Tiebout-Oates Model." *Journal of Political Economy* 82 (5, September/October): 941–54.

Epple, D., and A. Zelenitz. 1981. "The Implications of Competition among Jurisdictions: Does Tiebout Need Politics?" *Journal of Political Economy* 89 (6, December): 1197–1217.

Epple, D., A. Zelenitz, and M. Visscher. 1978. "A Search for Testable Implications of the Tiebout Hypothesis." *Journal of Political Economy* 86 (3, June): 405–25.

Fischel, D. R. 1982. "The 'Race to the Bottom' Revisited: Reflections on Recent Developments in Delaware's Corporation Law." *Northwestern University Law Review* 76 (6): 913–45.

Friedman, M. 1953. "The Case for Flexible Exchange Rates." In *Essays in Positive Economics*, edited by M. Friedman. Chicago: University of Chicago Press.

Friedrich, C. J. 1968. *Trends of Federalism in Theory and Practice.* New York: Praeger.

Gramlich, E. M., and D. L. Rubinfeld. 1982. "Micro Estimates of Public Spending Demand Functions and Tests of the Tiebout and Median-Voter Hypotheses." *Journal of Political Economy* 90, (3, June): 536–60.

Gray, V. 1973. "Innovation in the States: A Diffusion Study." *American Political Science Review* 67 (4, December): 1174–85.

Hamilton, B. W. 1976. "The Effects of Property Taxes and Local Public Spending on Property Values: A Theoretical Comment." *Journal of Political Economy* 84 (3, June): 647–50.

Hofferbert, R. I. 1966. "Ecological Development and Policy Change in the American States." *Midwest Journal of Political Science* 10 (4, November): 464–83.

Kenyon, D. A. 1988. "Interjurisdictional Tax and Policy Competition: Good or Bad for the Federal System?" Washington, D.C.: U.S. Advisory Commission on Intergovernmental Relations, January. Draft.

Keohane, R. O. 1984. *After Hegemony: Cooperation and Discord in the World Political Economy*. Princeton: Princeton University Press.

Kindleberger, C. P. 1986. *The World in Depression, 1929–39*, rev. and enl. ed. Berkeley: University of California Press.

Lancaster, K. 1974. *Introduction to Modern Microeconomics*, 2nd ed. Chicago: Rand McNally.

Leland, H. E. 1979. "Quacks, Lemons, and Licensing: A Theory of Minimum Quality Standards." *Journal of Political Economy* 87 (6, December): 1328–46.

Mansfield, E. 1963. "The Speed of Response of Firms to New Techniques." *Quarterly Journal of Economics* 77 (2, May): 290–311.

McVoy, E. C. 1940. "Patterns of Diffusion in the United States." *American Sociological Review* 5 (2, April): 219–27.

Meadows, G. R. 1976. "Taxes, Spending, and Property Values: A Comment and Further Results." *Journal of Political Economy* 84 (4, pt. 1, August): 869–80.

Mills, E. S. 1980. *Urban Economics*, 2nd ed. Glenview, Ill.: Scott, Foresman.

Nurkse, R., with W. A. Brown, Jr. 1944. *International Currency Experience*. New York: League of Nations.

Oates, W. E. 1969. "The Effects of Property Taxes and Local Public Spending on Property Values: An Empirical Study of Tax Capitalization and the Tiebout Hypothesis." *Journal of Political Economy* 77 (6, November/December): 957–71.

Oster, S. M., and J. M. Quigley. 1977. "Regulatory Barriers to the Diffusion of Innovation: Some Evidence from Building Codes." *Bell Journal of Economics* 8 (2, Autumn): 361–77.

Pauly, M. V. 1976. "A Model of Local Government Expenditure and Tax Capitalization." *Journal of Public Economics* 6 (3, October): 231–42.

Reinganum, J. F. 1981. "On the Diffusion of New Technology: A Game Theoretic Approach." *Review of Economic Studies* 48: 395–405.

————. 1983. "Technology Adoption under Imperfect Information." *Bell Journal of Economics* 14 (1, Spring): 57–69.

Report, Royal Commission on Dominion-Provincial Relations. (Ottawa: King's Printer, 1940).

Reschovsky, A. 1979. "Residential Choice and the Local Public Sector: An Alternative Test of the Tiebout Hypothesis." *Journal of Urban Economics* 6 (4, October): 501–20.

Romano, R. 1985. "Law as a Product: Some Pieces of the Incorporation Puzzle." *Journal of Law, Economics, and Organization* 1 (2, Fall): 225–83.

Rose-Ackerman, S. 1979. "Market Models of Local Government: Exit, Voting, and the Land Market." *Journal of Urban Economics* 6 (3, July): 319–37.

Rosen, H. S. 1985. *Public Finance*. Homewood, Ill.: Irwin.

Rosen, K. T. 1982. "The Impact of Proposition 13 on House Prices in Northern California: A Test of the Interjurisdictional Capitalization Hypothesis." *Journal of Political Economy* 90 (1, February): 191–200.

Salmon, P. 1987a "Decentralization as an Incentive Scheme." *Oxford Review of Economic Policy* 3 (2, Summer): 24–43.

———. 1987b. "The Logic of Pressure Groups and the Structure of the Public Sector." *European Journal of Political Economy* 3 (1–2): 55–86.

Samuelson, P. A. 1953. *Foundations of Economic Analysis*. Cambridge, Mass.: Harvard University Press.

Savage, R. ed. 1985. "Policy Diffusion in a Federal System." *Publius: The Journal of Federalism* 15 (4, Fall): entire issue.

Schumpeter, J. A. [1942] 1975. *Capitalism, Socialism, and Democracy*. New York: Harper & Row.

Scott, T. M. 1968. "The Diffusion of Urban Governmental Forms as a Case of Social Learning." *Journal of Politics* 30 (4, November): 1091–1108.

Sharkansky, I. 1968. "Regionalism, Economic Status, and the Public Policies of American States." *Southwestern Social Science Quarterly* 49 (1, June): 9–26.

Stigler, G. J. 1964. "A Theory of Oligopoly." *Journal of Political Economy* 72 (1, February): 44–61.

Stiglitz, J. E. 1977. "The Theory of Local Public Goods." In *The Economics of Public Services*, edited by M. S. Feldstein and R. P. Inman. London: Macmillan.

Sutherland, E. H. 1950. "The Diffusion of Sexual Psychopath Laws." *American Journal of Sociology* 56 (2, September): 142–48.

Telser, L. G. 1980. "A Theory of Self-Enforcing Agreements." *Journal of Business* 53 (1, January): 27–44.

Tiebout, C. M. 1956. "A Pure Theory of Local Expenditures." *Journal of Political Economy* 64 (5, October): 416–24.

Walker, J. L. 1969. "The Diffusion of Innovations among the American States." *American Political Science Review* 63 (3, September): 880–99.

Westhoff, F. 1979. "Policy Inferences from Community Choice Models: A Caution." *Journal of Urban Economics* 6 (4, October): 535–49.

Winter, R. K. Jr. 1977. "State Law, Shareholder Protection, and the Theory of the Corporation." *Journal of Legal Studies* 6 (2, June): 251–92.

Chapter Three

HOW RELEVANT IS COMPETITION TO GOVERNMENT POLICYMAKING?

John E. Chubb

Can a federal system be expected to perform in a distinctive manner? Does a federal structure encourage the governments that comprise it to act in predictable ways? How should federalism be employed in policymaking? Questions such as these are more general than the sort that research on federalism has tended to raise. Impressed, if not overwhelmed, by the complexity of relations among governments, research has probed deeply into parts of the federal system, especially the workings of particular policies, but has usually not focused on the institution as a whole (although compare Oates 1972; Peterson 1981). Basic matters of federal system performance—most prominently, equilibria and stability—consequently remain unsettled. Albert Breton's paper (chapter 2) is a welcome contribution toward a settlement.

Breton strips federalism of most of its complexity, leaving behind a simple structure for investigation. The structure—a competitive market of subnational governments—is not novel (Tiebout 1956). However, since the general properties of the structure have never been determined (Rose-Ackerman 1983), the structure provides an appropriate framework for Breton's deceptively simple purposes: evaluating the empirical validity and equilibrium properties of a competitive model of federalism. Although Breton's research review is somewhat more successful than his theoretical investigation, both provide the kind of breadth too often lacking in work on federalism.

Breton examines the evidence for interstate or interjurisdictional competition in three kinds of research. He first notes that many studies of the timing of policy adoption reveal a pattern of diffusion across jurisdictions that is consistent with a competitive model. Governments that fear the loss of taxpayers to jurisdictions that offer more attractive services copy the innovations of neighboring governments. Apparently, the threat of citizens "voting with their feet" drives governments within federal systems to compete in public goods and services. So it may.

However, another mechanism of social control, democratic voting, may produce the same patterns of innovation, without exit—actual or potential—even coming into play. For example, research on the diffusion of policy innovations internationally (e.g., Collier and Messick 1975) discloses the same pattern as research on interstate diffusion. Yet, it is unlikely that the adoption of, say, social security programs in the United States had much to do with concerns about the relative attractiveness to U.S. citizens of European nations with more generous welfare systems. Competition may not account, then, for as much of the pattern of interjurisdictional policy diffusion as Breton suggests; political demands within jurisdictions may be at least as important.

An additional body of research relevant to the competition model is that on capitalization and property values. At one time taken as evidence of a competitive process, differences in property values attributable to differences in the benefit/cost ratios of local services ultimately came to be viewed as evidence against competition. If governments were really responsive to the demands of mobile taxpayers, excess demand for more favorable benefit/cost packages would be bid away by competing governments, and not capitalized in the property values of the more attractive jurisdictions. However, as Breton persuasively argues, this critique overlooks differences in jurisdictional resources that may explain the apparent capitalization of policy differences. Competition may yet be evident, then, in the variation in property values.

As with the evidence in patterns of policy diffusion, however, additional evidence tempers this conclusion. Specifically, research on the reciprocal relationship between government policy and taxpayer mobility (or the mobility of businesses and program beneficiaries) has generally not found an impressive connection between the two (e.g., Gramlich and Laren 1984; cf., Peterson and Rom 1990). This is all the more important because, whereas capitalization research looks for competition indirectly, mobility research looks for it directly. True, research on mobility is relatively scarce; nevertheless, Breton's case for competition would be stronger if it explained the weak findings of mobility research as well as it does the disconfirming results of capitalization research.

By contrast, I am in complete agreement with Breton's assessment of research on price rivalry. To his credit, he provides a forthright critique of the evidence that subnational governments effectively compete to attract new businesses or retain old ones. He could have pointed to a host of cities and states that have courted firms with tax breaks and assorted inducements. However, instead of building these cases into an argument for the existence of price rivalry, he exposes them as mere anecdotes. In fact, systematic research on price rivalry is in short supply and has produced no consistent results. The incidence and effects of price rivalry, even in much ballyhooed cases of its practice—the so-called "Massachusetts Miracle" of the 1980s—may be much less than expected.

In essence, Breton's reading of the empirical literature is that if it fails to provide convincing evidence of competition in any instance, it does offer broad support for the validity of the concept of interjurisdictional competition in some form. This is fair enough, although in my view the evidence is more problematic. The evidence does create something of a burden for Breton's theoretical analysis. If the validity of the competitive model is not transparent, theory ought to provide insights that justify and help account for the model's empirical shortcomings. Breton's theoretical analysis does not quite do this.

The analysis begins with great promise, employing Delaware's lenient incorporation laws to illustrate how complicated the consequences of interstate competition may be. The analysis also reveals that competition may not be unstable, even under conditions where a simple model of competition would predict instability. The pursuit of business has not led states into a mutually unbeneficial "race to the bottom" (Carey 1974: 666) in which the interests of taxpayers are sacrificed to attract business. Yet, after shedding doubt on common notions about competition and uncovering some of the intriguing subtleties of competition, Breton's analysis resorts to familiar simplifications (e.g., Oates 1972; Olson 1965). Likening interstate competition to oligopolistic competition, Breton suggests that the relationship between the states will produce unstable outcomes. Cooperation between states will arise periodically, but will ultimately be undone as individual states find an advantage in cheating on agreements. Price rivalry will prove to be a profitable short-term strategy for particular states, but a troublesome one for all states in the long term. No state's tax base will increase, and every state's tax rates will decrease, leaving inadequate revenue not only to meet the needs of less productive citizens but perhaps of the most productive ones as well.

Breton is evidently persuaded by the evidence of competition adduced in the beginning of his chapter, and by additional facts—urban crises stemming from "white flight" and global recession stemming from international trade wars—that he brings to bear in the theoretical analysis, for he turns quickly to remedies for unstable competition. This, too, is familiar (e.g., Oates 1972). He suggests that outcomes in which competition makes everyone worse off can best be avoided with the help of outside authorities to control cutthroat competition or promote cooperation. Thus, a federal system may benefit from a central government setting and enforcing minimum standards of performance, using grants to subsidize resource-poor jurisdictions, or discouraging jurisdictions from producing or ignoring externalities that impose costs on their neighbors. Of course, these are the kinds of functions that economists have long argued should be performed by a national government, and that the federal governments of the United States and Canada perform in varying ways already. Moreover, these remedies may be correct and proper. Even so, if there are reasons, empirical and theoretical, to doubt the intensity and instability of interstate competition—and Breton suggests some himself—the conclusions of Breton's paper do not adequately reflect them.

The reasons for doubt are considerable, and I would like to conclude by discussing two of them. Given that both reasons fall somewhat outside the domain of Breton's ambitious analysis, they do not point up weaknesses in it. However, both merit consideration because they address Breton's broader concerns—the specification of a more general model of federalism and the derivation of the basic properties of a model of competition.

Breton's model, like most models of federalism in the Tiebout tradition, assumes that states are individual actors. Like firms in an economic marketplace, they have objective functions that they seek to maximize. Where these objective functions originate is of no interest; in the case of governments, they are assumed to derive from a dominant party or, more commonly, a median voter. This notion is fine if the predictions that such simplifications produce are sufficiently interesting and accurate. In fact, the median voter assumption has worked effectively in research in public finance—for example, on intergovernmental grants (e.g., Inman 1979). Yet, given the kinds of empirical and theoretical problems encountered by the competitive model of federalism, the assumption that reduces state and local governments to "black boxes" may warrant reconsideration.

To illustrate the assumption's potential weakness, consider an analogous application of the competitive model to the behavior of the U.S. government acting as a competitor in the international economic system. The United States becomes a unitary "state," not a government divided into a Congress, an executive, and a bureaucracy. How much can such a model tell us about policies that affect the country's international competitiveness? Only a limited amount. It would not predict, for example, that the United States would reform its tax code in 1986 to the collective detriment of business, or that it would run large budget deficits that inflate interest rates. Of course, no model can explain everything. However, few observers would suggest that the fiscal policy of the U.S. government can be understood very well by focusing on the constraints of international competition. Even in the limited area of trade policy, the internal politics of the government cannot usefully be assumed away (e.g., Destler 1986).

The reason, in large part, is that even though the politicians who set U.S. policy may be concerned about the national business climate, overall economic conditions, and the influence of international economic competition, still other concerns may loom larger. If we assume that levels of political concern are determined by electoral repercussions, it is clear, for example, that the economic health and competitiveness of the national economy will be eclipsed by other concerns for most members of the U.S. Congress. Congressional elections are influenced by economic conditions, but with reelection rates that always exceed 90 percent, economic conditions are far from deterministic. If anything is deterministic in congressional elections, it is the member's service to the constituency—providing constituents and interest groups with particular programs and ensuring that they are administered properly. No one is surprised, therefore, when Congress votes for expensive bills that generate budget deficits or provide relief to unproductive citizens. True, the president may be acutely worried about general economic conditions and competitiveness; however, U.S. policy is not set by presidents unilaterally. It is negotiated between presidents and Congress.

Among state and local governments, especially the American states, politics is similarly organized and oriented. Indeed, my research (Chubb 1988) indicates that state legislators and even governors have less reason to fear the vicissitudes of economic conditions than national politicians. Their elections do not hinge on state economic performance, and to the small extent that economic conditions do come into play, it is the president's party, and not the governor's party, that is blamed or credited for them. In addition, state politicians are developing the same kind of insulation from electoral defeat as their congressional counterparts. This likely comes from comparable attention to constituencies, not from responding to voter exit or entry, actual or potential.

If all this is so, then the political forces within states that push policy in the direction of a range of (expensive) constituency concerns may be much stronger than the economic forces of competition that push policy in another direction. It may make hardly more sense, therefore, to conclude that competition forces states into destabilizing behavior than it does to reach the same verdict about international competition. This is not to suggest that a model of competition should not be pursued, only that it might more fruitfully be developed as a constraint on a well-developed model of intrastate decisionmaking.

Finally, there is a quite different reason to be dubious about the alleged consequences of competition. Even if individual states are regarded as black boxes and their decision making is placed in the hands of strategic maximizers, it is not clear that competition implies instability. The states, after all, are not engaged in a short-term battle for competitive advantage, but in an ongoing struggle for economic development. In game-theoretic terms, the states are not locked into a prisoner's dilemma in which their rational decision to refuse to cooperate dooms them to a suboptimal outcome. Rather, they are in a repeated-play version of that game, where they can learn about the problems of uncooperative behavior. In a seminal study, Robert Axelrod (1984) demonstrated that cooperation is the dominant strategy for rational players in such a situation, and that cooperation has emerged in a variety of historical instances. This is of more than theoretical interest, for in state politics today, governors, state budget officers, and legislators interact regularly in national associations and at national meetings, providing the kinds of regular relationships that ought to stabilize competition.

If cooperation is emerging from these kinds of interactions, and if state politicians are becoming more secure in their positions, there may be far less reason than Breton's analysis suggests for the national government to intervene in the federal system. The states may not require the full measure of protection against each other that economic analysis often recommends. Competition, in many respects a virtue of a federal system, may be stable.

References

Axelrod, Robert. 1984. *The Evolution of Cooperation.* New York: Basic Books.
Carey, William L. 1974. "Federalism and Corporate Law: Reflections upon Delaware." *Yale Law Journal* 83 (4, March): 663–705.

Chubb, John E. 1988. "Institutions, the Economy, and the Dynamics of State Elections." *American Political Science Review* 82, 1(March): 133–54.

Collier, David, and Richard E. Messick. 1975. "Prerequisites versus Diffusion: Testing Alternative Explanations of Social Security Adoption." *American Political Science Review* 69, 4(December): 1299–1315.

Destler, I. M. 1986. *American Trade Politics: System under Stress.* Washington, D.C.: Institute for International Economics.

Gramlich, Edward M., and Deborah S. Laren. 1984. "Migration and Income Redistribution Responsibilities." *Journal of Human Resources* 19: 489–511.

Inman, Robert P. 1979. "The Fiscal Performance of Local Governments: An Interpretative Review." In *Current Issues in Urban Economies*, edited by Peter Mieszkowski and Mahlon Straszheim. Baltimore: Johns Hopkins University Press.

Oates, Wallace E. 1972. *Fiscal Federalism.* New York: Harcourt Brace Jovanovich.

Olson, Mancur. 1965. *The Logic of Collective Action.* Cambridge, Mass.: Harvard University Press.

Peterson, Paul E. 1981. *City Limits.* Chicago: University of Chicago Press.

Peterson, Paul E. and Mark C. Rom. 1990. *Welfare Magnets: A New Case for a National Standard.* Washington, D.C.: Brookings Institution.

Rose-Ackerman, Susan. 1983. "Beyond Tiebout: Modeling the Political Economy of Local Government." In *Local Provision of Public Services: The Tiebout Model after Twenty-Five Years.* New York: Academic Press.

Tiebout, Charles M. 1956. "A Pure Theory of Local Expenditures." *Journal of Political Economy* 64(5, October): 416–24.

Chapter Four

COOPERATIVE FEDERALISM

Daniel J. Elazar

Cooperative federalism has been the dominant operational theory of American intergovernmental relations at least from the days of Franklin D. Roosevelt's New Deal (1933), if not from Woodrow Wilson's New Freedom (1913). It was the regnant normative theory from the Kennedy-Johnson administration (after 1961) to the Reagan years. During the 1980s, however, cooperative federalism came under increasing criticism. This criticism has been based, for the most part, on a confusion between operational and normative theory, and a simplistic assessment of the theory of cooperative federalism.

From a federalist perspective, the most important reason for the development of the theory of cooperative federalism was that it enabled federalism to survive in a period of growing federal-state interdependence. The argument was that dual federalism may have been an appropriate theory for an earlier age when it was possible to separate federal and state functions because the velocity of government (the amount of governmental activity relative to the total activity in civil society) was so much lower. However, with the quantum increase in the velocity of government, dual federalism could no longer sustain the federal system.

More recently, another theory, competitive federalism, has been proposed as an alternative to cooperative federalism.[1] Although competitive federalism is primarily an economic theory, it has been argued that the theory offers the best basis for preserving federalism altogether. The theory of competitive federalism recognizes the reality of the greatly increased velocity of government and the interdependence of all governments within the same system. It contends, however, that precisely for these reasons, governments have to be made more efficient by introducing marketlike mechanisms such as interjurisdictional competition.

The theory of competitive federalism, like its predecessors, is addressed to federal-state, interstate, and state-local relations. Unlike dual federalism, which emphasizes federal-state relations, or cooperative federalism, which emphasizes all three (with perhaps less of a focus on interstate relations), competitive federalism emphasizes interstate relations. The premier theoretician of competitive federalism, Albert Breton, was no doubt encouraged to explore this theory by the particular character of Canadian federalism to which his theory was initially addressed. The Canadian federal system is notable in that it includes a limited number of provinces with parliamentary systems of government that enable their heads of government to speak in the name of the province with a single voice. This situation has stimulated the growth of interprovincial relations to the point that the federal prime minister sits with the provincial premiers in a First Ministers Conference that meets regularly and effectively determines policy for the entire intergovernmental system in Canada.

Such a possibility is distinctly lacking in the United States. The existence of five times as many states; strong and often constitutionalized traditions of local home rule; separation-of-power arrangements in the state and federal governments, which prevent any American government from speaking with one voice, except on rare occasions; and a very large population with a strong tradition of interest-group activity—all make the Canadian model impossible of achievement. Hence, cooperative federalism is still a necessary theoretical framework. Indeed, competitive federalism, as portrayed by Breton and others, can be seen by theorists of cooperative federalism as an economic extension or variant of cooperative federalist theory, close to what theorists of cooperative federalism refer to as antagonistic cooperation, that is to say, intergovernmental competition within an interactive framework.

Under conditions such as those of the United States, interstate relations depend on state-federal relations. Given that interjurisdictional competition revolves principally around taxing and secondarily around spending, the existence of a substantially independent sphere of state-local taxation makes interstate competition feasible in that field. In almost every other policy field, the heavy involvement of the federal government, even after the Reagan revolution, makes it difficult to talk about an entirely or even substantially separate sphere of interstate or "horizontal interjurisdictional" relations.

SOME POINTS ON THE HISTORY OF AN IDEA

Until the 1930s, the regnant theory of federalism in the United States, as elsewhere, was what Edward S. Corwin (1934, 1936, 1937) referred to as "dual federalism." The theory of dual federalism held that a proper federal system is one constructed on the basis of two separate spheres of authority—federal and state—that overlap only minimally where absolutely necessary, as in the conduct of elections or perhaps in the administration of a few critical programs. Corwin and others, particularly Jane Perry Clark (1938), V. O. Key (1937), and William Anderson (1946, 1955), noted that under the conditions of expanded government activity in this century, the states and the federal government had to share responsibility for many if not most functions, bringing their concurrent powers into play rather than emphasizing their separate spheres of authority. Morton Grodzins, who became known as the leading proponent of the theory of cooperative federalism, popularized one understanding of the differences between the two through a now-famous metaphor in which he described the federal system according to dual federalist theory as a layer cake and according to the cooperative federalist theory as a marble cake. In the former, the separate layers are clearly distinct, linked by the frosting; in the latter, everything is swirled together (Grodzins 1966).[2]

The theory of cooperative federalism became popular among academics in the half-generation between the end of World War II and the presidency of John F. Kennedy, and became the dominant theory in the United States and increasingly in the rest of the world during the 1960s.[3] Following Grodzins's model, the theory of cooperative federalism as it had evolved by the mid-1960s can be summarized as follows: The American system of government is functionally analogous to a marble cake of shared activities and services, even though it is formally structured (like a layer cake) in three planes. Despite the great increase in the velocity of government in the 20th century, the system remains noncentralized, democratic, and responsive to the public because there is a little chaos built into it. On one level, this chaos promotes sharing because it prevents any single government or governmental plane from gaining exclusive jurisdiction and power in any area of governmental concern. On a second level, the chaos allows citizens to utilize multiple cracks (in the double sense of wallops from outside the system and fissures inside the system) to gain their ends. This has the consequence of involving (at least potentially) government on every plane in the same problem. On the national plane, in particular, the existence of a public-private continuum, which is used to mobilize local influence, helps to translate citizen benefits from the multiple crack into benefits for the states and localities.

The sharing system is maintained in large measure by the nation's undisciplined political parties, which are almost caricatures of the system they serve. The constitutionality of the sharing system has been ratified by United States Supreme Court decisions, which tend to divert questions about the precise measures and forms of sharing from the courts to the political arena. The sharing system is effective because channels of sharing exist that bring some order to the process. These include the constitutionally defined mechanisms of federalism and the mixture of laws that lies at the root of the sharing process.

In a system of this kind, there are perpetual tensions and problems, including a perennial search for balance between the centers of power, a constant need to deal with squeak points in the system, and a continuing effort to harmonize special interests with the general (or national) interest. These problems can lead to antagonistic cooperation between governments (and other elements) in the system, but it is inevitably cooperation, or sharing, nonetheless. The existence of these problems is not a sign of the system's deficiencies but, rather, a reflection of its vigor and health (Grodzins 1966).

By the end of the 1960s, the academic study of cooperative federalism was increasing in sophistication while the theory was being transformed by policymakers in the Washington, D.C., community into what actually was coercive federalism (Elazar et al. 1969; Kincaid 1990a). Policymaking was no longer a matter of basically equal governments cooperating to achieve common ends or to serve the same citizens, but a hierarchical system whereby the federal government was to make policy. If the states and localities did not carry out this policy, they were being "uncooperative" and were subject to federal sanctions. This led, in turn, to a reexamination and rejection of cooperative federalism in both the academic and public affairs communities (Hawkins 1982).[4] In part, this is because the theory was often presented in simplistic ways and with Pollyannaish expectations, with the so-called theoretical discussion rapidly becoming a contest to invent new metaphors for cooperative federalism rather than to develop a systemic theory (Stewart 1984).

As a result, some scholars dismiss cooperative federalism as a passing fad, as an explanation of federalist principles and processes designed as an apologia for New Deal and Great Society centralization, but inadequate operationally as well as normatively. Yet, if critics seriously confronted one of the systematic theories of cooperative federalism, they would have great difficulty maintaining their position.

A SYSTEMIC THEORY OF COOPERATIVE FEDERALISM

Let me begin by laying to rest several simplistic assumptions.

First, "marble cake" is not a theory. Grodzins never used it as a theory but only as a metaphor.[5]

Second, the adjective *cooperative* in *cooperative federalism* does not imply that intergovernmental relations are always peaceful and friendly. Grodzins (1966) used the phrase "antagonistic cooperation" to describe situations in which governments must work together, but not always willingly or in a friendly spirit, or where they pursue different and contradictory goals. *Cooperative* refers to the fact that governments must co-operate, that is, work and function together. It is not a statement of how they work and function together. There can also be coercive cooperation, which is the antithesis of a normative view of cooperation as a matter of mutuality among partners.[6]

Third, cooperative federalism is not a theory that, ipso facto, endorses big government. In principle, cooperative federalism does not relate to the velocity of government per se.

Fourth, the sum and substance of federal theory is not embodied in either dual or cooperative federalism, or in any of the other current slogans.

What, then, is a proper theory of cooperative federalism?

Federalism as a Compact and a Partnership

The starting point of any theory of federalism is to be found in the derivation of the term itself, from the Latin *foedus*, meaning covenant. By definition, federal relationships emphasize partnership between individuals, groups, and governments; cooperative relationships that make the partnership real; and negotiations among the partners as the basis for sharing power. The entire history of the covenant idea in any of its several forms has emphasized these three elements.[7]

The roots of our understanding of cooperative federalism thus lie in the origins of the covenant idea. For Americans, that means looking at the idea's biblical origins through the prism of the Puritans' adaptation of their federal theology to political life, as well as the secular political adaptations of covenant by the British compact theorists (especially Thomas Hobbes and John Locke), Montesquieu, and the philosophers of the 18th-century Scottish Enlightenment. Their ideas matched the realities of American political life in the colonial and revolutionary periods. Much, if not most, of the colonial founding, as well as the national founding, involved entering into covenants and/or compacts by people who saw themselves as equal partners from a political and theological standpoint, embarked on a common errand into the wilderness, and requiring the development of new institutions for survival and for building a city upon a hill.[8]

The realities of American life during the colonial era led to the development of political theories of covenant and compact before Hobbes and Locke—the theories put into practice in various ways from the Mayflower Compact (1620) to the New England Confederation (1643). The result was that the United States was born with a pervasive set of federal principles and practices already in place, and supported by an appropriate political culture, a firm commitment to maintaining the diverse integrities of the various constituents of the union, the constitutional forms for such preservation, and the habit of working together to achieve common ends. All of these elements have continued to inform the American federal system. In turn, they led to the idea of partnership or constitutional noncentralization, whereby power was to be diffused among many centers and the diffusion was to be entrenched and protected constitutionally.

The American system is a federal-state-local-private partnership, a super complex of institutions and actors that combine in different ways in connection with different policy games within the framework of the American constitutional system. The way they share or divide responsibility within those games is the essence of American federalism. This sharing and dividing is determined in part by constitutional arrangements and in part by pragmatic considerations.[9]

Noncentralization differs from decentralization in that decentralization requires a center where decisions are made about what is to be decentralized. Furthermore, those who can decentralize can also recentralize. Noncentralization requires that there be no single center but, rather, a dispersal of power among many centers that must coordinate with one another to make the body politic work. This reality requires us to consider what models are proper for describing federalism and which are not.

The proper model of a federal polity is a matrix of constitutionally equal cells within a common frame. All polities and other inter-organizational arrangements are organized along the lines of one or another of three models: they are either organized as hierarchies, as centers with peripheries, or as noncentralized matrices. Each model is a classic expression of an ideal type. Although elements of the three models may be somewhat mixed in a real polity, in fact, every polity is essentially constituted on the basis of one or another model, which remains its form of government if and until a fundamental reconstitution takes place.

The pyramid is the classic expression of the hierarchical model. Organizational authority and power are distributed among levels linked by a chain of command. The hierarchical model has its origin in some form•of conquest, and the use of force (a possibility in all polities) is implied in its constitution. Thus, it is the military model of government par excellence. It goes without saying that, in the hierarchical model, the top level must be the most important and governs the actions of the lower levels.

The center-periphery model is one in which authority is concentrated in a single center that is more or less influenced by its periphery, depending upon the situation in which the center finds itself. Such polities or organizations tend to develop organically, either around a center or by developing one over time. They tend to be oligarchic in character, with power resting in the hands of those who control the center. Power is either concentrated or dispersed according to decisions made in the center, which may or may not include significant representation from the peripheries.

The matrix model reflects a polity compounded of arenas within arenas held together by common framing institutions (the general, or federal, government) and a shared communications network. Its origins are to be found in the deliberate coming together of equals to establish a mutually useful framework within which all partners can function on an equal basis, usually as defined by a pact. Consequently, the model reflects the fundamental distribution of powers among multiple centers across the matrix, not the devolution of powers from a single center or down a pyramid. Each cell in the matrix represents an independent political actor and an arena for political action. Some cells are large and some are small. The powers assigned to the various cells may reflect that size difference, but no cell is "higher" or "lower" in importance than any other. This matrix organization is quite unlike an organizational pyramid where "levels" are distinguished as higher or lower as a matter of constitutional design.

The matrix model is singularly appropriate for theories of competitive federalism because it clearly demonstrates what is conventionally referred to in the literature as the horizontal divisions within federal systems, offering graphic ways to project their relationships. By presenting the federal government as a framing institution rather than as the center of power or the top of the pyramid, the matrix model emphasizes the interjurisdictional relations among the cells. Thus, analysis based on federalism concepts can be translated into different "power loadings" within the matrix.

Needless to say, each model carries with it certain implications for the organization, distribution, and exercise of power or authority. At the same time, the nature of politics is such that various groups, parties, and interests give the system life. The interaction between them and the institutional framework among them represent the substance of the political process.

The federal government provides the framework uniting the constituent units, each of which has its own governing institutions. In the matrix model, there can be cells within cells, reflecting the various arenas of political and governmental organization. The matrix model reflects the way in which federalism is based on the premise that there are no higher or lower arenas of government, only larger or smaller ones; also, that good fences make good neighbors. At the same time, there must be interaction among the cells if the system is to work. Such interaction is what is referred to generally as cooperative federalism.

The matrix model stands in opposition to the center-periphery and hierarchical models. To the extent that those involved in governance now conceive of the American federal system as a pyramid with federal, state, and local "levels," they have opened the door to the transformation of cooperative federalism into coercive federalism. In any hierarchy, the top is expected to have more authority and power than the middle or the bottom. Such an arrangement contradicts the basic principles of federalism. A proper understanding of the theory of cooperative federalism requires the rediscovery of the authentic theory of federalism, not the center-periphery model characteristic of parliamentary systems or the hierarchical model characteristic of bureaucratic structures.[10]

Much of the shift in intergovernmental relations in the last 20 years results from this conceptual error. Beginning in 1886 with Woodrow Wilson's *Congressional Government* academics proposed the hierarchical and center-periphery models came to replace the original matrix model of the American founders. Those models opened the doors to thinking in decidedly unfederalistic terms, for example, by expecting the federal government to take the lead in areas in which it is not constitutionally expected or entitled to do so. Thus, in measuring the changes in the character of cooperative federalism in different epochs in American history, one needs to look at the strength of the fences within the matrix, how permeable the boundaries between the cells are, and the character of the communications between and among the cells. The matrix model lends itself to a cybernetic understanding of federalism which, as Martin Landau (1973) has argued, is more accurate than any other in describing how a federal system works. In a cybernetic model, what counts are the channels of communication that link the cells. In sum, the federal system is a matrix, not a marble cake; there is real separation between the cells or arenas but, because the smaller cells sit within the larger ones, there also is permeation and intermixture.

Elements of Cooperative Federalism

Cooperative federalism rests, in addition, upon the idea that within the American federal system more interests are shared than not. A dynamic society, such as that of the United States, generates shared public demands. In seeking governmental action, people do not easily distinguish among governmental arenas. Moreover, the nature of the American division of powers almost inevitably requires shared governmental responses if anything is to be done. The alternative would be unilateral action by one arena of government. Experience tells us that the arena likely to assert itself most vigorously is the federal government. For many reasons, were federalism not cooperative, the states and localities would have little defense. That this has not happened is because cooperative federalism has been the norm.

Also central to the idea of cooperative federalism is the notion that cooperation is negotiated. If there is no negotiation, then cooperation becomes either coercive or antagonistic. Negotiated cooperation has two dimensions—sharing and bargaining. Sharing reflects the assumption that intergovernmental cooperation is a good thing. It also assumes that sharing should be patterned and not random. The way to achieve proper patterns of sharing is through bargaining.

In other words, cooperative federalism introduces into a system of government—which like all governments ultimately rests on its ability to resort to the exercise of coercive powers—a marketplace dimension that serves to minimize the amount of coercion exercised and, through negotiation, to maximize the degree of consent. Under such circumstances, the establishment of intergovernmental programs and their funding through intergovernmental transfers are bases, almost licenses, for bargaining.

Viewing the American federal system as the game of games, it is possible to determine how each governmental arena pays the ante to sit in on the game. The federal government uses its superior resources and better ability to attract public attention; the states use their constitutional position as the keystones in the governmental arch; and local governments use their ability to exist as constituted governments, normally with the power to tax, and their direct connections with the citizenry. Once having paid the ante, these governments have the right and the duty to bargain over what is to be shared and how. They are, in essence, "licensed" and expected to do so.

In describing the relationship between all of these elements, another Grodzins metaphor is useful. For the citizen, the system is one of "multiple cracks" in which open access as well as representation are vital parts of the formal as well as informal process of negotiation. All political systems, even the most hierarchical and rigid, have some room for negotiation and bargaining, even if only through "court politics." A key aspect of the American system is that negotiation and bargaining are accepted as legitimate and are conducted openly so as to increase equality of access to the maximum.

The drawback is that through sharing and bargaining, cooperative federalism can become cartel-like. Government officials working together on a continuing basis try to establish monopolies or oligopolies in different games. In reality, these cartels are limited by (1) the existence of the multiple crack, which continually opens new doors for access and influence, (2) frequent elections that change the people involved, and (3) the formal "fences" of separation of powers and arenas.

What is striking about the American system is its essential consistency since the inauguration of the federal government in 1789. That consistency manifests itself in the pervasiveness of sharing as provided by the constitutional framework, with its emphasis on concurrent or cooperative functions—the former open to sharing and the latter requiring it. So pervasive is sharing that even so-called exclusive functions have been shared functions.

Sharing is accomplished through politics, professionalization, and proximity, as well as by design. Although observers tend to focus on the latter mode—namely, the formal intergovernmental programs, as the most visible form of sharing—the other three modes are at least equally important. Today, sharing by design is probably the safest form with regard to the health of the federal system. It is where politics, professionalization, and proximity are involved that coercive elements sometimes come into the picture, precisely because less attention is paid to the necessity to systematize and constitutionalize the sharing that takes place in those areas.[11]

In its 1985 *Garcia* v. *San Antonio Metropolitan Transit Authority* decision, the United States Supreme Court formally endorsed sharing through politics as the only way to protect the states in matters of interstate commerce. Although, in making this decision, the Court may have abdicated its constitutional role, it was correct in its assessment of the empirical reality. Politics, especially congressional politics, has been a major arena for shaping the character of American federalism.

Until the 1960s, the political influence of the states meant that Congress would favor and protect the states in any federal legislation, even in seemingly unilateral federal programs. Subsequently, the political power of local, especially big-city and private interests in Congress, led to a weakening of the states' position in the national political process. Lately, there seems to have been a reversal in the state-local-private balance, but it is accompanied by a Congress that is more assertive of federal powers because its members are less likely than in the past to come from state-oriented political environments and to have experience in state government and politics before entering Congress (Kincaid 1990b). Thus, sharing through politics has undergone possibly substantial changes in the past generation.

However, in one way or another, the cooperative system has reinforced intergovernmental sharing within politics. Thus, if the state political party organizations have lost power in choosing presidents through the primary and caucus system, the people as citizens of their states have become very influential.

Sharing through professionalization was particularly important during the days of governmental expansion, beginning with the New Freedom and accelerated by the New Deal. Professionalization is an extremely important dimension of cooperative federalism, since professionals in various fields share experiences and standards regardless of the governments they serve, and regardless of whether they serve in governmental, public nongovernmental, or even private organizations.

Sharing through proximity ranges from the simplest kind of sharing of services by adjacent governments (e.g., fire-fighting equipment and services) to state involvement in foreign affairs. With reference to the latter, the states have become involved with foreign economic activity because, in their efforts to maintain jobs and strengthen their economies, they have found themselves willy-nilly in proximity to Washington, D.C., in dealing with foreign trade and investment issues. The federal government has recognized this and encouraged further state involvement.[12]

With regard to the varieties of sharing, several typologies are now available to help refine our understanding of cooperative federalism. The simplest division is to examine forms of cooperation as informal collaboration (e.g., conferences and consultations), channels for simple sharing (e.g., crop reports), interchanges of personnel (e.g., police), interdependent activities (e.g., regulation of elections), transfers of payments, grants-in-aid, tax offsets, and shared revenues. On a different level, there is the typology of intergovernmental political relationships developed by Fritschler and Segal (1972): (1) joint policymaking, (2) mutual accommodation, (3) innovative conflict, and (4) disintegrative conflict.

Donald Rosenthal (1980) has suggested yet another way to look at bargaining relationships within cooperative federalism by examining the values inhibiting bargaining, the distributive and regulatory aspects of bargaining, the existence and influence of zones of indifference, the indeterminacy problem, and the floating actor as a factor.

Requisites of Cooperative Federalism

Cooperative federalism is based on four principal requisites:

1. There must be a federalist theory of government. This theory emphasizes a noncentralized approach to governance that combines national supremacy, including broad national legislative and appropriation powers, with maximum local control.

2. There must exist a dualistic governmental structure with separate government institutions for each plane, sufficiently comprehensive so that the states as well as the federal government can be complete governments in their own right. These must be reinforced by a noncentralized, nondisciplined party system that strengthens the noncentralized distribution of power and prevents the de facto concentration of power in a de facto center. Finally, the states and localities must be the primary managers of domestic programs, whether intergovernmental or not.

3. Cooperative federalism must be manifested through specific cooperative programs developed through a system of contractual

relations. In the United States, this has led to a smorgasbord of co-operative programs. Other federal systems are able to maintain co-operative relationships through general revenue-sharing devices. These have not worked in the United States. Rather, they have led to greater centralization as Congress has utilized fiscal assistance to set general conditions binding on state and local governments beyond the conditions required for specific programs.

4. Finally, the system rests on a set of administrative techniques for collaboration, including regular intergovernmental consultation and negotiation, routinized legislative "interference" in program administration, and the development of new or revised programs on a cooperative basis.

It is the combination of these four requisites that makes cooperative federalism viable in the United States.

Changing Patterns of Cooperative Federalism

Although cooperative federalism has been a constant, the character of the federal system has shifted at various times in American history. Any proper theory of cooperative federalism must have a dynamic dimension; in other words, it must be able to track the sources of change in the system. Four basic internal sources of change can be identified: (1) increases or decreases in the velocity of government; (2) the growing complexity and interconnectedness of government activities; (3) the progressive routinization of administrative procedures; and (4) shifts in the character of recruitment into political life. Taken together, the foregoing shape the relative importance of the several planes of government at any given time.

The basis for determining the character of federalism at any particular time is through an examination of the basic trends in American political life, including the forms and fields of intergovernmental collaboration. With this general formula, we can identify four principal periods, each two generations in length: the formative period (1789–1848); the era of national infrastructure development (1848–1913); the period of federal intervention (1913–77); and a new period beginning in 1977 whose character is not yet clear. Each period represents responses to the basic economic, social, political, and intellectual trends in American life at the time, especially as shaped by the then-dominant frontier of development. Each period has developed its own forms of and devices for intergovernmental collaboration, and each emphasized certain fields of cooperative activity as principally important.

Constitutional Basis of American Federalism

One of the principal characteristics of the American system is its emphasis on constitutional design. One of the virtues of cooperative federalism as a theory is that it goes beyond simple concern with constitutional law to treat larger issues of constitutionalism and constitutional design.

A proper theory of cooperative federalism rests on the understanding that a constitution has three components: (1) the frame of government dealing with the governmental and political structure and component institutions; (2) the socioeconomic distribution of power as reflected in the system of games and complexes; and (3) the moral basis of the constitution as reflected in the political culture and norms that shape the people's conceptions of justice. With this in mind, the theory addresses the problem of constitutionalism in a dynamic system, including the role of institutions and structures as related to political behavior, the problem of measuring constitutional change, and the differences between perception and reality. Cooperative federal theory understands that the American constitution consists of the federal and state constitutions together, that the federal Constitution is incomplete without the state constitutions upon which it rests, and that the latter are incomplete without the former (Lutz 1988).

The sources of American constitutionalism are to be found in the colonial charters, covenants, and constitutions and in the early state constitutions adopted at the time of the Revolution, as well as the Articles of Confederation. The Articles of Confederation established the principle that the United States of America came into existence with independence. The Articles also forged the permanent federal linkage of the states. In the case of both the Articles and the Constitution of 1787, the motives of national constitution-making were to make a more perfect federal union. Both documents reflected the founders' understanding of this as coming about through necessary intergovernmental collaboration. The Articles of Confederation required such collaboration because the Confederation government could only operate through the states. To the extent that the Constitution of 1787 deliberately provided for direct connections between the federal government and the citizens of the United States, it introduced a dimension of dual federalism absent in the Articles. Even so, in view of the fact that it provided for so many cooperative or concurrent powers, the idea of dual federalism should not be exaggerated.

Perceptions of the Federal System

Any proper theory of cooperative federalism must also reckon with the perceptions of the system on the part of the general public, political and civic leaders, and disciplined observers. In the case of each of these groups, perceptions come in both abstract and concrete forms, and the two are often contradictory. Thus, among the general public, there is an abstract perception of what Li'l Abner used to call "the gummint" out there without distinction as to plane or arena. On the other hand, there are concrete perceptions derived from political interest, which are almost invariably developed under conditions of conflict. This leads to a perception of the system principally through a conflict model whereby individual governments may appear as separate entities striving for autonomy or blocking some worthy governmental activity.

The abstract perceptions of political and civic leaders tend to be more sophisticated, but, at any given time, to be drawn from the currently conventional model. Thus, in the days of dual federalism, the system was perceived as one in which the federal and state governments each functioned within their own spheres with a minimum of contact and overlapping. Once the cooperative model became the norm, the system began to be seen as a marble cake in which there were no separations between the federal and state governments. When their concrete interests are involved, the perceptions of political and civic leaders tend to shift to one of intergovernmental interaction to a greater or lesser extent, depending on the nature of the issue and the degree and character of the interaction affecting the issue. Their involvement enables them to see this and also to see that the system has elements of both cooperation and conflict.

The disciplined observers were once drawn almost entirely from selected political leaders such as James Madison, Albert Gallatin, and John C. Calhoun, whose special abilities or interests led them to develop disciplined views of the federal system. Today this group generally consists of academics or quasi-academics, such as the staff of the U.S. Advisory Commission on Intergovernmental Relations. They tend to perceive the system as it is in light of their detached observations, but those observations often rest on a conception of what the system ought to be, based on some normative theory, explicit or implicit.

COOPERATIVE FEDERALISM AND THE FUTURE OF THE FEDERAL SYSTEM

Were cooperative federalism the simplistic theory its critics make it out to be, they would certainly be correct in suggesting that it is inadequate to explain the workings of a federal system. A more sophisticated understanding of cooperative federalism, on the other hand, appreciates the theory as a dynamic contruct that can take into account changes in political and administrative behavior and constitutional interpretation. Any appropriate theory must be able to deal with the current problems in the preservation of the system's structural integrity, which are exacerbated by the fact that most decisions affecting the system's structural integrity do not make federalism their primary concern.

Curiously enough, after cooperative federalism became the dominant theory, the question of separate and concurrent powers took a turn that led to a new kind of dual federalism, owing to the full federal preemption of fields previously deemed to be concurrent and the placing of limitations on reciprocal tax immunity.

Where does this leave us with regard to the contemporary distribution of the great constitutional powers? In matters of commerce, the U.S. Supreme Court has abjured any role in determining the boundaries between the federal government and the states. Under present Court doctrine, Congress has plenary powers in matters of interstate commerce, which have been so extended as to include essentially all commerce. More problematic, judicial doctrine has in many cases become a preemptive policy, appropriating fields for the federal government even where Congress has not indicated an intention to do so. Yet, the changing situation of the United States on the world scene has led the states to become increasingly involved in matters of foreign commerce in barely anticipated ways. To sum up, there seem to be few if any barriers to federal intervention in state affairs in matters of interstate commerce, even while there are progressively fewer limitations on state involvement in foreign commerce and economic development.

In the field of individual rights, the Supreme Court under Chief Justice Earl Warren (1953–1969) inaugurated a period of protection of individual rights against all governments, grounded in a doctrine that closely resembled the substantive due process of the Court under Melville Weston Fuller in matters of commerce. That absolutist position has been somewhat eroded during the past two decades but, by and large, the Court still stands behind the restriction of all governments in matters interfering with individual freedom, even to the point of preventing the adoption of certain otherwise useful social policies on a collective basis. In this respect, one might say that neither the federal nor the state governments have the powers they once had, since those powers have flowed to the courts, particularly the U.S. Supreme Court.

With regard to the general welfare, after a generation and a half of federal dominance, a redistribution has been taking place in favor of the states as the federal government has lost the initiative. In part, this has been by public choice, reflecting a strong sense that federal initiatives have been wasteful and unsuccessful, and in part resulting from the more focused and deliberate efforts of President Ronald Reagan. Although this could simply be a cyclical matter (the late 1970s and 1980s are parallel in the cycle of American politics to the late 1940s and 1950s, when state and local activity was more important than federal activity in meeting new challenges), there are signs that it may be more far-reaching. With the growth in the size and resources of the states and the excessive size of the federal government, the states may simply be more capable of responding to new challenges than the federal government, provided the states are not shackled and prevented from doing so. This, indeed, would be a sea change in American government.

Cooperative federalism per se does not lead to fiscal centralization or decentralization. From approximately 1968 to 1979, there was a trend toward fiscal centralization in the federal government's relationship with the states and localities. In the decade following, however, from 1979 to 1989, cooperative federalism persisted despite the Reagan administration's efforts to revive dual federalism. Fiscal centralization diminished, and the thrust was distinctly in the other direction. In essence, decisions regarding fiscal centralization or decentralization stand independently of the existence of cooperative federalism, although the direction of the thrust at any given time certainly influences the character of intergovernmental cooperation.

In terms of state-local relations, cooperative federalism has encouraged an almost uninterrupted fiscal centralization since the early 1930s, the one possible exception being the period between 1946 and 1961. In a sense, this centralization is a reflection of the difference between the federal-state and the state-local relationship. The federal-state relationship is a federal one, whereas states are what might best be described as unions of localities. Although the U.S. Supreme Court has proclaimed states to be unitary governments, most state constitutions include home rule provisions that maintain their states as unions. That is, local governments are constitutionally protected and are granted substantial home rule. Of course, this generalization must be qualified by noting that each state is different. Some states have had no significant fiscal centralization, while others have moved from decentralization to centralization in the past decade.

It seems inevitable that the basic federal-state-local relationship will continue to be cooperative. Ronald Reagan did his best to reintroduce dual federalism of the kind he perceived (correctly or incorrectly) as operative in the towns of northwestern Illinois in his youth, when the historical 19th century (roughly from Waterloo to World War I) was giving way to the 20th. Although Reagan did succeed in reducing many of the coercive elements introduced by his immediate predecessors, the end result was to restore a more truly cooperative federalism than to separate functions as he had intended. This was no mean achievement. On the contrary, it has given new life to American federalism. It has also demonstrated the basic truth of the theory of cooperative federalism.

Today American cooperative federalism is again more like it was intended to be—namely, a means for encouraging nationwide efforts to meet particular problems without national government dominance, and a means for using the federal government as a backstop for state efforts, rather than making the states administrative arms of a dominant Washington, D.C. Indeed, these are the two great operative principles of a properly cooperative federalism.[13] Americans should develop a more sophisticated understanding of cooperative federalism, one that does not allow the call for cooperation to justify a concentration of power in Washington, D.C., or the employment of coercive measures by the federal government against states and localities. Although empirically one can describe that as coerced cooperation, in normative terms it is not cooperation.

Here, in particular, the theory of competitive federalism is helpful as a means of anchoring within the larger framework of federal theory what in cooperative federal theory has been referred to as antagonistic cooperation, while at the same time integrating the new theories of competitive federalism that relate primarily to interstate and interlocal relations. Here one enters the realm of normative theory.

One can accept cooperative federalism on normative grounds and build normative rules for intergovernmental collaboration. These rules would include the maintenance of the fourfold elements of theory, structure, programs, and techniques; the two principles of state initiative and federal backstopping; and perhaps most of all, the principle of federal self-restraint, especially where constitutional barriers have been lifted or substantially reduced by the courts.

Beyond that, a proper theory of cooperative federalism that can be used for normative as well as descriptive purposes must recognize the problem of diversity in a nationalizing society and the social forces that shape political life. If the mass communications media are centralized, then it is very difficult to focus public attention away from Washington and the White House (except for the never-ending presidential campaigns). If the tendency in education, religion, commerce, and industry is toward consolidation, then the states may become even more important bulwarks against the concentration of power than in the past.[14]

At the same time, there seems to be a reversal or a shifting of all these trends toward a deconcentration of power and a growing pluralism in each of these areas. Along with the new pluralism is a new participation, a new desire on the part of the activist stratum in society to be involved in governmental decision making in every arena. This new participation has led to everything from more active involvement in local affairs to an expansion of the use of constitutional choice mechanisms in state affairs. These activists prefer to hold things in their hands, which probably is another force favoring present trends.

All of this has resulted in a new academic and government interest in theories of public and constitutional choice to support new participation. Not surprisingly, there has been a growing integration of theories of cooperative federalism with those of public and constitutional choice, for the mutual benefit of both. The emerging synthesis is giving cooperative federalism a theoretical foundation and a philosophic justification that it has never had in quite the same way.

Notes

1. See, for example, Breton (1985: 486–526).
2. See Elazar (1979).

3. See Sundquist (1969).

4. See also Beer (1973, 1978).

5. See also Elazar (1984).

6. President Richard M. Nixon presented this theory in a paper coauthored with William Safire that was circulated early in his administration as "New Federalist Paper No. 1" under the pseudonym "Publius." This paper and the three responses it drew were published in *Publius: The Journal of Federalism* in 1972. See also Fritschler and Segal (1972) and Rosenthal (1980).

7. This theory was first formulated by me in a comprehensive manner in January 1970 and published in *American Federalism: A Working Outline*.

8. See Elazar (1987c).

9. On games and complexes, see Elazar (1984).

10. On the matrix model, see Elazar (1984, 1987b), where the model is also contrasted with the other two models. See also Landau (1961, 1973), Vincent Ostrom (1969, 1974, 1987), and Elinor Ostrom (1976).

11. Grodzins deals with this in great detail in *The American System* (1966). Although his research is now 30 years old, the picture he paints still stands, except in the case of the political parties where the weakening of the parties-qua-parties requires modification of his analysis.

12. The first comprehensive examination of the role of the states in foreign affairs was that of Dennis Palumbo (1969: 377–87). For a more recent analysis, see John Kincaid (1984).

13. See Elazar (1987a).

14. I dealt with this at length in "Cursed by Bigness or Toward a Post-Technocratic Federalism" (1973).

References

Anderson, William. 1946. *Federalism and Intergovernmental Relations: A Budget of Suggestions for Research.* Chicago: Public Administration Service.

————. 1955. *The Nation and the States: Rivals or Partners?* Minneapolis: University of Minnesota Press.

Beer, Samuel H. 1973. "The Modernization of American Federalism." *Publius: The Journal of Federalism* 3 (Summer): 49–96.

————. 1978. "Federalism, Nationalism, and Democracy in America." *American Political Science Review* 72 (March): 9–21.

Breton, Albert. 1985. "Supplementary Statement." In *Report of the Royal Commission on the Economic Union and Development Prospects for Canada.* Ottawa: Minister of Supply and Services. Reprinted, 1987, as "Towards a Theory of Competitive Federalism." *European Journal of Political Economy* 3: 263–329.

Clark, Jane Perry. 1938. *The Rise of a New Federalism: Federal-State Co-*

operation in the United States. New York: Columbia University Press.

Corwin, Edward S. 1934. *The Twilight of the Supreme Court*. New Haven, Conn: Yale University Press.

————. 1936. *Commerce Power versus States' Rights*. Princeton, N.J.: Princeton University Press.

————. 1937. "National-State Cooperation—Its Present Possibilities." *Yale Law Journal* 46: 599–633.

Elazar, Daniel J. 1970. *American Federalism: A Working Outline*. Philadelphia: Center for the Study of Federalism.

————. 1973. "Cursed by Bigness or Toward a Post-Technocratic Federalism." *Publius: The Journal of Federalism* 3 (Fall): 239–98.

————. 1979. *The Federal Polity*. New Brunswick, N.J.: Transaction Books.

————. 1984. *American Federalism: A View from the States*, 3rd ed. New York: Harper & Row.

————. 1987a. *Building Cities in America*. Lanham, Md.: Hamilton Books.

————. 1987b. *Exploring Federalism*. Tuscaloosa, Ala.: University of Alabama Press.

————. 1987c. "Our Thoroughly Federal Constitution." In *How Federal Is the Constitution?* edited by Robert Goldwin and William Schambra. Washington, D.C.: American Enterprise Institute.

Elazar, Daniel J., R. Bruce Carroll, E. Lester Levine, and Douglas St. Angelo, eds. 1969. *Cooperation and Conflict*. Itasca, Ill.: F. E. Peacock.

Fritschler, A. Lee, and Morley Segal. 1972. "Intergovernmental Relations and Contemporary Political Science." *Publius: The Journal of Federalism* 1 (Winter): 95–122.

Garcia v. San Antonio Metropolitan Transit Authority 1985. 469 U.S. 528.

Grodzins, Morton. 1966. *The American System: A New View of Government in the United States*, edited by Daniel J. Elazar. Chicago: Rand McNally.

Hawkins, Robert B., ed. 1982. *American Federalism: A New Partnership for the Republic*. San Francisco: Institute for Contemporary Studies.

Key, V. O. 1937. *The Administration of Federal Grants to the States*. Chicago: Public Administration Service.

Kincaid, John. 1984. "The American Governors in International Affairs." *Publius: The Journal of Federalism* 14 (Fall): 95–114.

————. 1990a. "From Cooperative to Coercive Federalism." *Annals of American Academy of Political and Social Science* 509 (May): 139–152.

————. 1990b. "How Much Does Federalism Matter in the U.S. Senate?" *Intergovernmental Perspective* 16 (Spring): 35–42.

Landau, Martin. 1961. "On the Use of Metaphor in Political Analysis." *Social Research* 38 (Autumn): 331–53.

————. 1973. "Federalism, Redundancy, and System Reliability." *Publius: The Journal of Federalism* 3 (Fall): 173–96.

Lutz, Donald S. 1988. "The United States Constitution as an Incomplete

Text." *Annals of the American Academy of Political and Social Science* 496 (March): 23–32.

Nixon, Richard M., and William Safire. 1972. "New Federalist Paper No. 1" [and three responses]. *Publius: The Journal of Federalism* 2 (Spring): 98–137.

Ostrom, Elinor. 1976. "Size and Performance in a Federal System." *Publius: The Journal of Federalism* 6 (Summer): 33–74.

Ostrom, Vincent. 1969. "Operational Federalism: Organization for the Provision of Public Services in the American Federal System." *Public Choice* 6 (Spring): 1–17.

————. 1974. "Can Federalism Make a Difference?" *Publius: The Journal of Federalism* 3 (Winter): 197–238.

————. 1987. *The Political Theory of a Compound Republic: Designing the American Experiment.* Lincoln: University of Nebraska Press.

Palumbo, Dennis. 1969. "The States in the Conduct of American Foreign Relations." In *Cooperation and Conflict,* edited by Daniel J. Elazar, R. Bruce Carroll, E. Lester Levine, and Douglas St. Angelo. Itasca, Ill.: F. E. Peacock.

Rosenthal, Donald B. 1980. "Bargaining Analysis in Intergovernmental Relations." *Publius: The Journal of Federalism* 10 (Summer): 45–76.

Stewart, William H. 1984. *Concepts of Federalism.* Lanham, Md.: Center for the Study of Federalism and University Press of America.

Sundquist, James L. 1969. *Making Federalism Work.* Washington, D.C.: Brookings Institution.

Wilson, Woodrow. 1956. *Congressional Government.* Reprinted. New York: Meridian.

Chapter Five

THE COMPETITIVE CHALLENGE TO COOPERATIVE FEDERALISM: A THEORY OF FEDERAL DEMOCRACY

John Kincaid

Current interest in competitive federalism represents another phase in the continuing attempt, especially by Americans and Canadians, to come to grips with federalism in terms compatible with modes of social thought that seem able to address contemporary problems. In this case, the mode of thought is economic theory, the model is the free market, and the central concept is competition. In simple terms, just as competition is a remedy for monopoly in the marketplace, so too is competition a possible remedy for the contemporary problem of American federalism that is variously called big government, centralization, and Leviathan.[1]

Competitive federalism is being viewed more favorably today than in the 1890s, when cooperative federalism was first advanced as a remedy for the social problems created by big business, trusts, combinations, and monopolies. These market failures and their anti-democratic consequences were seen as being intractable so long as the nation's governments were constrained by competition with each other and by the U.S. Supreme Court's notion of dual federalism. The federal system, in the view of many Progressives, had to be transformed into a cooperative commonwealth that would strengthen and unify government, especially to allow the federal government to regulate big business and reintroduce competition into the marketplace (e.g., trustbusting).

Today, the situation is different. Issues such as the savings and loan scandal, the U.S. government's $2.8 trillion debt, and annual interest payments on the debt that exceed annual grants-in-aid to state and local governments suggest that a key problem lies in government failure. Given that most states and many local governments are "big businesses" too, issues of limits and efficiency arise throughout the federal system.

Condoning competition in the public sector is controversial, however, mainly because of concern that competition will (1) unduly limit government's ability to perform redistributive and regulatory functions and (2) trade social equity for public efficiency. Since the rise of cooperative federalism, moreover, competition in the federal system has usually been seen as conflict, and therefore as unhealthy.[2]

Whether, in the midst of intergovernmental stress, competitive federalism can displace cooperative federalism as the normative view of American federalism is a matter of conjecture. Whether competitive federalism should displace cooperative federalism is a matter of concern. The historical experience with cooperative federalism is instructive. Cooperative federalism so thoroughly displaced dual federalism by the 1960s that the constitutional and political barriers to concentrations of power in the federal government that characterized dual federalism were dismantled to the point where it can be argued that cooperative federalism is now yielding to coercive federalism (Kincaid 1990: 139–52). A wholesale embrace of competitive federalism could have its own undesirable consequences.

A theory of effective and benign federalism must, therefore, be more complex. An approach to such a theory can be found in The Federalist, which does not land squarely on dual, cooperative, or competitive federalism. Instead, the political theory of the "compound republic" (The Federalist, nos. 39, 51, and 62) articulated by James Madison, Alexander Hamilton, and John Jay in the late 1780s contains elements of all three conceptions of federalism. The complexity of The Federalist model is due partly to design—the desire to promote republican liberty and commercial prosperity—and partly to differences among the authors, especially Madison's penchant for competition and Hamilton's penchant for centralization. This complexity has enabled interpreters to pick out elements of The Federalist model to support dual, cooperative, or competitive federalism.

The argument to be made here, and drawn from The Federalist, is that federalism is a uniquely dynamic mode of democratic governance in which institutional elements are intentionally held in tension, thus making relationships more important than structure per se. This system has seemingly paradoxical requirements. Cooperation is necessary for competition, and competition is necessary for cooperation. Cooperation is required at the very outset to transform anarchy into competition. Competition is required to prevent the rise of a monopoly government, which would have no incentive to cooperate. In turn, dualism is needed to have cooperative or competitive relationships; that is, there must be two or more semiautonomous governments able to cooperate and compete with each other. These seemingly paradoxical requirements stem from the seemingly contradictory values of federalism: unity and diversity (Elazar 1987)—a theme captured partly by the phrase e pluribus unum.

Dual federalism stresses the need for a constitutional distribution of powers that maintains coordinate, semiautonomous governments able to perform exclusive and concurrent functions. Dualism also recognizes the need for an umpire to referee the competitive and cooperative relations that arise among those coordinate governments. In the American system, the sovereign people, acting through their 51 constitutions, are the final arbiter. Cooperative federalism addresses the need for governments to cooperate and coordinate to perform certain functions and to counteract the centrifugal forces of diversity and competition, which can degenerate into anarchy. Competitive federalism addresses the need for governments to be restrained by more than the "parchment barriers" (The Federalist, nos. 25, 47, 49, 73) of constitutions and to counteract the centripetal forces of unity and cooperation, which can drift into collusion and culminate in monopoly. Both competition and cooperation, however, can promote coordination. Although intergovernmental coordination is usually seen as requiring cooperation, competition also coordinates human activities. Market competitors coordinate even when they do not cooperate.

Before elaborating on this theory, however, two basic distinctions are made in the following two sections.

INTERGOVERNMENTAL AND INTERJURISDICTIONAL COMPETITION

One usually thinks of competition in a federation as being interstate or interlocal, but federal-state-local competition is more important, both for its antimonopolistic effects and for its interactions with interstate and interlocal competition. These two types of competition are designated here as intergovernmental and interjurisdictional.

Intergovernmental competition (sometimes called vertical competition) involves competition between governments having different powers—namely, competition between the federal government and the states, between a state and its local governments, between a county and other local governments within its territory, and between general-purpose and special-purpose local governments.

Interjurisdictional competition (sometimes called horizontal competition) entails competition between governments having comparable powers—namely, competition among states and competition among similar types or classes of local governments—in short, interstate and interlocal competition.

Both types of competition are embedded in federal systems. As one scholar has argued:

> . . . one of the more important features of federal constitutions is their role in constraining the ability of governments to use in an exploitative way the coercive powers that are necessarily given to them. . . . the coercive powers of central governments are, and are intended to be, constrained both by the constitutionally defined limits on their roles and functions and by the fact that they are in effect put into competition with subnational governments that are given essentially equal rights in their own domains and given concurrent access to major revenue sources. The coercive powers of subnational governments are further constrained by their being put into political competition with one another, voters (and businesses) having the power to vote with their feet as well as through the ballot box (Walsh 1989: 219).

Interjurisdictional competition has been subject to criticism at least since the Federalists first sought to create a stronger union. Criticism again became acute in the late 19th century, when certain Progressives sought to enhance federal power to promote a more national, majoritarian democracy better able to serve the common good.[3] With the rise of cooperative federalism, interjurisdictional competition fell into disrepute.

Comparatively little attention has been given to intergovernmental competition, perhaps because: (1) the federal government in the United States and some other federations has become so fiscally and politically predominant as to render intergovernmental competition seemingly obsolete and even dangerous; (2) intergovernmental competition conflicts with the tendency to view federalism as either a cooperative system or a hierarchy of "levels" of government, with higher levels having higher authority and different levels having different responsibilities; and (3) intergovernmental competition even more than interjurisdictional competition runs counter to the drive for national unity characteristic of the age of nation-states.

Nevertheless, intergovernmental competition is a de facto reality in many federal and unitary systems. Where the legitimacy of the national government is weak (e.g., the Soviet Union, Yugoslavia, Nigeria, and India) intergovernmental competition is intense because most constituent governments enjoy more public support than the national government. In the Soviet Union and Yugoslavia, of course, intergovernmental competition was only recently unleashed as a real force because those previously monopolistic regimes only recently abandoned and decentralized certain powers. As a result, these coerced federal unions may dissolve and, in so doing, unveil the fundamental purpose of intergovernmental competition: preventing tyranny and inefficiency. These experiences suggest that when a national government is established with sufficient power to restrain the anarchic tendencies of interjurisdictional competition, then, among other things, provisions should be made for intergovernmental competition to restrain the monopolistic impulses of that national government.

MEDIATED AND UNMEDIATED COMPETITION

Another important distinction is between mediated and unmediated intergovernmental and interjurisdictional competition. Unmediated competition is direct competition between governments in the open market, as when states compete directly for tourists and firms. Mediated competition occurs through the institutions of a government, often a third-party government, as when states compete in the U.S. Congress for grant-in-aid funds, and localities compete in the state legislature for highway funds.

Unmediated competition is not unregulated. The federal and state governments do set ground rules for many facets of such competition. Within those rules, however, outcomes are decided by open competition, not by a government institution picking the winner. Mediated competition, in which a government institution does pick the winner, is largely unregulated. With few formal rules governing state and local lobbying, governments are largely free to win whatever is politically possible.

Models of federalism must account for both forms of competition because losers in unmediated competition are tempted to win through mediated competition. Since the days of the Federalists, critics of unmediated interjurisdictional competition have sought to mitigate that competition by promoting interstate compacts and preempting state and local powers. Limited in their ability to compete directly, however, localities and states will vote with their intergovernmental feet, so to speak, by competing for resources through and from the state and federal governments. Indeed, one scholar has labeled the high point of cooperative federalism as "competitive," precisely because of state and local competition over grant monies in Washington, D.C. (Wright 1988: 81–83).

In assessing the costs and benefits of unmediated competition, therefore, it is important to assess the costs and benefits of mediated competition as well, because there is often an inverse relation between the two. As unmediated competition is reduced, mediated competition is likely to increase. States and localities will feel even more pressed to compete in the Congress for resources. A typical but also unusual case, because it provoked controversy, was a $500,000 fiscal year 1991 congressional appropriation to Strasburg, North Dakota, to develop Lawrence Welk's birthplace into a tourist attraction (Kenworthy 1990). A key question, then, is whether legislative lobbying, logrolling, and pork barreling produce more efficient outcomes than, say, state and local tax incentives offered to businesses in open-market competition.

Mediation of federal-state competition is highly charged politically because there is no true third party. Federal-state competition is mediated in the Congress, the executive branch, and the U.S. Supreme Court—long viewed as the "umpire" of the federal system. Hence, there is a question of partiality because federal institutions have interests in expanding their own powers. All such expansions need not occur at the expense of states, because society and the economy expand too, but in a system of shared and divided powers, issues of encroachment do introduce elements of zero-sum competition.

State-local competition is often mediated in Washington, D.C., as well. Since the 1890s, local governments have competed with states for access to Washington. Under President Lyndon B. Johnson's Creative Federalism in the mid-1960s, local governments were finally legitimized as the "third partner" in the federal system, thus enabling them to bypass states and go directly to Washington. More federal funds flowed directly to local coffers, and local officials often obtained leverage over state officials through conditions attached to federal grants.

The states objected to this bypassing. In 1978, the governors petitioned President Jimmy Carter to stop "the ongoing attempts to bypass state governments." The governors argued "that the issue here is not competition between state and local governments, but rather the most effective management of government and the use of scarce public resources" ("A Letter to the President" 1979). Although Carter's New Partnership was aimed at helping distressed communities, since 1978, direct federal aid to local governments has declined sharply. Under the New Federalism of the 1980s, President Ronald Reagan virtually ignored local officials. Under President George Bush, local governments have had only limited success in trying to reclaim their status as "third partner."

FEDERAL DEMOCRACY AND COMPETITION

With these distinctions in mind, I turn now to the origins and theory of federal democracy, and to the roles of competition, cooperation, and dualism.

A *federal democracy* can be defined as a constitutional union of separate democratic polities (e.g., states) within an overall democratic polity in which power is distributed and shared "among general and constituent governments in a manner designed to protect the existence and authority of both" (Elazar 1984: 2). In contrast to a *unitary democracy*, which relies on national majority rule, a federal democracy relies on complex majoritarianism in which (1) separate majorities have self-governing authority within the constituent polities, (2) national majority rule is constitutionally and structurally limited (i.e., Madison's "extended republic"), and (3) extraordinary majority consent is required to change constitutional rules (e.g., three-fourths of the states). A federal democracy, therefore, seeks to avert, according to Madison, the principal "diseases" of unitary democracy, namely, majority tyranny or a Leviathan erected in the name of the people. Given diverse constituent majorities and limited national majoritarianism, a federal democracy requires cooperation to produce adequate governance and maintain itself. Competition, as will be seen, is a more complex requirement.

Covenants and Competition

The word *federal* comes from the Latin *foedus*, meaning *covenant*. As such, federalism connotes cooperation, but it also requires dualism and elicits competition. The paradigmatic Western covenant, that between God and the federated tribes of Israel at Sinai, did not create a unitary entity. It established a dynamic perpetual relationship characterized by dualism (i.e., God and Israel are not one being), cooperation (e.g., Israel is led to the promised land), and competition (e.g., Israel periodically worships idols), as well as conflict and apostasy. These ever-present facets of the covenantal relationship provide much of the drama of the Hebrew Bible.

The biblical idea of covenant, which was revived as a theological and political concept by Reformed Protestants in the 16th century, served as a reactive backdrop for three influential secular theories of covenanted political life in the modern era (Kincaid and Elazar forthcoming).

The first theory was the Leviathan model developed by Thomas Hobbes (1651). In this theory, humans are driven into a civil covenant, which establishes a monolithic regime that enforces the covenant because individuals cannot be relied on to honor their covenants voluntarily. Anarchy is the evil Hobbes sought to defeat with Leviathan. Hence, dualism, competition, and even cooperation are excluded from his regime.

The second theory was the now classic, liberal democracy model developed by John Locke (1690), who rejected Hobbes's Leviathan as tyrannical. In Locke's theory, humans willingly consent to a civil compact, which establishes a liberal majoritarian regime characterized by cooperation based on mutual advantage, competition within democracy and the economy, and dualism between "state" and "society." Tyranny and penury—both functions of political and economic monopoly—are the evils Locke sought to defeat through the bourgeois, parliamentary, protocapitalist polity.

The third theory was the communal model developed by Jean-Jacques Rousseau (1762). In this theory, humans wake up to their exploitation by civilization, especially the institution of private property, and consent to a social contract that establishes a communal polity governed by the people's General Will. Competition and dualism are not so much excluded by this model as rendered irrelevant by the General Will. Tyranny and alienation are the evils Rousseau sought to defeat with pacific communalism.

The practical fates of these theories reveal something about the political value of competition. Hobbes's anticompetitive Leviathan has little normative appeal because its built-in monopoly power is a recipe for tyranny. Most nation-states in the modern era—from the absolute monarchies to more recent fascist, communist, military, and one-party dictatorships—have been ruled by Leviathan-like regimes.

Rousseau's noncompetitive communal democracy has had considerable appeal. History has produced many visions, including Marxism, of the communal society that heals the hostilities and alienation that produce anarchy and monopoly. Yet, no noncompetitive democracy has ever been institutionalized in a nonauthoritarian manner in societies larger than a village or town. Even village democracy is often either more adversarial or more stultifying than it appears to be on the surface.

A key problem is that Leviathan and communalism define competition as conflict arising from egoism and alienation; hence, they drive competition out. "Competition of riches, honor, command, or other power," wrote Hobbes ([1651] 1958: 87), "inclines to contention, enmity, and war." By excluding competition, however, these models also exclude cooperation and dualism. Cooperation signifies a relationship between entities capable of noncooperation—of divorce (or secession), competition, or conflict. Thus, Leviathan subordinates the individual will to that of the sovereign, whereas communalism merges the individual will with the General Will. There is no dualism to give rise to cooperation or competition. Although both models presuppose that a person cannot surrender basic rights (e.g., to life), in the end, liberty for Hobbes lies in "the silence of the law" and for Rousseau, in the harmonious oneness of the individual will and the General Will.

Only Locke's model, with later modifications, has survived as a theoretical underpinning for polities characterized, in reasonable degrees, by liberty, democracy, and prosperity. Locke held that competition is not necessarily conflict, and that egoism channeled in productive directions can reduce alienation. However correct or appealing in principle, the Leviathan and communal models promote monopoly. For Locke, liberty lies in the protection of individual rights. This protection is grounded in the competition and cooperation necessitated by electoral democracy as well as in the competition and coordination required for economic prosperity.

Competition and Democracy

The controversy over competitive federalism is somewhat puzzling, therefore, because competition has long been viewed as essential for liberal democracy (Schumpeter 1942). Competition for wealth, power, and prestige restrains the hierarchical tendencies, evident in all polities, for goods and power to be monopolized by the few—the antithesis of democracy, which is rule by the many. If the many cannot compete against the few (as in Leviathan), then democracy is subverted by the tyranny of the minority. If the few cannot compete against the many (as in communalism), then democracy is subverted by the tyranny of the majority. In either case, argued Madison (like Locke before him), the cure is to stimulate competition, in part by organizing political life so that ambition will "counteract ambition" (*The Federalist*, no. 51). Such competition keeps wealth, power, and prestige fluid. In effect, competition in a democracy undercuts monopolies organized by the few and cartels organized by the many.

Virtually every liberal democracy rests on majoritarian adherence to six covenants of competition:

☐ Party competition (maintained by the right to vote and affiliate);
☐ Interest-group competition (maintained by rights of speech, press, association, and petition);
☐ Competition between the sacred and the secular (maintained by religious freedom and non-establishment);
☐ Competition between the government and its citizenry (maintained by state-society dualism and restrictive rules of treason);
☐ Competition between the public and private sectors (maintained by limited government and property rights); and
☐ Competition in the economic marketplace (maintained by various public devices, including limited government).

Of these six types of competition, only the last two have been subject to significant controversy since settlement of the religious question. Many theorists hold that the first four types of competition sufficiently protect democracy, and that a popularly elected government should be free to limit and regulate economic competition. Others argue that economic competition is detrimental to democracy because it immiserates a portion of the population, and effectively disenfranchises lower classes. For other theorists, however, capitalist competition goes hand in hand with democracy, linking individualism and liberty in the private sector to individualism and liberty in the public sector, thus supplying another social foundation for democracy. It has also been argued that the very pluralism and competitiveness of democratic institutions promote economic growth (Baechler 1975; Berman 1983; Hayek 1988; Jones 1981; Rosenberg and Birdzell, Jr. 1986). Key concerns, then, are whether expansions of government power to regulate economic competition can place the "state" in a monopoly position in society, depressing both democracy and prosperity.

Economic and public-private competition, therefore, have occupied a more ambiguous position in the modern democratic tradition. In the United States, the state constitutional tradition, although not hostile to economic competition, has always shown a willingness to intervene in market affairs. For much of American history, the U.S. constitutional tradition was associated with protections of private property and the promotion of domestic capitalist commerce. The

U.S. Constitution was intended, in part, to lower state barriers to free trade so as to establish a common market in which entrepreneurial competition could undercut mercantilistic interjurisdictional competition. The commerce clause, therefore, gives the Congress unqualified authority to regulate interstate and foreign commerce, but not commerce simply (i.e., intrastate commerce). Congressional authority to regulate commerce "among the several States" was directed not at market failure but at government failure, namely, "the conflicting, and often ruinous regulations of the different States" (Story [1840] 1986: 140).

In short, modern democracy is inconceivable without competition. Competition is not an accidental or undesirable by-product of democracy; it is a constitutionally protected value. Competition, therefore, must be considered within this constitutional framework, and not only in terms of economic efficiency, because the primary purpose of competition in democratic theory is to protect liberty.

Competition and Federal Democracy

Because of its constitutional distribution of powers between governments, federalism adds two other forms of competition to democracy: intergovernmental and interjurisdictional. Although the creation of the American federal system was, in part, a practical concession to 13 powerful states, a logic lay behind it. That logic included: (1) preventing one party or faction from monopolizing or "cartelizing" power nationwide or regionally; (2) preventing any one government from monopolizing power nationwide or regionally; (3) allowing governments to check and balance each other; (4) providing citizens with multigovernmental and multijurisdictional choices for advancing their interests; (5) establishing unity while preserving diversity; and (6) enhancing national as well as local self-government.

American federal democracy, however, institutionalizes competition more thoroughly than most federations because it adds (1) intragovernmental competition (i.e., the separation of powers), (2) intrainstitutional competition (e.g., bicameralism in the Congress and 49 state legislatures), and (3) dual legislative authority where initiative, referendum, and/or recall rules allow citizens themselves to make law or unseat lawmakers.

A major function of these arrangements, according to Madison, is to "render an unjust combination of a majority of the whole very improbable." Working properly, a federal system with separations of powers within governments ensures that "a coalition of a majority of the whole society [will] seldom take place on any other principles than those of justice and the general good" (*The Federalist*, no. 51). In the view of *The Federalist*, one cannot rely entirely on extraconstitutional competition, such as party and interest-group competition, to preserve liberty; one must also build competition into the constitutional structure so that all government instrumentalities cannot easily be captured by forces eager to suppress competitors.

At the same time, competition bolsters cooperation. At base, a federal democracy is a voluntary association of persons and jurisdictions. The right of persons to emigrate is fundamental. However, because emigration is costly, citizens must have effective choices within the polity. Here, competition performs a dual function. It allows citizens to migrate from one group or jurisdiction to another in search of satisfaction, and it encourages public and private institutions to satisfy their constituents so that they stay put voluntarily. Governments and their component institutions are rendered cooperative because competition compels them to focus on their respective missions and constituencies, and to appeal continually for public support.

Some federations also permit jurisdictions to emigrate (i.e., secede). Secession, however, hedges the federal covenant and continually threatens a union's life. Americans, since the Civil War, have viewed their union as perpetual (as stipulated in the Articles of Confederation). The federal union, argued Abraham Lincoln in his first inaugural address, is like a regular marriage, except that there can be no divorce. For him, "secession is the essence of anarchy." Without a right of divorce, however, the constituent jurisdictions must be protected "by constitutional checks and limitations" against formation of a national monopoly power, namely, "despotism."

Lincoln's point is often overlooked. The Union's victory did not ensure the supremacy of the national government, which would have made it the monopoly party to the federal covenant; it ensured the perpetuity of the union, of the covenantal relationship itself. As the U.S. Supreme Court held in 1869: "The Constitution, in all its provisions, looks to an indestructible Union, composed of indestructible States" (*Texas* v. *White* 1869). In short, competition is a barrier to monopoly, which can drive a federal union into tyranny or provoke anarchy.

Given that the United States has some 83,217 governments, that approximately 38,000 of those governments embody a separation of powers, and that party and interest-group competition, public-private competition, and denominational and economic competition operate on those governments, the potential for competition is astronomical.

A THEORY OF FEDERAL DEMOCRACY

The formation of federal democracy in the United States was shaped significantly by the teachings of John Locke and by the indigenous covenantal political tradition extending back to the Mayflower Compact (formally a covenant) of 1620 (Lutz 1980: 101–33). In terms of competition and cooperation, Locke's teachings fall on the side of competition and individualism, whereas the covenantal tradition falls on the side of cooperation and communitarianism. These conceptions underlie what one scholar has termed the tension in American political culture between "marketplace" and "commonwealth" visions of the good polity (Elazar 1984: 112).

Anarchy versus Monopoly in Federalism and Antifederalism

These conceptions also underlay differences between the Federalists and Anti-Federalists. The former argued for a competitively structured federal republic rooted in individualism; the latter argued for a cooperatively structured confederal republic rooted in communitarianism. Although the Federalists gained the upper hand, the U.S. Constitution—with the Bill of Rights added at Anti-Federalist insistence—institutionalized both conceptions. The general (i.e., United States) government is structured along Federalist lines, though not to the degree desired by Madison and Hamilton. The states are free to structure their political systems along Anti-Federalist lines, though not with the degree of freedom desired by many Anti-Federalists who believed that the new government would become a "consolidated" monopoly.

In essence, the Federalists were concerned with anarchy, which they saw as the effectual condition of the Confederation. Hence, *The Federalist* depicts horrendous hostility, conflict, and competition among the states. The Anti-Federalists were concerned with monopoly, which they saw lurking in the proposed constitution. Consequently, using equally inflated rhetoric, they portrayed the constitutional plan as an imperialistic plot that would, in Patrick Henry's words, "destroy the state governments, and swallow the liberties of the people" (in Tyler [1887] 1962: 324).

At the same time, the Federalists saw a different monopoly problem. Because the states and their citizens could not be compelled by confederal law to support the union fiscally or militarily, or to restrain their economic and potential military competition, the states held a monopoly position that put the confederation at the mercy of their goodwill. Being in a monopoly position, the states were not especially cooperative. For example, of $15,670,000 requested by the confederal Congress between 1781 and 1786, only $2,419,000 was contributed by 11 states (Ferguson and McHenry 1967: 52).

Some Federalists, especially Madison, saw still another monopoly problem: tyranny in the states. Madison argued that communitarian republicanism often degenerated into factional strife, or produced nothing more than a tyranny of the majority or of a clever minority. Hence, *The Federalist* paints a bleak picture of democracy and competence in the states. In turn, state-based tyranny exacerbated anarchy in the confederation.

Some Anti-Federalists, however, saw anarchy in Madison's vision of ambition counteracting ambition. They predicted that such individualistic competition in the proposed "consolidated" government would degenerate into a naked scramble for power and its economic benefits. Republican virtue would be subverted by aggressive egoism, rational deliberation would succumb to raw competition, and the states would be undone by interest-group factionalism. In the end, either the republic would explode from factionalism or power would be consolidated nationally by a Leviathan faction.

Competition and Cooperation versus Monopoly and Anarchy

The Federalists realized that implementation of their constitutional plan required an extraordinary act of cooperation. To obtain the consent of the people through their states, the Federalists had to steer between these complex concerns about anarchy and monopoly.

The U.S. Constitution addresses the problem of anarchy, as manifested in unmediated and unregulated interjurisdictional competition, in three basic ways. First, the Constitution gives the federal government civil and criminal authority over persons, thus enabling it to enforce its laws, regulate interjurisdictional competition, and compete directly with state governments for public esteem, tax resources, policy supremacy, and other goods. This, more than the policy powers delegated to the federal government, is one of the great innovations of the U.S. Constitution.[4] Second, the policy powers delegated to the federal government fall into two areas most adversely affected by unbridled interjurisdictional competition: (1) national defense and foreign affairs and (2) union land and commerce. The Federalists believed that such competition had ruinous consequences for Americans' "political prosperity" because it weakened national defense, posed a constant danger of civil war, and thwarted economic development. The federal government's policy powers, therefore, allow it to act unilaterally in some cases and to preempt some state powers to preserve the union and its common market. Third, the U.S. Constitution permits and requires, in some cases, the federal government to mediate interjurisdictional competition that spills over into conflict.

The U.S. Constitution did not abolish competition or the constituent competitors (i.e., the states); instead, it created a countervailing power able to regulate interjurisdictional competition and compete directly with state governments. As such, the U.S. Constitution deprived states of their monopoly position, but did not elevate the federal government to a monopoly position. Both parties to the covenant were obliged to compete and cooperate to achieve many of their objectives.

The U.S. Constitution addresses the problem of intrastate monopoly political establishments in a variety of ways. First, by creating a countervailing power, the Constitution allows citizens to migrate intergovernmentally to seek redress from the federal government for certain grievances against states. Such migration became a flood after the 1920s when the U.S. Supreme Court began "incorporating" much of the U.S. Bill of Rights into the Fourteenth Amendment (1868). Second, by having state governments surrender certain military and economic powers, the U.S. Constitution deprives intrastate factions of key tools of monopolistic domination. Third, the Constitution guarantees each state a republican form of government (Art. IV, Sec. 4). Fourth, such provisions as the full-faith-and-credit clause and such prohibitions on the states as nonimpairment of the obligations of contracts and no granting of titles of nobility all weaken monopolistic opportunities.

The U.S. Constitution did not, in part because it could not, assault intrastate tyranny across the board—slavery being the conspicuous example. Even after the Civil War amendments to the U.S. Constitution, the federal government not only declined to disturb white supremacy for nearly a century but upheld it (*Plessy v. Ferguson* 1896). Furthermore, for much of the late 19th and early 20th centuries, most states had one-party regimes, although the federal government also remained under one-party control for long periods.

Having addressed interjurisdictional competition and intrastate monopoly politics, the Federalists also had to address Anti-Federalist concerns, as well as problems created by the constitutional plan. During the ratification debates, the Federalists sought to assuage their opponents' fears. Hamilton wrote, for example, "that the State governments will too naturally be prone to a rivalship with that of the Union . . . and that in any contest between the federal head and one of its members, the people will be most apt to unite with their local government" (The Federalist, no. 25).

Anti-Federalist fears of national monopoly power are addressed in numerous ways. One is through the constitutional checks and limitations placed on the federal government, which possesses limited, delegated powers, which, in turn, are separated and shared among three branches. The Bill of Rights, especially the Tenth Amendment, amplified these limits because, originally, it applied only to the federal government. Second, the states make up the Congress, and are indirectly represented in the executive and judicial branches. Third, certain restrictions are placed on federal powers, in part to protect the states (e.g., "No Tax or Duty shall be laid on Articles exported from any State" [Art. I, Sec. 9]). Fourth, the provision for admitting new states to the union implies that the federal government cannot hold territories as conquered provinces and, therefore, as sources of wealth to enhance national power. On the contrary, land grants became the first grants-in-aid to states, and were among the earliest expressions of cooperative federalism. Finally, if states believe that the balance of power has shifted decidedly to the federal government, they can appeal to the people, the only third-party umpire available for federal-state contests, by asking the Congress to call a constitutional convention.

However, as The Federalist argued, constitutional provisions are mere "parchment barriers" to monopoly. Auxiliary barriers are needed in the form of structures rooted in, but not wholly dependent on, the Constitution. The first is Madison's famous theory of the extended federal republic in which factions are so diverse, so dispersed, and so institutionally constrained as to make a monopoly power grab virtually impossible (The Federalist, especially nos. 10, 51). The second is to divide power within and between governments so as to stimulate competition by giving officeholders incentives to exercise power as well as selfish motives to protect their power against other power centers. "In the compound republic of America," wrote Madison, the power surrendered by the people is first divided between two distinct governments, and then the portion allotted to each sub-divided among distinct and separate departments. Hence a double security arises to the rights of the people. The different governments will control each other, at the same time that each will be controlled by itself (*The Federalist*, no. 51).

The theory of federal democracy developed in *The Federalist*, then, regards intergovernmental competition as a key structural barrier to monopoly, not only on the part of the federal government but also on the part of the states (as during confederation). Through the U.S. Constitution, the Federalists sought to supply the general government with sufficient powers and incentives to compete against the parochial loyalties and centrifugal forces of the states. This feat first required an act of voluntary cooperation, namely, ratification of the Constitution. In turn, by establishing a competitive relationship rather than another monopoly power, the U.S. Constitution created pressure for intergovernmental cooperation.

Madison carried the competitive argument a step farther by welcoming intergovernmental competition in a kind of public-choice fashion.

If . . . the people should in future become more partial to the federal than to the State governments, the change can only result from such manifest and irresistible proofs of a better administration, as will overcome all their antecedent propensities. And in that case, the people ought not surely to be precluded from giving most of their confidence where they may discover it to be most due; but even in that case the State governments could have little to apprehend, because it is only within a certain sphere that the federal power can, in the nature of things, be advantageously administered (*The Federalist*, no. 46).

At the same time, the Federalists seemed to recognize the limits of competition and cooperation. Competition on every front would be debilitating, whereas cooperation on every front would be impossible. Thus, there is a dualistic distribution of exclusive and concurrent powers that allows the federal and state governments to carry out essential functions, such as taxation, independently.

These solutions to the problems of anarchy and monopoly produced two other problems, however. One is the problem of federal neutrality with respect to continuing interjurisdictional competition. This is addressed through such constitutional provisions as equal representation of the states in the U.S. Senate and the requirement that "no preference shall be given by any Regulation of Commerce or Revenue to the Ports of one State over those of another" (Art. I, Sec. 9). The second problem is that of reducing incentives for persons and jurisdictions to compete in the Congress for resources because of federal restraints on interjurisdictional competition. This problem is addressed through bicameralism in the Congress, the separation of powers, fixed and relatively short terms of elected office (also to promote electoral competition), and limits on federal powers, especially revenue-raising powers (prior to the Sixteenth Amendment of 1913).

Economic Competition and Political Prosperity

More fundamentally, by establishing a competitive relationship limiting both federal and state powers, the Federalists endeavored to channel some of the competitive and rent-seeking energies of citizens into the private sector by depriving them of certain governmental opportunities for wealth-getting. If the Constitution could make it impossible to compete for military power and less rewarding to use government to compete for wealth, then ambitions would be diverted, to that extent, from rent-seeking careers in government to entrepreneurial careers in a national market, thus unleashing forces needed to raise everyone's living standard, and also blunting fears that individualistic competition in an extended republic would produce a naked scramble for power.

Thus, the Federalist desire to restrain anarchic interjurisdictional competition in the 1780s was tied to a larger constitutional scheme of creating an extended commercial republic of peace, prosperity, and liberty. By restraining interjurisdictional competition, the U.S. Constitution would not only mute beggar-thy-neighbor state policies and prevent fratricidal war but also minimize the ability and incentive for citizens to use state government to acquire wealth and power over each other and the citizens of other states. This, in turn, would reduce men's propensity to treat state power as an economic prize, and would open state government to broader citizen participation.

By creating a stronger federal government, but still one of limited, delegated powers, the Federalists also endeavored to keep relatively small the number and value of national prizes available to rent seekers. Further, given that nearly all of the policy powers delegated to the federal government are either common-interest powers (i.e., national defense and foreign affairs) or common-market powers (i.e., interstate and foreign commerce), the Federalists sought to channel the exercise of national power away from policies that benefit insular interests and toward policies that benefit general interests. It is partly because of the anticipated effects of these provisions that the authors of *The Federalist* argued that "fit characters" rather than rent seekers would be more attracted to federal offices.

Continuing Interjurisdictional Competition

Finally, the Federalists did not find it desirable to abolish interjurisdictional competition. For one thing, abolition would transform unmediated competition into mediated competition. The federal government is designed to mediate interstate conflict (e.g., over state boundaries and navigation on interstate waterways) and to set ground rules for interstate competition, but not to be a major mediator of that competition. Second, abolition of interjurisdictional competition would require such an expansion of federal powers and deprivation of state powers as to place the federal government in a monopoly position. Thus, indirectly, interjurisdictional competition complements the antimonopoly functions of intergovernmental competition. Third, interjurisdictional competition diverts state attention to some degree from intergovernmental competition—a major concern for the Federalists because most believed that the new federal government would be competitively weak for some time. Thus, interjurisdictional competition relieves some of the pressure that would otherwise heat up both intergovernmental competition and federal mediation of interjurisdictional competition. Fourth, interjurisdictional competition, especially for economic resources, pressures state and local governments to perform more efficiently and attract immigrants—a major concern of those Federalists who envisioned a continental republic.

In certain respects, then, the U.S. Constitution encourages interjurisdictional competition so as to reduce monopolistic tendencies and promote economic growth. The privileges-and-immunities clause is a Tiebout-like mechanism (Tiebout 1956), later expanded by U.S. Supreme Court guarantees of the right to travel. Reapportionment of the U.S. House of Representatives after each decennial census rewards states that attract residents. The admission of new states increases the number of competitors (by 285 percent since 1789) in the multijurisdictional marketplace, stimulating similar dynamics locally. On average, for example, a unit of local government has been created or abolished every hour of every working day during the past 50 years.

In summary, the theory of federal democracy sketched here is, to paraphrase Madison, a compound of competition and cooperation. Cooperation among independent states creates a union in which a general government and constituent governments are intentionally held in dualistic tension. The principal purpose is to protect liberty by creating unity out of anarchy, while not destroying liberty and diversity by monopoly. Monopoly is the more acute danger, however, because the insecurity of anarchy can drive people into cooperation. Persons in a monopoly position have no incentive to cooperate and every incentive to suppress competition. Thus, intergovernmental and interjurisdictional competition within a covenantal framework perform an antimonopoly function that creates conditions conducive to intergovernmental and interjurisdictional coordination and cooperation.

FROM COMPETITION TO COOPERATION

If competition is central to the design of American federal democracy, then why the normative emphasis on cooperation today? The root answer is market failure. The old Federalists of the 1780s were preoccupied with massive government failure under the Articles of Confederation. The new Federalists emerging in the 1890s were preoccupied with massive market failure induced, in part, by flaws in the old Federalists' design. A key problem was that the U.S. Constitution produced what Alexis de Tocqueville called "an incomplete national government" ([1835] 1969: 157). The new Federalists, therefore, set out to complete the founders' handiwork.

The campaign for cooperative federalism had many facets, so I can focus on only a few most relevant to competition. Essentially, by the late 19th century, the competition built into the political system by federalism and the separation of powers came to be seen as vices that fragment power, making it difficult for government to counteract a gigantic market failure: the rise of economic monopolies and cartels, which created vast inequalities of wealth and power. Consolidation of private wealth and the apparent transfer of power from the public to the private sector were seen as requiring a countervailing consolidation of power in the public sector and a transfer of wealth from private to public hands.

The states were seen as increasingly obsolete in the face of an expanding *national* economy (Laski 1939: 367–69). States could not control large corporations individually, or coordinate regulation among themselves. Interjurisdictional competition, moreover, undercut each state's power, allowing "robber barons" to divide and conquer state governments. Reformers also argued that interjurisdictional competition diminished social equity, as in the case of "competition in convict-made goods." Alone, each state was "powerless to prevent the dumping upon it of goods made in the prisons of other states" and, thus, to prevent "the products of prison labor from competing unfairly with those made by free men" (Clark 1938: 124).

Intergovernmental competition was especially criticized because it was so successful. It did more than prevent formation of a national monopoly power; it debilitated what reformers now called the "national" government. This perception contributed to the appeal, for example, of Charles Beard's argument in 1913 that the Federalists were economic elites who designed the U.S. Constitution to advance their class interests. The intergovernmental competition embedded in dual federalism was seen as blocking government action. The "relationship which . . . prevailed with the [Supreme] Court [under dual federalism] was a competitive conception," wrote a prominent legal scholar. Given that "the National Government and the states [were seen] as rival governments bent on mutual frustration," it was "the supreme duty of the Court to maintain the two centers of government in theoretical possession of their accustomed powers, however incapable either might be in fact of exercising them" (Corwin 1941: 98).

Although there were many calls to nationalize the federal system, cooperative federalism prevailed because, politically, a consolidation of federal power could not be advanced under the name of centralization or socialism. As President Theodore Roosevelt said in his last State of the Union address, enhancement of national power "does not represent centralization." In 1910, Woodrow Wilson expressed as a basic tenet of his New Freedom: "Cooperation amidst variety is what we seek." Jane Perry Clark summarized the case in 1938 in *The Rise of a New Federalism*: "Cooperation between the federal and state governments is one solution of the difficulties caused by the governmental attempt to regulate the centripetal forces of modern industrial life and the centrifugal elements of state interest and tradition" (p. 7)—in short, oppressive monopoly in the private sector and paralyzing anarchy in the public sector.

Reformers promoted cooperation in two basic ways. One was to increase the competitive position of citizens against both corporate and party bosses by, for example, allowing them to organize unions and vote in primary elections so as to exert greater control over parties, elected officials, and corporations. This approach also produced a major change in the operation of federalism: the direct election of U.S. senators in 1913 so as to free them from the clutches of state legislatures corrupted by big business. The second approach was to enhance the competitive position of government against business by increasing the power of the national government—mainly through a strong presidency, a professional bureaucracy, and an activist judiciary—and by giving the national government revenue-raising authority to extend its reach and redistribute income. This approach resulted in another major change in federalism: the federal income-tax amendment of 1913.

Thus, the private sector was to be made more internally competitive and business rendered more socially cooperative by a strong national government composed of popularly elected officials, backed by unions and other public-interest groups, funded by a progressive income tax, and operated by professional administrators. The separation of powers was to be made cooperative by a strong president embodying the national will and backed by professional bureaucrats and a united party anchored in the general electorate. Federalism was to be made cooperative by expanded national power coupled with grants-in-aid (i.e., carrot-and-stick federalism), which were deemed necessary in an era when states' rights had strong appeal. Cooperative federalism also aimed to prevent disastrous and cut-throat competition, induce state implementation of national policies, and allow the national government to preempt state authority, all while preserving state administrative responsibility—another concession to states' rights.

Underlying this vision of cooperative federalism was a rejection of the complex majoritarianism of *The Federalist* in favor of national majority rule as the legitimate expression of the public good. Cooperative federalism, therefore, leaned toward a decentralized unitary democracy in which policymaking would be lodged in the national government, and implementation would be the province of state and local governments. About this time, reformers began to speak of "levels" of government and of state and local governments as "service deliverers." The emphasis on national majority rule also led to an emphasis on a strong presidency—a trend that lasted until the rise of "the imperial presidency" of the Johnson-Nixon years (Schlesinger 1973). Other reformers advocated parliamentary democracy as a way to surmount the competitive impediments to national majority rule posed by federalism and the separation of powers.

Despite the emphasis on majority rule, cooperative federalists also turned to the least democratic branch, the U.S. Supreme Court—the bastion of dual federalism. Given the extraordinary votes required for constitutional amendments (which enable minorities to defeat a majority), reformers advanced the idea of a "living Constitution" subject to creative interpretation. When, after President Franklin D. Roosevelt tried to pack the Court, the justices held that the Tenth Amendment to the U.S. Constitution "states but a truism" (*United States* v. *Darby* 1941), dual federalism came to an end, thus dropping barriers to expanded federal power. This trend was powerfully reinforced by the civil rights revolution, which so discredited the states and, thereby, federalism, as to lead one scholar to write that "if in the United States one disapproves of racism, one should disapprove of federalism" (Riker 1964: 155). Then, when the Court accelerated its nationalization of the U.S. Bill of Rights, thus lending strong legitimacy to the entitlements revolution of the 1960s and its broad distribution of benefits to citizens, cooperative federalism reached its peak.

FROM COOPERATION BACK TO COMPETITION?

The question one might ask today is: Have the reforms of the cooperative era made federalism safe for competition again and rendered the federal government unsafe for cooperation? The evils attacked by cooperative federalism were real, but, like every reform, changing conditions require reevaluation.

One altered condition is the general reform of state governments and many local governments since World War II. Far from being obsolete, the states have emerged as competent, innovative, and energetic governments. The defects of state governments that helped to drive cooperative federalism are less and less evident. Many states also are ahead of the federal government in such areas as individual rights, environmental, and consumer protection—so much so that business increasingly presses Congress to preempt state authority in many of these fields.[5]

Another new condition is an extensive array of federal, state, and local social welfare and social service programs, plus a substantial federal floor of rights protection. These developments help to compensate for the equity liabilities of competition.

Economic conditions also are different. Cooperative federalism responded to the nationalization of the U.S. economy. Today, the nation must address the internationalization of its economy. Because states were said to be unable to cope with a national economy, co-operative federalists shifted power to the national government. To-day, the national government has comparable difficulties coping with the international economy. Hence, state and local governments have entered the global economy on their own as direct competitors with jurisdictions worldwide.[6] Domestic interjurisdictional competition is being augmented by globalized interjurisdictional competition.

At the same time, the federal government has assumed monopo-listic characteristics, making it less cooperative. For example, it ap-pears that more than 50 percent of all preemptions of state and local authority enacted by Congress since 1789 have been enacted only since 1969—the last 10 percent of U.S. history (U.S. Advisory Com-mission on Intergovernmental Relations 1991). Conditions attached to federal grants, mandates on state and local governments, and other sanctions, such as threatened withholdings of funds for noncompli-ance with federal policies, have also increased dramatically.[7] Of the more than 1,140 state and local acts declared unconstitutional by the U.S. Supreme Court since 1789, more than 35 percent have been nullified since 1964 (Kincaid 1969).

A great political shock to cooperative federalism came from the Reagan administration. The shock came not so much from Reagan's drive to cut federal aid and knock local governments out of the intergovernmental loop, but from the fact that Reagan was the first real conservative to capture the White House since the rise of co-operative federalism. Reformers had assumed that expanded federal powers would not produce tyranny because the national electorate would elevate progressives—like the two Roosevelts, Wilson, and Johnson—to the presidency. Having Reagan at the helm of a powerful national government, therefore, prompted reconsideration of the dangers of monopoly. Hence, many prior advocates of cooperative federalism have sought to restimulate both intergovernmental com-petition, by turning to state and local governments for reform, and intragovernmental competition, by reinvigorating the separation of powers through congressional challenges to presidential policies.

From the New Deal to the Great Society, expanded federal power seemed to produce more cooperation, but expansion also made the federal government a magnet for interest groups. Fragmentation was reintroduced as "the centrifugal elements of state interest" (Clark 1938: 7) created by governmental competition were replaced by the centrifugal elements of atomized interest-group competition and clientelism. This occurred, in part, because, by suppressing state centrifugalism, the federal government eroded state and local powers that had diffused many elements of interest-group competition across jurisdictions. National centripetalism then pulled competition into the federal government and intensified it by raising the stakes.

In turn, by restraining unmediated interjurisdictional competition, cooperative federalism increased mediated competition—producing, among other things, a fragmented array of some 538 grant programs. More fundamentally, the rise of mediated interjurisdictional competition produced a "state and local government lobby" that is viewed as "just another interest group," a concept sanctioned by the U.S. Supreme Court in the 1980s (*Garcia* v. *San Antonio Metropolitan Transit Authority* 1988; *South Carolina* v. *Baker* 1988). This outcome suggests that unmediated interjurisdictional competition was a sign of the vitality of states as polities rather than interest groups.

Finally, cooperative federalism has not had uniformly beneficial effects on interjurisdictional competition. Federal policies that gave suburbs a competitive edge over central cities, and sunbelt states an edge over snowbelt states, are prime examples. Defense spending, farm subsidies, tax laws, business regulation, and many other national policies shape every jurisdiction's competitive position. Such policies may introduce distortions and inefficiencies in the state-local marketplace comparable to those that get introduced into the economic marketplace. It is also likely that the lack of coordination among the myriad national policies that affect interjurisdictional competition weakens the "invisible hand" coordination that may arise from unmediated competition. Nor has cooperative federalism remedied the interjurisdictional inequities said to be produced by unmediated competition; federal grants have not equalized jurisdictional fiscal and service capacities. Furthermore, with declining federal aid and rising federal mandates, government costs are being shifted onto arguably less progressive tax systems. In turn, mandates have diminished accountability as federal officials take credit for popular policies while slipping costs to state and local governments.

CONCLUSION

It is not self-evident that cooperative federalism, in its current form, is uniformly superior to dualistic competitive federalism. Invigoration of intergovernmental and interjurisdictional competition could, with safeguards, help to resolve the problems created by the centralizing consequences of cooperative federalism. If safeguards included consensual agreement on basic rights, environmental protection, individual welfare, and market competition, the principal objections to competitive federalism could be met. At the same time, genuine intergovernmental cooperation could be reinvigorated by the pressure of competition.

Notes

1. The literature on the growth of government and Leviathan is enormous. For perspectives, see Higgs (1987) and Wildavsky (1980).

2. For a range of views, see U.S. Advisory Commission on Intergovernmental Relations (1988).

3. See, for example, Croly (1910).

4. See *The Federalist*, nos. 15 and 16, and Ostrom (1987).

5. See Moore (1990).

6. See Michelmann and Soldatos, "State and Local Governments in International Affairs" (1990) and "Federated States and International Relations" (1984).

7. See U.S. Advisory Commission on Intergovernmental Relations (1984) and Fix and Kenyon (1990).

References

Baechler, Jean. 1975. *The Origins of Capitalism*. Oxford, England: Basil Blackwell.

Beard, Charles. 1913. *An Economic Interpretation of the Constitution*. New York: Macmillan.

Berman, Harold. 1983. *Law and Revolution: The Formation of the Western Legal Tradition*. Cambridge, Mass.: Harvard University Press.

Clark, Jane Perry. 1938. *The Rise of a New Federalism: Federal-State Cooperation in the United States*. New York: Columbia University Press.

Corwin, Edward S. 1941. *Constitutional Revolution Ltd*. Claremont, Calif.: Claremont Colleges.

Croly, Herbert. 1910. *The Promise of American Life*. New York: Macmillan.

Elazar, Daniel J. 1984. *American Federalism: A View from the States*, 3rd ed. New York: Harper & Row.

_____. 1987. *Exploring Federalism.* Tuscaloosa: University of Alabama Press.

"Federated States and International Relations." 1984. *Publius: The Journal of Federalism* 14 (Fall): 1–152.

Ferguson, John H., and Dean E. McHenry. 1967. *The American Federal Government,* 9th ed. New York: McGraw-Hill.

Fix, Michael, and Daphne A. Kenyon, eds. 1990. *Coping with Mandates: What Are the Alternatives?* Washington, D.C.: Urban Institute Press.

Garcia v. San Antonio Metropolitan Transit Authority. 1985. 469 U.S. 528.

Hayek, F. A. 1988. *The Fatal Conceit: The Errors of Socialism,* edited by W. W. Bartley, III. Chicago: University of Chicago Press.

Higgs, Robert. 1987. *Crisis and Leviathan: Critical Episodes in the Growth of American Government.* New York: Oxford University Press.

Hobbes, Thomas. [1651] 1958. *Leviathan.* Indianapolis, Ind.: Bobbs-Merrill.

Jones, E. L. 1981. *The European Miracle: Environments, Economies, and Geopolitics in the History of Europe and Asia.* Cambridge, England: Cambridge University Press.

Kenworthy, Tom. 1990. "Kansan Targets Pork Barrel Projects." *Washington Post,* December 19: A21.

Kincaid, John. 1969. "A Proposal to Strengthen Federalism." *Journal of State Government* 62 (January/February): 139.

_____. 1990. "From Cooperative to Coercive Federalism." *Annals of the American Academy of Political and Social Science* 509 (May): 139–152.

Kincaid, John, and Daniel J. Elazar, eds. Forthcoming. *The Covenant Connection: Federal Theology and the Origins of Modern Politics.* Durham, N.C.: Carolina Academic Press.

Laski, Harold J. 1939. "The Obsolescence of Federalism." *New Republic* 98 (May): 367–69.

"A Letter to the President from the National Governors' Association." 1979. *Publius: The Journal of Federalism* 9 (Winter): 91–95.

Locke, John. [1690] 1960. *Two Treatises of Government.* Cambridge, England: Cambridge University Press.

Lutz, Donald S. 1980. "From Covenant to Constitution in American Political Thought." *Publius: The Journal of Federalism* 10 (Fall): 101–33.

Michelmann, Hans J., and Panayotis Soldatos. 1990. *Federalism and International Relations: The Role of Subnational Units.* Oxford: Clarendon Press.

Moore, W. John. 1990. "Stopping the States." *National Journal,* 22 July 21: 1758–62.

Ostrom, Vincent. 1987. *The Political Theory of a Compound Republic: Designing the American Experiment.* Lincoln: University of Nebraska Press.

Plessy v. Ferguson. 1896. 163 U.S. 537.

Riker, William H. 1964. *Federalism: Origin, Operation, Significance.* Boston: Little, Brown.

Rosenberg, Nathan, and L. Z. Birdzell, Jr. 1986. *How the West Grew Rich: The Economic Transformation of the Industrial World.* New York: Basic Books.

Rousseau, Jean-Jacques. [1762] 1978. *On the Social Contract.* New York: St. Martin's Press.

Schlesinger, Arthur M., Jr. 1973. *The Imperial Presidency.* Boston: Houghton Mifflin.

Schumpeter, Joseph A. [1942] 1975. *Capitalism, Socialism, and Democracy,* 2nd ed. New York: Harper & Row.

South Carolina v. Baker. 1988. 56 USLW 4311.

"State and Local Governments in International Affairs." 1990. *Intergovernmental Perspective* 16 (Spring): 5–34.

Story, Joseph. [1840] 1986. *A Familiar Exposition of the Constitution of the United States.* Lake Bluff: Ill.: Regnery Gateway.

Texas v. White. 1869. 74 U.S. 700.

de Tocqueville, Alexis. [1835] 1969. *Democracy in America.* Garden City, N.Y.: Doubleday/Anchor.

Tiebout, Charles M. 1956. "A Pure Theory of Local Expenditures." *Journal of Political Economy* 64 (5, October): 416–24.

Tyler, Moses Coit. [1887] 1962. *Patrick Henry.* Ithaca, N.Y.: Cornell University Press.

United States v. Darby. 1941. 312 U.S. 100.

U.S. Advisory Commission on Intergovernmental Relations. 1984. *Regulatory Federalism: Policy, Process, Impact, and Reform.* Washington, D.C.: Author.

————. 1988. *Interjurisdictional Competition in the Federal System: A Roundtable Discussion.* Washington, D.C.: Author.

————. 1991. *Federal Preemption of State and Local Authority.* Washington, D.C.: Author.

Walsh, Cliff. 1989. "An Economic Perspective." In *Australian Federalism,* edited by Brian Galligan. Melbourne: Longman Cheshire.

Wildavsky, Aaron. 1980. "The 1980s: Monopoly or Competition?" *Intergovernmental Perspective* 6 (Summer): 15–18.

Wright, Deil S. 1988. *Understanding Intergovernmental Relations,* 3rd ed. Pacific Grove, Calif.: Brooks/Cole.

Part Two

EFFECTS OF INTERJURISDICTIONAL COMPETITION

Chapter Six

FEDERALISM'S "INVISIBLE REGULATOR"—INTERJURISDICTIONAL COMPETITION

John Shannon

The continuing debate about the efficacy of interjurisdictional competition has long emphasized the fiscal "braking" effect of *tax* competition but has not focused sharply on the "accelerator" effect of
expenditure (public service) competition. This chapter examines these
two countervailing forces and makes the case that together they serve
as the "unseen hands" preventing a state from either pushing too far
ahead of its neighbors on the tax front or lagging too far behind them
in the public service area.

TAX COMPETITION: THE FISCAL BRAKE

Interstate tax competition stands out as a "hot button" issue guaranteed to trigger sharply differing responses from liberals and conservatives.

The Liberal Position

Interjurisdictional tax competition for jobs and economic development cuts against the liberal grain because it calls for tax and
spending policies specifically designed to retain and to attract
upper-income taxpayers and business payrolls. Liberals have long
argued that interjurisdictional tax differences do not figure importantly in business location decisions, and they point to the
findings of many academic studies to buttress their case.

They also claim that interjurisdictional tax competition creates
a "beggar-thy-neighbor" environment that leaves in its wake un-
warranted tax concessions, anemic revenue systems, regressive tax
policies, and underfunded public programs. In short, they contend
that interjurisdictional tax competition is both unnecessary and
harmful.

The Conservative Position

Most conservatives view tax competition as twice blessed. First, it places powerful constraints on the "soak-the-rich" and "stick-big-business" tendencies of liberal populists. Second, concerns about tax competition strengthen the hands of those urging a conservative spending policy and a pro-business approach to taxes.

Conservatives have long argued that a "good business tax climate" stands out as a strong plus factor in the interstate competition for jobs and economic development. They then define a good tax climate as the absence of those tax policies they deem especially hurtful to economic development in general and to business firms in particular. The six tax "sore thumbs" most often cited are:

- An overall state-local tax burden that is well above the national and regional averages.
- A state individual income tax that is both heavy and quite progressive.
- Any major state business tax that is definitely "out of line" with those of neighboring states. (The state corporation income tax, the workers' compensation tax, and the unemployment compensation tax are all subjected to this "out-of-line" test.)
- A property tax on business realty that is quite heavy and/or discriminatory in character.
- A property tax on business personalty—machinery, inventories, and goods in process.
- A general sales tax that imposes a levy on a significant number of business purchases.

Most conservatives concede that the absence of all or most of these "sore thumbs" will not automatically ensure strong economic development. They do contend, however, that their presence can and does work against job creation.

It should be noted that the more "sore thumbs" a jurisdiction exhibits, the greater the likelihood that its policymakers will resort to a wide variety of temporary painkillers—business tax concessions—as the most expedient way to deal with these competitive problems.

The Liberal-Conservative Agreement

Although liberals and conservatives differ sharply on both the need for and efficacy of interjurisdictional tax competition, they agree on its effects. The bitterness of their debate underscores one area of consensus. Both sides believe that competitive taxation can put a damper on the growth of the state and local sector in general and on the adoption of progressive tax policies in particular.

EXPENDITURE (PUBLIC-SECTOR) COMPETITION—THE ACCELERATOR EFFECT

Although keenly concerned about the fiscal braking power of competitive taxation, students of public policy have paid considerably less attention to the fiscal accelerator effect of competitive emulation on the public service front. Much of this acceleration effect can be traced to two factors—the pacesetter phenomenon and the "catch-up" imperative.

The Pacesetter Phenomenon

State and local innovation is an oft-cited value of federalism. Thus, if a jurisdiction successfully pioneers in a new public service area, it then becomes only a question of time before detailed information about this new public service filters through the state-local sector. As this filtering process occurs, the forces of competitive emulation convert yesterday's expensive novelty (or public service "frill") into today's standard budgetary fare. For example, not too long ago, kindergarten services were nonexistent in many parts of the country; now this tax-supported service is virtually universal. Also, until quite recently, the heavily subsidized community college was something of a rarity. Now it has become a standard public education fixture in most states.

These expensive innovations usually originated in the "liberal" pacesetter states noted for their high tastes for public goods and services—Massachusetts, New York, Michigan, Wisconsin, Minnesota, and California. Once the beachhead is secured in these liberal states, the proponents of this new public service then carry their message into the more conservative bastions and to the less-affluent jurisdictions.

The "globalization" of the U.S. economy has added new pacesetters—foreign jurisdictions. A recent *Washington Post* article (August 30, 1988) highlighted both the dramatic shift of decision making from Washington, D.C., to the state capitals, as well as the liberal pacesetter role of Sweden:

Because legislatures often act fast, business interests have often found themselves playing catch-up on some legislation, said Conference Board's McGuire. "We have this kind of 'Stockholm Syndrome' where a piece of radical legislation gets passed by the Swedes, then it's flown directly to the U.S. and is passed into law in California. Then it's flown to Wisconsin. Then to New York. By the time it gets to Mississippi, which is about four years later, it's a national birthright."

The American federal system is now confronting the fact that our states and localities have another and more significant foreign pacesetter in education—Japan, our increasingly powerful economic competitor. To become more "competitive," states and their local school boards will come under increasing pressure to spend more tax dollars for longer school terms and more substantive educational offerings.

The fiscal accelerator effect of pacesetting governments is also apparent in a very costly area—the negotiation of public employee pay schedules and fringe benefit packages. If, for example, rich Fairfax County, Virginia, raises the minimum annual salary of junior high school principals from $59,000 to $64,000, the other school districts in the Washington, D.C., metropolitan area will soon come under competitive pressure to meet that higher salary standard. In fact, the representatives of state and local employees are constantly citing the higher salary levels of the pacesetters to buttress their case for pay comparability.[1]

The "Catch-Up" Imperative

The accelerating fiscal effect of interjurisdictional competition is only partially explained by the pacesetter phenomenon. In critical and costly economic development areas, such as education and public infrastructure, the more conservative and the poorer jurisdictions confront a harsh reality. They dare not allow themselves to fall too far behind their more liberal and affluent neighbors—to become written off as "banana republics." In short, they are forced by the catch-up imperative to keep their service levels fairly close to their pacesetting neighbors.

This catch-up imperative is dramatically illustrated by the economic development strategies of many of the poorest states in the federation—Mississippi, South Carolina, Arkansas, and Tennessee. In virtually every recent account highlighting the resurgence of the states, these southern jurisdictions are cited for their willingness to

raise taxes—the price they have to pay to keep their education systems competitive. Their leaders are convinced that both their short-
and long-range economic development interests leave them no alternative. Just as many northern states are trying to shake free from
their bad tax-climate reputation by flattening their personal income
tax rates, many southern states are opting to raise taxes for education
as a way to overcome a poor public school image. William Raspberry,
writing in the *Washington Post* (May 30, 1988), quoted Mississippi
Governor Ray Mabus as emphasizing the pacesetter role of North
Carolina, the competitive character of teachers' pay, and the catch-
up determination of Mississippi.

> The governor in an interview picked up the theme: "Look at a state
> like North Carolina, which in the late 50's and early 60's was
> pretty much neck-and-neck with Mississippi. Then they elected
> Terry Sanford governor. He plowed a lot of money into education
> and now it's a tradition there. A succession of governors have
> made education a priority and now, 30 years later they're in great
> shape."
>   Mabus, in office only since January, has succeeded in selling his
> program of improved teachers' pay (to avoid the drain of Missis-
> sippi-trained teachers to other states) and major new investments
> in education from preschool to community college to univer-
> sity. . . .

Many less-affluent local governments are also willing to pay the
competitive tax price to keep their schools and public services
within at least hailing distance of their wealthier, pacesetting
neighbors. In the Washington, D.C., metropolitan area, Prince
George's County, Maryland, raised taxes to finance the creation of
"magnet" schools and justified this action in no small part on
competitive grounds. The first-rate school systems of Montgomery
County, Maryland, and Fairfax County, Virginia, are widely believed to be the magnets that help attract upper-income taxpayers
and high-tech employers to their jurisdictions. Prince George's
County's new magnet schools have certainly attracted the attention
of its citizens. Local newspapers have carried pictures of parents
camped out all night waiting to register their children for atten-
dance in these new "super" schools.

Admittedly anecdotal, these examples nevertheless underscore an
interjurisdictional fiscal reality: state and local elected officials are
under unremitting competitive pressure to approximate the public
service standards of the pacesetters.

THE COUNTERVAILING COMPETITIVE FORCES—
THEIR FISCAL EFFECTS

Has the accelerating fiscal effect of expenditure competition proved stronger than the restraining or braking effect of tax competition? Although it is impossible to answer this question directly, an examination of historical trends can provide insights into the relative power of the progrowth and antigrowth forces.

Since the end of World War II, state and local own-source revenue has grown steadily and at a faster clip than the economy. According to the U.S. Bureau of the Census, total state-local own-source general revenue rose from 5.4 percent of gross national product (GNP) in 1946 to 12.8 percent of GNP in 1989.

This remarkable real growth in state-local own-source revenue supports two general conclusions about the countervailing power of interjurisdictional tax and expenditure competition. First, the accelerating fiscal power of interjurisdictional public service competition *and* that of its progrowth allies (i.e., post–World War II baby boom, the stimulating effect of federal matching grants, the partial write-off of state and local tax payments against the federal income tax) has proved stronger than the restraining power of interjurisdictional tax competition and that of its principal ally— the taxpayers' revolt of the late 1970s and early 1980s. Second, this steady growth in state-local own-source revenue since the end of World War II has also knocked into a cocked hat the old conventional wisdom that states and localities were destined to have anemic revenue systems because they were "crippled by fears" of tax competition.

THE COUNTERVAILING COMPETITIVE FORCES—
FEDERALISM'S REGULATOR

Although the braking power of interjurisdictional competition has not proved as effective as most conservatives would like, interjurisdictional competition has provided a valuable regulating service for our federal system. Interstate tax *and* expenditure competition serve jointly as the two "unseen hands" that set the outer limits on how far any state can push ahead of other states on the tax front or lag behind them in the public service area.

The Convoy Analogy

The behavior of our states resembles 50 ships sailing in a great naval convoy during wartime. The farther any state moves ahead of the convoy on the tax side, the greater becomes the risks of tax evasion, taxpayer revolts, and the loss of economic development to states pursuing more conservative tax and spending policies. By the same token, the farther any state falls behind the convoy in the public service area, the greater becomes the risk that it will lose economic development to states providing a higher quality of life, especially in the area of public education.

Our 50 ships of state differ from the wartime naval convoy in at least three important respects: First, the passengers and crew members elect their captain and officers and can toss them over-board (politically speaking) every two or four years and select in their stead a new set of officers. Second, the passengers and crew members are free both to move to any other state that is more to their liking and to take with them their possessions, investments, and their payrolls. In fact, a primary responsibility of the convoy's protecting supercarrier (the federal government) is to make sure that there is a free flow of persons and commerce between the states. Third, and most significant, there is no visible central control system that sets the fiscal speed and the public service course for each state in the convoy.

A close examination of this 50-state convoy also reveals that there are regional clusterings within the convoy. The smaller states are concerned lest they get too far out of line—on taxes or public services—with the other states in their own region. The officers of the larger states have a more difficult navigational assignment. Although often pacesetters, these states must keep a close competitive eye both on their regional neighbors and on the other major states in the convoy. For example, New York competes for certain types of business with the distant "megastates"—Florida, Texas, Illinois, and California—as well as with the other states in the mid-Atlantic region. In 1989, New York State's concern for its competitive position in general and its poor national tax image in particular prompted it to buy full-page ads in the *New York Times* and the *Wall Street Journal* to announce that the state was getting back in line with a dramatic cut in its relatively heavy and highly progressive state personal income tax.

Diversity—Setting the Outer Limits

Another oft-cited virtue of our federal system is the great diversity in tax and public service policies in the 50 states and thousands of local governments. This diversity, in turn, permits mobile citizens to vote with their feet as well as with their ballots, thereby forcing elected officials to be more responsive to varying public service concerns and more cautious about imposing taxes.

But even this virtue of diversity has its limits. Some institution in a federal system must prevent jurisdictions from drifting too far apart, especially in the critical areas of taxation and public service provision. In the American federal system, interjurisdictional competition has traditionally performed this critical and delicate regulator task—that of preventing states and localities from moving too far apart. This power to contain interjurisdictional diversity is clearly reflected in countervailing competitive pressures. Competitive tax concerns, for example, were forcing New York policymakers to bring their progressive income tax policies closer to the national norm at the very time that competitive public service concerns were prompting Mississippi officials to raise taxes and narrow the educational distance that separates that state from the pacesetting North Carolina.

Admittedly, serious shortcomings are associated with regulation by competition. It is to be hoped that the federal government will soon provide special financial assistance to the poorest states and thereby enable them to compete on more equal terms with the wealthier states. By the same token, state governments should reduce competitive disparities by providing special financial aid to those localities handicapped by anemic revenue bases or extraordinary expenditure requirements, or both.

Despite these competitive shortcomings, the forces of tax and public service competition are providing the necessary regulator service. The interests of our federal system are well served by leaving the delicate and critical task of setting the outer limits of interjurisdictional diversity where it now resides—with elected state and local officials operating in a highly competitive environment. Why? Because the light and "invisible hands" of tax and public service competition are clearly preferable to the heavy and visible hand of Washington, D.C.

Note

1. See, also, U.S. Advisory Commission on Intergovernmental Relations (1988: 9).

References

Hamilton, Martha. 1988. "States Assuming New Powers as Federal Policy Role Ebbs." *The Washington Post*, August 30: A1.

Raspberry, William. 1988. "Mississippi Moving Up." *The Washington Post*, May 30: A27.

U.S. Advisory Commission on Intergovernmental Relations. 1988. *Interjurisdictional Competition in the Federal System: A Roundtable Discussion*. Washington, D.C.: Author.

Chapter Seven

THE ALLOCATIVE AND DISTRIBUTIVE IMPLICATIONS OF LOCAL FISCAL COMPETITION

Wallace E. Oates and Robert M. Schwab

There can be little doubt that state and local jurisdictions actively compete against one another for jobs, investment, and other assets that promote economic growth. The intense bidding for the General Motors Saturn plant and the competition for the federal government's supercollider are two obvious examples.

The implications of this competition, however, are much less clear. The debate over the merits of interjurisdictional competition is long-standing, often acrimonious, and far from resolution. Proponents would have us believe that competition offers both protection from self-seeking bureaucrats and assurances that public goods will be provided efficiently; opponents tell us that competition necessarily leads to inadequate local government budgets, regressive local taxes, and insufficient social services for the poor.[1]

Our goal in the chapter is to step back from the fray and address the question: What does economic theory tell us about the implications of interjurisdictional competition? Two themes emerge from our work.

First, if many local governments compete against one another, then all local taxes become benefit taxes. That is, the taxes that consumers and businesses pay in such a setting would exactly equal the value each places on the publicly provided goods and services they receive. In particular, we would not expect to find that the revenue from local taxes levied on businesses would be used to fund social programs, parks, education, and the like. In a competitive setting, communities will actively bid against one another for new firms so that in the limit (as in the world of perfect competition in the private sector), there will be no net fiscal gains from such competitive pur-

Department of Economics, University of Maryland. Oates is also a University Fellow at Resources for the Future; Schwab was recently a Gilbert White Fellow at Resources for the Future while working on this paper.

suits. Any attempts to attract new business investment by lowering taxes below the cost of providing local services or by offering subsidies to firms would fail in the sense that the cost to the community of such programs would more than offset any gains in increased jobs and income or tax revenues. Communities (like competitive firms) would behave as "price takers"; they would take as given the going rate of return to capital and would select tax and expenditure policies in light of this parameter.

The second theme is that the outcome would be, in economic terms, efficient; that is, it would consist of an allocation of society's scarce resources, which would involve no waste in the sense that no one could be made better off without reducing the level of welfare of someone else. Firms and households would balance the value of local public goods and taxes offered by communities when choosing a location. Given that local taxes will reflect the cost of providing these goods, economic units would make use of locally provided public services to the point where their value at the margin equaled the marginal cost to society of providing them.

These results emerge from a model that shares many of the strengths and weaknesses of the perfect competition paradigm of the private sector. The model abstracts from a wide range of sources of distortions in economic outcomes; from this perspective, it offers a clear description of the outcome one should expect if jurisdictions compete against one another under perfect conditions. This characterization of fiscal competition thus provides a useful benchmark in the debate over interjurisdictional competition.[2]

These models of private and public competition also lead to similar conclusions: the outcomes in both models are efficient, but not necessarily equitable. In particular, local taxes on capital are not effective instruments for the redistribution of income; as George Stigler (1957) argued, "Redistribution is intrinsically a national policy."[3] Thus, our analysis suggests that we should applaud interjurisdictional competition on efficiency grounds whenever the federal government has fulfilled the redistributive function. Where this is not the case, the argument in favor of interjurisdictional competition is much less compelling.

A MODEL OF INTERJURISDICTIONAL COMPETITION

This section of the chapter sets forth a simple model for examining some of the important issues in the debate over interjurisdictional

competition. The model is similar in spirit to models we have presented earlier (Oates and Schwab (1988a, b)). In this model, jurisdictions compete for a mobile capital stock by lowering taxes and providing public inputs to firms, such as roads and police and fire protection. In return for a larger capital stock, residents receive higher wages. A community must, however, weigh the benefits of higher wages against foregone tax revenues and the cost of public services.

Consider a society that consists of n jurisdictions. Firms in each jurisdiction produce a private good (Q), which is sold in a national market. Production requires private capital (K), labor (L), and a publicly provided input (X). We assume that the production function for the private good exhibits constant returns to scale. If we define k and x as the capital-labor and public input-labor ratios, we can write the production function for a particular jurisdiction as

$$Q = F(K, L, X) \tag{7.1}$$
$$= Lf(k, x).$$

This society has a fixed stock of capital, which is perfectly mobile (at least in the long run) and which can therefore be allocated among the n jurisdictions. We assume that labor is immobile and thus fixed for each community in the aggregate.[4] We also assume that all of the workers in each community are identical. It is easiest to think of the third input, X, as being acquired from a different society at a fixed exchange rate of p_x units of Q in exchange for a unit of X.[5]

The labor market in each community is perfectly competitive; therefore, the wage (w) in each community will equal the value of the marginal product of labor. Thus, if we let the private good Q be the numeraire and use subscripts to denote partial derivatives, then

$$w = f - kf_k - xf_x. \tag{7.2}$$

Workers also receive nonwage income y.[6]

The public input is distributed among firms in proportion to each firm's capital stock; thus, the ratio x/k will be the same for all firms in the community.[7] The gains to a firm from hiring an additional unit of capital is the sum of, first, the marginal product of capital f_k and, second, the additional output from the increase in the publicly provided input $(x/k)f_x$; thus, firms will continue to hire capital until $f_k + (x/k)f_x$ equals the rental price of capital gross of local taxes. Capital will be distributed so as to maximize its earnings, implying that the return to capital net of local taxes will be equated across communities.

In the spirit of perfect competition, we assume that all of the communities are small in the sense that they treat this rate of return as a parameter. Therefore, given a tax rate t, public input-labor ratio x, and net rate of return available in other communities r, the stock of capital in a community will adjust so that

$$f_k + (x/k)f_x - t = r. \tag{7.3}$$

In this formulation, we leave open the possibility that the community will choose to subsidize capital and thus choose a tax rate that is negative.[8]

The community also chooses a second local public good g, which yields utility to consumers; g is purchased at a cost of p_g per unit. The public budget constraint requires that the cost of providing public goods equal the sum of revenue from the taxation of capital and taxes levied on consumers. We assume that the community is free to set a head tax h; as we discuss here, the ability to tax residents is an important issue in the theory of interjurisdictional competition.[9] The public-sector budget constraint (expressed in per capita terms) thus requires

$$h + kt = p_g g + p_x x. \tag{7.4}$$

We assume that local government's sole objective is to maximize the welfare of its constituents subject to the relevant resource constraints. Let c be per-capita consumption of the privately produced good and let $u(c, g)$ be the utility function of a representative consumer. The local government's problem is to maximize $u(c, g)$ subject to the private budget constraint

$$y + w = c + h, \tag{7.5}$$

the labor market requirement in (7.2), the rate of return constraint in (7.3), and the public budget constraint in (7.4).

Market Equilibrium

The appendix to this chapter shows that the solution to this problem requires

$$u_g/u_c = p_g \tag{7.6a}$$

$$f_x = p_x \tag{7.6b}$$

$$t = (x/k)f_x. \tag{7.6c}$$

Equation (7.6a) states that the local government should provide consumers with local public goods such that their marginal rate of substitution between the public and private goods equals the ratio of their prices. Equation (7.6b) states that government should continue to provide public goods to firms up to the point that the marginal product of the public input equals its price. Equation (7.6c) states that the tax on capital should equal the benefit the owners of capital receive from local public goods. Together, equations (7.6b) and (7.6c) imply, first, that kt will equal $p_x x$ (i.e., business taxes will equal the cost of providing public goods to business); and, second, that together with the public budget constraint, taxes on individuals must equal the cost of the public goods they consume.[10]

Therefore, under interjurisdictional competition, all local taxes become benefit taxes; they are fees for goods and services provided. To see this point in the clearest light, suppose for the moment we were to replace the local governments in our model with perfectly competitive profit-maximizing firms that produced the two public goods at a constant cost of p_g and p_x per unit. Households would continue to purchase g until their marginal rate of substitution between the public and private good equaled the ratio of their prices; firms that produced the private good would continue to hire x until the marginal product of x equaled its price. Firms would pay the full cost of providing x, and households would pay the full cost of providing g. This is precisely the outcome that has emerged in our model of interjurisdictional competition; the role of local governments in such a setting is equivalent to that of a firm that offers goods and services to households and intermediate inputs to firms.

Efficiency in the Market System

Efficiency in our model requires us to maximize the utility of a representative resident of one community subject to three constraints: (1) we allow a representative consumer in all other communities to reach a specified level of utility (which may vary across communities), (2) aggregate production in society equals the sum of aggregate consumption and cost of purchasing x and g, and (3) we allocate society's fixed stock of capital among the n communities.

Let superscripts denote community. The solution to this efficiency problem requires

$$u_g^i/u_c^i = p_g \qquad i = 1, 2, \dots\dots\dots\dots\dots, n \qquad (7.7a)$$

$$f_x^i = p_x \qquad i = 1, 2, \dots\dots\dots\dots\dots, n \qquad (7.7b)$$

$$f_k^i = f_k^j \qquad i, j, = 1, 2, \dots\dots\dots\dots\dots, n. \qquad (7.7c)$$

Clearly these efficiency conditions are satisfied in our model of interjurisdictional competition. Equations (7.7a) and (7.7b) are equivalent to equations (7.6a) and (7.6b). Equation (7.7c) tells us that efficiency requires that society's capital stock must be distributed among the communities so that the marginal product of capital is the same everywhere; if this were not true, then it would be possible to move capital from low-productivity communities to high-productivity communities and thus increase aggregate output. Because the rate of return must be the same everywhere, equation (7.6c) implies that equation (7.7c) will be satisfied.

These results should not be surprising. We argued earlier that the outcome that emerges under interjurisdictional competition is identical to that which would emerge if perfectly competitive firms were to provide local public goods. Since it is well known that perfect competition (in the absence of externalities) leads to an efficient outcome, our model must also imply efficiency.

A Diagrammatic Approach

Figure 7.1 helps to clarify these points. The figure shows the demand and supply of capital in one of the communities in our model. The supply curve is perfectly elastic in the diagram, reflecting our assumption that each community takes the market rate of return r as given. The demand curve (i.e., the marginal product of capital) is downward sloping, given diminishing marginal returns. For simplicity, we ignore the local public good that enters firms' production functions, thus ruling out benefit taxes.

Suppose initially that this community decides not to tax capital. The market will clear when the marginal product of capital f_k equals r; the equilibrium capital stock in this case will be K^*. The community will produce goods worth $abcd$ (the integral under the marginal product of capital curve). The income from the sale of these goods will be divided as follows. Capital will receive $ebcd$, or rK^*. Under constant returns to scale, payments to factors of production exhaust revenues, and profits equal zero. Thus, the other factors of production (labor in our model) receive the residual abe.

Now suppose that the community in figure 7.1 sets a tax on capital of t. The demand curve for capital shifts down to $f_k - t$. The new equilibrium stock is K^{**} and the value of goods produced in the community falls to $aifd$. Capital's gross income now includes net income of $egfd$ and local taxes of $hige$. Thus, capital's net income

Figure 7.1 Demand and Supply of Capital in a Community

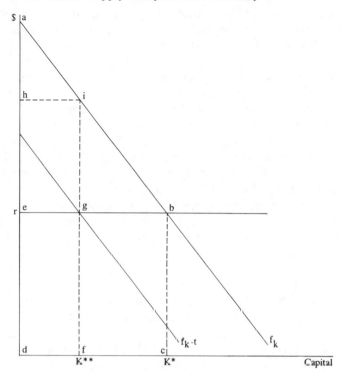

falls by *gbcf*, the product of the constant r and the change in the capital stock ($K^* - K^{**}$), as a result of the tax. However, these ($K^* - K^{**}$) units of capital can earn r in other communities; consequently, this tax, though nominally on capital, has no effect on capital income. This is a further application of the general proposition that a tax on a factor of production or a good that has a perfectly elastic supply curve will always be shifted onto other factors of production or consumers.[11]

Labor's wages fall by the sum of *hige* and *ibg*, or *hibe*. The area *hige*, as already noted, equals the taxes nominally paid by capital but which, in fact, are shifted to labor. It is thus impossible to use local taxes on capital to redistribute income from capital to the residents of a community; any taxes paid by capital are immediately offset by lower wages.

Thus, *ibg* equals the decrease in wages that is not offset by the taxes paid by capital. This is consistent with our result that the optimal tax on capital for a community is zero; *at any positive tax rate, the decrease in wages will be greater than the taxes collected.*

The wedge between lost wages and tax revenues, area *ibg*, has a further interpretation. Clearly, as argued earlier, area *ibg* represents the private loss from the imposition of the tax. It is not difficult to see that it also represents the social loss. If the tax were removed, output in the community would rise by *ibcf*. Output would fall by *gbcf* in other communities (given our assumption that the marginal product of capital remains constant at r elsewhere) and, therefore, aggregate output would rise by *ibg*. Thus, interjurisdictional competition promotes an efficient allocation of the capital stock by leading communities to forego the taxation of mobile capital.

Taxation of capital can take only the form of benefit taxation. A community can tax capital for any services that increase the marginal product of capital—but only to the extent of the increment in productivity.

Figure 7.1 also allows us to put our results in the context of the literature on tax incidence. Our assumption that communities are perfect competitors implies (as shown in figure 7.1) that the supply of capital to a community is perfectly elastic at the market-determined rate of return, r. The incidence literature tells us that a tax on a factor of production that is perfectly elastic in supply will never in the end fall on that input; it will always be passed on to consumers or to other inputs. From the incidence literature, we should expect taxes to fall on factors that are in relatively inelastic supply. The supply of labor in a community in our simple model is perfectly inelastic; consequently, it is not surprising to find that labor bears the full burden of a local tax on capital. Our model suggests that communities understand the incidence literature, that they will foresee the futility of trying to impose taxes on mobile capital, and that, therefore, they will not tax capital.

MARKET FAILURE

Competition among firms need not always lead to efficiency; private markets sometimes fail. This section examines market failure in the public sector.

Externalities

Clearly, if production or consumption generates externalities, one would not expect competition in the private sector to lead to efficiency. Similar issues arise in the analysis of public sector competition. To offer a concrete example, suppose a park built in Community A yields benefits to the residents of Community B as well as to those of A. If we allow A to choose its own level of spending, it will provide a suboptimal level of parks because the interests of those outside the community will be ignored.

This problem is well understood in the literature.[12] One solution, as Oates (1972) argued, is for the federal government to offer a Pigouvian subsidy in the form of a matching grant equal to the benefits received by others.

There is also an intertemporal aspect to this issue. It has been argued that local governments, in their eagerness to attract new firms, will ignore the interests of future generations who will live in the community, just as they ignore the interests of current residents of other communities. According to this argument, one might expect to find, for example, that communities offer public workers generous future pension benefits in return for lower current wages and then pass the cost of these benefits on to future generations by failing to fund public pension plans; similarly, current residents may defer maintenance of the public capital stock and ignore the impact of current policy on future environmental quality in their efforts to attract new firms. These issues presumably would not arise in federal policy. We would all want the federal government to take into account the interests of our children when setting policy, because it is likely that our children will live somewhere in this country; it is unlikely, however, that our children will live in our current community.[13]

As we have argued elsewhere (Oates and Schwab 1988b), however, this argument is not altogether persuasive. An extensive literature has found that many of the factors that determine "the quality of life" in a community are reflected in property values.[14] If this literature is correct, our concern that the interests of future generations will be ignored in interjurisdictional competition may be somewhat misguided. For example, suppose a community were considering allowing a new firm to locate in that community, and suppose further that this firm will cause $100 of environmental damages at some point in the future. If the capitalization argument holds, then property values would fall by the present value of $100 if the firm were allowed to enter; the community would have to take into account the anticipated decline in property values, and thereby acknowledge the interests of future generations when making its decision. We thus find that the intertemporal issue is very different in its implications for efficient decisions than the more standard case of interjurisdictional externalities.

Market Power

Competition in the private sector will not, in general, produce efficient outcomes if firms in one or more sectors hold a substantial degree of market power. Most models of the public sector, including ours, look at the perfect competition analog; consequently, little is known about competition among a "few" jurisdictions. It would not be surprising, however, to find that competition in a strategic setting, where officials react to the policies of other jurisdictions, leads to systematic distortions in fiscal decisions.

Jack Mintz and Henry Tulkens (1986) have made a careful study of this issue in a two-region model in which each jurisdiction places a tax on a single private good. Because consumers can purchase the good in either region (subject to transport costs), the tax rate set in one jurisdiction affects the revenues in the other; there is a kind of fiscal externality present. In this setting, Mintz and Tulkens found that a noncooperative (Nash) equilibrium (should it exist) will not, in general, be efficient. They showed that the equilibrium outcome is likely to display tendencies toward suboptimality, in that efficiency-improving tax changes can never involve a reduction in tax rates in both regions; such changes must imply higher taxes in at least one (and perhaps both) region(s).

The Mintz-Tulkens model is, of course, only one of a large class of models of strategic fiscal interaction. However, the presumption must be that where there is such explicit interplay of fiscal choices, fiscal externalities will exist that can be the source of distortions in tax and expenditure choices. In thinking about fiscal competition in the United States, this is a useful juncture at which to raise the distinction between such competition among states and among localities. Within a metropolitan area, for example, where there are a large number of communities competing against one another, our competitive version of fiscal competition may represent a reasonable approximation to actual fiscal behavior. For states, however, strategic interaction may be more prevalent. State officials often justify fiscal measures in terms of policies in neighboring states. Yet, the really important question is the *magnitude* of the distortions introduced by such strategic interaction. On this, we have virtually no evidence.

Imperfect Information

In the past decade, economists have come to recognize imperfect information as a potential source of market failure in the private sector. Consider the labor market. Suppose firms cannot monitor their employees perfectly and, as a result, are unable to know with certainty who is working hard and who is shirking. Under these circumstances, proponents of the efficiency-wage theory have argued that it is in the firm's interest to offer high wages so that all of the firm's employees have an incentive to work hard. But if firms offer high wages to prevent shirking, some people who are willing to work at the market wage will not be hired. This difficulty in acquiring information about workers' effort thus results in unemployment, an outcome that is surely not efficient.

Information problems can also lead to inefficiencies in the public sector. Our model, for example, assumes implicitly that firms can always evaluate the tax and expenditure packages offered by various communities. Clearly, an extreme version of this assumption is heroic, but it seems reasonable to expect firms to take public policy "into account," even if somewhat imperfectly, when making location decisions. This view is consistent with the empirical evidence on firm location discussed later here. Moreover, there is good evidence that households take public policy into account when choosing a community of residence (see Oates 1969 and the subsequent capitalization literature), and there is no reason to believe that firms have less incentive than households to acquire such information.

Taxation of Mobile Capital

A number of economists, including John Wilson (1987a, b), George Zodrow and Peter Mieszkowski (1986), and David Wildasin (1989), have argued that *if communities must rely entirely on taxes on mobile capital* (at least at the margin) to fund public goods, the outcome will not be efficient; we show in the appendix that a similar result emerges in our model. The basic argument is as follows. Communities realize that as they raise the tax rate, they will drive capital out of the community. Thus, they raise the tax rate only to the point at which the cost of the public good to the community, including the negative effects of the smaller capital stock, equals the benefits.

But as Wildasin (1986) has explained, the social cost of public goods in this setting will be less than the private cost because capital that leaves one community will be deflected to another. Therefore, public goods will be underprovided.

This result is sensible, given the assumption that only mobile capital can be taxed. Charles McLure (1986) offered the following "tale" to illustrate this point. Suppose Gloucester, Massachusetts, were to finance a school lunch program by taxing the fishing fleet that docks there. The tax would effectively raise the cost of fishing for boats choosing to dock in Gloucester; the fishing fleet would tend to seek less expensive docking sites in competing ports. Thus, competition from neighboring communities would prevent the cost of school lunches in Gloucester from being borne by those who eat fish or (except in the very short run) the owners of boats. Instead, one would expect to find that boats would be docked elsewhere, with little revenue being collected. The burden of the tax would be borne by owners of the least mobile factors in Gloucester—most likely the owners of the docks. Finally, we would expect to find that too few lunches would be provided. Given this unfortunate outcome, McLure continues, it would be surprising to find that the residents of Gloucester (or any other community) would favor such a plan; they would be better off taxing themselves to pay for the lunch program, as our analysis suggests.

A good case can be made that McLure's point has not been lost on local governments. Given the myriad of inducements that jurisdictions offer to potential new firms, it is hard to believe that the moral of the story of the unhappy people of Gloucester has gone unnoticed.

IMPLICATIONS FOR EMPIRICAL RESEARCH

The theoretical model we have presented has some interesting implications for empirical research on the impact of local taxes on firm location and economic growth. The results of existing empirical research have been very mixed. The early literature, as summarized by John Due (1961), found that taxes had virtually no effect on the local economy. Some of the recent work on this problem, including that of Dennis Carlton (1983) and Timothy Bartik (1985), reached similar conclusions; others have found the expected negative effect of taxes on firms' location decisions, though the effects tend to be small.[15]

For a number of strong reasons, one should not be surprised to find that it is difficult to identify the impact of local taxes on growth. First, simultaneity problems may plague some studies. Suppose firms are less likely to locate in communities where taxes are high. Suppose further, however, that communities where growth is high because of unobservable (or at least unobserved) reasons set high taxes to fund the public infrastructure investment made necessary by that growth. In such a case, it would be very difficult to sort out these two effects econometrically; if they were of roughly the same magnitude, it would be easy to conclude mistakenly that taxes have no effect on firms' decisions.

Second, nearly all studies have had to rely on a crude measure of local taxes. The correct measure is the tax burden on the *marginal* firm. Such a measure would reflect all of the various provisions of the community's tax code, all tax incentives for new firms (e.g., property tax abatement, tax exemptions), and the operating characteristics of the firm. These data would be extremely difficult to collect, especially since fiscal packages for potential new firms are often designed on a case-by-case basis. Most studies therefore rely on some measure of the average tax rate. Average and marginal rates, however, are likely to diverge significantly for new firms; hence, one should treat all studies of the effects of taxes on location very cautiously.[16]

Third, local taxes are a fairly small part of the total costs of most firms. Consequently, it may be difficult to find the effects of taxes on location decisions; they may be swamped by the effects of differentials in other variables, such as the level of wages.

Our analysis lends support to an additional explanation raised by several other authors.[17] Typically, studies of firm location include measures of the local taxes that firms pay but no measure of the benefits they receive in return. Carlton (1983), for example, included a weighted average of the corporate and personal income tax rates in his model, but did not include any measure of the local public goods provided to firms.

We might then ask the following question. If our argument is correct and all local taxes on capital are in fact benefit taxes, what would be the effect of omitting local public services from an equation that tries to explain firm location decisions? A likely answer to this question is that the coefficient on the tax variable in such an equation would capture both (1) the direct effect of taxes on profits as well as (2) the product of the correlation between business taxes and local public goods and the direct effect of local public goods on profits. Our model suggests that an increase of $1 in a firm's local taxes will always be accompanied by $1 of extra benefits. If this is true, then the coefficient on taxes will be zero, since the negative effect of higher taxes will be exactly offset by the positive effect of better public services.

Helms (1985) presented interesting evidence on this point. His model was specified so that the coefficient on a tax variable represented the effect of a 1 percentage point increase in that tax if the proceeds were used to increase transfer payments; similarly, the coefficient of an expenditure variable showed the effect of a 1 percentage point increase in that expenditure category financed by a cut in transfer payments sufficient to leave the local budget intact. Helms's results are broadly consistent with our argument. He found that increasing business taxes to finance transfers has a negative and significant effect on a state's economic growth. On the other hand, increases in business taxes to finance services that benefit firms and firms' workers by improving a state's infrastructure or educational system had a positive effect on growth.

SUMMARY AND CONCLUSIONS

Our analysis suggests that the theory of state and local public finance offers three basic insights into interjurisdictional competition. First, if communities compete against one another to attract new business investment and jobs, then local taxes are equivalent to user fees.

Second (and basically a corollary to the first point), localities in a competitive setting are unable to redistribute capital income through taxation because taxes are nothing more than payments for goods and services received. When communities compete, one should expect to find that firms are required to pay for the police protection, public utilities, and roads that they require. Any attempts by localities to extract additional revenues from local business firms will fail in the sense that the loss in local wages associated with the departure of capital will more than offset any increments to local tax revenues. Likewise, subsidies to attract new business investment would, in our model, produce less in the way of additional wage income than the cost of the subsidies. The community best promotes its interests by avoiding such subsidies and by taxing local business only to pay for the benefits provided by local public services to these firms.

Third, interjurisdictional competition fosters efficiency. To see this, it is sufficient to note that the outcome under interjurisdictional competition is identical to the outcome that would emerge if one were to replace local governments with perfectly competitive firms that supplied local public goods to firms and households at marginal cost. Local taxes, in this setting, play the same role as prices. They do not distort economic decisions. Instead, they provide exactly the same information that prices provide; they represent the marginal social cost of the goods that households consume and firms use in production.

How should one evaluate these results? We contend that the answer to this question hinges on the policies of the federal government; it is impossible to evaluate interjurisdictional competition in a vacuum. Specifically, we would support such competition on efficiency grounds if we were certain that the federal government would fulfill the distribution function. If, for example, the federal government were to provide adequate support for low-income households throughout the country, then the case for local fiscal competition based on its efficiency-enhancing properties is compelling.

The problem arises if the federal government fails to fulfill its distribution function and communities are forced to compete against one another; in this case, our evaluation of competition is much less favourable. The attempt by local governments to institute needed redistributional measures may depend for its success on curbing to some extent the forces of interjurisdictional competition. Otherwise, the mobility of capital (and in a broader context the mobility of households) may largely frustrate the efforts to transfer income to poorer households. Such measures will, at the very least, introduce distortions in resource allocation, thereby compromising the case for unfettered competition among local jurisdictions. If we insist that state and local governments assume a major role in providing aid to the poor, then it is no longer clear that the solution that emerges under competition is desirable. There may then be a case, on second best grounds, for restricting such competition.

APPENDIX

In this appendix we derive the necessary conditions for the optimal community decisions presented in equations (7.6a), (7.6b), and (7.6c) in the text. It is easiest to begin by substituting the labor market condition in equation (7.2) into the private budget constraint in equation (7.5). Let λ_1, λ_2, λ_3 be the Lagrange multipliers associated with the private budget constraint, the public budget constraint in equation (7.4), and the constraint on the rate of return in (7.3). Then the solution to the community's maximization problem, assuming an interior solution, requires

$$u_c - \lambda_1 = 0 \tag{7.A1}$$

$$u_g - \lambda_2 \, p_g = 0 \tag{7.A2}$$

$$-\lambda_1(x f_{kx} + k f_{kk}) + \lambda_2 t \tag{7.A3}$$

$$+\lambda_3[f_{kk} - (x/k^2)f_x + (x/k)f_{kx}] = 0$$

$$-\lambda_1(k f_{kx} + x f_{xx}) - \lambda_2 p_x \tag{7.A4}$$

$$+\lambda_3[f_{kx} + (1/k)f_x + (x/k)f_{xx}] = 0$$

$$-\lambda_1 + \lambda_2 = 0 \tag{7.A5}$$

$$\lambda_2 k - \lambda_3 = 0. \tag{7.A6}$$

Equations (7.A1), (7.A2), and (7.A5) lead directly to equation (7.6a) in the text. Similarly, equations (7.A4), (7.A5), and (7.A6) together imply (7.6b), whereas equations (7.A3), (7.A5), and (7.A6) imply (7.6c).

Suppose we now add the additional constraint that the head tax must be equal to or less than some specified level h^*. Let λ_4 be the Lagrange multiplier associated with this new constraint. Optimization then requires us to replace (7.A2) with:

$$u_g - \lambda_2 p_g - \lambda_4 = 0. \tag{7.A2'}$$

If this head tax constraint is effective, then λ_4 must be positive. In that case, (7.A2') and (7.A1) show that the consumer's marginal rate of substitution between the public and private good u_g/u_c must be greater than p_g (i.e., public goods will be underprovided).

Notes

1. See U.S. ACIR (1991) for a review of the major issues in this debate.

2. The point of departure for the theory of local public finance is the famous Tiebout (1956) model. In a Tiebout world, mobile consumers choose among communities offering a diverse arry of local public goods; the basic insight emerging from this body

of work is that by "voting with their feet," consumers sort themselves out according to their demands for local public goods and produce an outcome that is marketlike in spirit and in its efficiency-enhancing properties. See Zodrow (1983), for a collection of papers on this approach to local public finance. Our approach here differs from the Tiebout setting in that we envision communities with stable populations that compete for a mobile stock of capital to generate higher employment and wage income. The motivation with which we are concerned is thus somewhat different from that in a Tiebout world in which individuals' incomes are often taken to be exogenously determined. Nevertheless, the outcome in our model shares some of the marketlike spirit of a Tiebout world. In addition, as we note, it is easy to extend our model to allow for mobile households without changing the basic results.

3. See Brown and Oates (1987) for a discussion of the redistributive function in a federal system.

4. It is not difficult to show that all of our results would continue to hold if we were to allow for labor mobility. In such a model, we would have to introduce land markets, where the price of land in each community would adjust so that in equilibrium, identical workers would realize the same level of utility everywhere.

5. This fictitious trading partner simplifies the problem by allowing us to focus on a one-sector model.

6. We assume that the ownership of capital in this society has been determined exogenously. There is no requirement that people necessarily own capital in their community; capital is traded in a national market.

7. The publicly provided input, X, is not a pure public good in the Samuelson sense; it is subject to congestion to the full extent of a private good. Thus, if a community's capital stock and labor force were to double, the community would have to double its inputs for local services in order for output to double. We assume, in addition, that units of this input are allocated among producers in proportion to their capital stock; larger facilities will thus require and receive proportionally more in the way of such things as sewer services, police protection, and training services.

8. Conceptually, it makes little difference whether we think of this tax as a property tax or a corporate income tax. In practice, however, the distinction might be important. For example, an income tax would treat firms that earn a profit (as defined by the state or local tax code) differently than firms that realize losses, but a property tax would draw no such distinctions.

9. In our model, the taxes households pay (h) and the services the community provides (g) do not influence business location decisions, but in a richer model this would not necessarily be the case. Suppose, for example, the labor is mobile and can, therefore, choose among communities. Workers would be willing to accept a lower wage in communities that have low taxes or superior public services. Firms would also prefer such communities, since labor costs would be lower there. Our model does not capture these important issues because it is a "closed city" model (labor in each community is fixed); it would be interesting to explore these matters further in an "open city" model (where labor is mobile).

10. Note that this rule that taxes on businesses should equal the cost of providing public goods to businesses is independent of the decisions of other communities. In particular, if for some reason Community A were to extract a fiscal surplus from firms, it remains optimal for Community B to set taxes exactly equal to costs. This result might at first seem paradoxical, but it follows logically from the structure of the model. The only thing that matters to Community B is r, the after-tax rate of return available in Community A; the composition of that return is irrelevant.

11. This argument is not quite correct. The economywide rate of return r must fall to allow the markets to absorb the capital leaving the community that imposed the

tax. Thus, figure 7.1 is a correct analysis of the partial equilibrium effects of a local tax on capital, but it misses some general equilibrium issues.

12. See Gordon (1983), for example.

13. Thus, the Barro (1974) model might be applicable to the federal government but not to local governments.

14. See, for example, Freeman (1979) on environment quality, Epple and Schipper (1981) on unfunded pension plans, and Oates (1969) on taxes and spending.

15. See U.S. ACIR (1991) and Newman and Sullivan (1988) for reviews of the literature in this field.

16. Papke (1987) offers some interesting evidence. Her tax variable is probably the best measure of local marginal tax rates. In a study of investment in 20 industries in 20 states, this variable had the correct sign and was statistically significant; two alternative measures of the average tax rate were insignificant.

17. See, for example, Papke (1987), Carlton (1983), Newman and Sullivan (1988), and Helms (1985).

References

Barro, R. J. 1974. "Are Government Bonds Net Worth?" *Journal of Political Economy* 82 (November/December): 1095–1117.

Bartik, Timothy J. 1985. "Business Location Decisions in the United States: Estimates of the Effects of Unionization, Taxes, and Other Characteristics of States." *Journal of Business and Economic Statistics* 3 (1, January): 14–22.

Brown, Charles C., and Wallace E. Oates. 1987. "Assistance to the Poor in a Federal System." *Journal of Public Economics* 32:307–30.

Carlton, Dennis. 1983. "The Location and Employment Choices of New Firms: An Economic Model with Discrete and Continuous Endogenous Variables." *Review of Economics and Statistics* 65 (3, August): 440–49.

Due, John F. 1961. "Studies of State-Local Tax Differences on Location of Industry." *National Tax Journal* 14 (June): 163–73.

Epple, D., and K. Schipper. 1981. "Municipal Pension Funding: A Theory and Some Evidence." *Public Choice* 37: 141–78.

Freeman, A. Myrick. 1979. *The Benefits of Environmental Improvement: Theory and Practice.* Baltimore and London: Resources for the Future and Johns Hopkins University Press.

Gordon, Roger. 1983. "An Optimal Taxation Approach to Fiscal Federalism." *Quarterly Journal of Economics* 97: 567–86.

Helms, L. Jay. 1985. "The Effect of State and Local Taxes on Economic Growth: A Time Series–Cross Section Approach." *Review of Economics and Statistics* 67 (November): 574–82.

McLure, Charles E. 1986. "Tax Competition: Is What's Good for the Private

Goose Also Good for the Public Gander?" *National Tax Journal* 39 (3, September): 341–48.

Mintz, Jack, and Henry Tulkens. 1986. "Commodity Tax Competition between Member States of a Federation: Equilibrium and Efficiency." *Journal of Public Economics* 29: 133–72.

Newman, Robert J., and Dennis H. Sullivan. 1988. "Econometric Analysis of Business Tax Impacts on Industrial Location: What Do We Know, and How Do We Know It?" *Journal of Urban Economics* 23 (March): 215–34.

Oates, Wallace E. 1969. "The Effects of Property Taxes and Local Public Spending on Property Values: An Empirical Study of Tax Capitalization and the Tiebout Hypothesis." *Journal of Political Economy* 77 (6, November/December): 957–71.

————. 1972. *Fiscal Federalism*. New York: Harcourt Brace Jovanovich.

Oates, Wallace E., and Robert M. Schwab. 1988a. "Economic Competition among Jurisdictions: Efficiency Enhancing or Distortion Inducing?" *Journal of Public Economics* 35 (April): 333–54.

————. 1988b. "The Theory of Regulatory Federalism: The Case of Environmental Management." Working Paper 88-26. College Park: University of Maryland, Department of Economics.

Papke, Leslie A. 1987. "Subnational Taxation and Capital Mobility: Estimates of Tax-Price Elasticities." *National Tax Journal* 40 (June): 191–204.

Stigler, George. 1957. "The Tenable Range of Functions of Local Government." In *Federal Expenditure Policy for Economic Growth and Stability*, U.S. Congress, Joint Economic Committee. 85th Cong., 1st sess. Washington, D.C.: U.S. Government Printing Office.

Tiebout, Charles. 1956. "A Pure Theory of Local Expenditures." *Journal of Political Economy* 64 (5, October): 416–24.

U.S. Advisory Commission on Intergovernmental Relations. 1991. *Interjurisdictional Tax and Policy Competition: Good or Bad for the Federal System?* Washington, D.C.: U.S. ACIR.

Wildasin, David E.. 1989. "Interjurisdictional Capital Mobility: Fiscal Externality and a Corrective Subsidy." *Journal of Urban Economics* 25 (March): 193–212.

Wilson, John D. 1987a. "Trade, Capital Mobility, and Tax Competition." *Journal of Political Economy* 95 (4, August): 835–56.

————. 1987b. "Trade in a Tiebout Economy." *American Economic Review* 77 (3, June): 431–41.

Zodrow, George R., ed. 1983. *Local Provision of Public Services: The Tiebout Model after Twenty-five Years*. New York: Academic Press.

Zodrow, George R., and Peter Mieszkowski. 1986. "Pigou, Tiebout, Property Taxation, and the Underprovision of Local Public Goods." *Journal of Public Economics* 19: 296–315.

Chapter Eight

HOW CLOSELY DOES STATE AND LOCAL GOVERNMENT BEHAVIOR CONFORM TO A PERFECTLY COMPETITIVE MODEL?

Andrew Reschovsky

Wallace E. Oates and Robert W. Schwab, in chapter 7, have offered important insights in helping to clarify the debate over the advantages and disadvantages of interjurisdictional competition.

The major outcome of their chapter is that on the basis of a competitive model of local government behavior, all local taxes become benefit taxes, with both businesses and consumers paying for publicly provided goods and services an amount exactly equal to the value they place on these public goods. Thus, there are no possibilities for local governments to finance redistributive public expenditures. An advantage of this model is that it emphasizes the fact that both consumers (or voters) and businesses benefit directly from the public goods provided by local government.

The authors conclude that their competitive model of local government behavior results in an efficient provision of local public goods. I believe their conclusion is correct, and as the authors assert, the model creates a useful benchmark for evaluating actual competition between governments. The major question, however, is the applicability of the perfectly competitive model to the actual competitive behavior of local governments.

Under the competitive model, local governments compete for firms by providing them with public goods that serve as inputs into their production processes. In equilibrium, local governments provide public goods to firms up to the point where the marginal product of the public input equals its price. I am not at all sure, however, that this competitive analog provides a good explanation of how most local governments operate. From the perspective of local governments, the link between the marginal productivity of public goods and the taxes on businesses is not crystal clear. Governments generally do not know how important public education, and even police and fire services, are to individual firms. In the private market analogy, this is not a problem because firms are assumed to be price takers. They reveal the value of the marginal product of any factor by equating it to the price of the factor. However, for several reasons, many firms may not be price takers with respect to local or state governments.

Even where governments provide goods and services that are essentially private, the collective financing of publicly provided goods can weaken the link between tax prices and the consumption of public goods. The price that a firm pays for public goods is equal to its share of the total local government cost of providing the public good. Firms can often reduce their share of the total cost by influencing the local political process. This can occur by a firm's threatening to move if tax rebates or other tax preferences are not granted, or by financing the election campaigns of politicians who agree to lower the firm's tax share. Governments tend to be susceptible to pressure from businesses because they fear the political damage created by firms that make good on their threats to move. In fact, the political damage created by a firm that leaves a community because it has not been granted preferential tax treatment may outweigh the real economic costs of the firm's departure. Governments tend to be particularly sensitive to the demands of businesses because they have no way of judging the credibility of threats to leave, and are uncertain of whether they can attract other firms willing to pay a larger share of costs than firms already within the jurisdiction.[1]

Although one might expect the competitive model to apply to small firms with little market power and low levels of employment, in many states, business firms have banded together in lobbying groups that, in effect, allow them to act like monopsonists with respect to both state and local governments. In Massachusetts, for example, a group called Citizens for Limited Taxation, which sponsored both Proposition 2½ in 1980 and a voter initiative to place a tight cap on state spending in 1986, is funded primarily by business groups, such as the High Tech Council. Other groups, such as the Massachusetts Taxpayers Foundation (representing commercial and banking interests) and the Associated Industries of Massachusetts, have been very successful in influencing tax policies in Massachusetts. To the extent that these groups act like monopsonists, there is no longer a guarantee that governments will be able to provide the efficient level of public services.

In chapter 7, Oates and Schwab show that the taxation of mobile capital to finance public (redistributive) goods is inefficient. They illustrate this point by citing an example from Charles McLure (1986) involving taxation of the fishing fleet by Gloucester, Massachusetts, in order to finance a school lunch program. McLure argues that neither fish eaters nor the owners of the fishing boats would (in the long run) bear the cost of the lunch program because the boats would simply move to a neighboring harbor. In reality, however, capital may be significantly less than perfectly mobile because its use is often linked to a specific location. In fact, McLure's example of capital mobility is not an especially good one. It turns out that Gloucester fishing boat owners probably have no alternative harbors that are both well protected from winter storms and in which they would be welcome. The shores of most neighboring harbors are now lined with fancy private homes and condominiums, and the available commercial space is usually taken up by yacht marinas and by seafood restaurants with dining terraces overlooking the harbor. The fishing industry is no longer welcome. Although the fishing boats themselves are mobile, docking rights, to say nothing of fish processing plants, can no longer outbid alternative land uses in most if not all of Massachusetts' ports. The lesson from this example is that the owners of dock space in Gloucester are earning location rents, and taxing these rents may in fact be an efficient way of financing a school lunch program.

Although not essential for their results, the authors assume that labor is immobile between communities. It is interesting to point out that some recent research indicates that tax policy does in fact influence the locational decisions of individuals. Some research (Advisory Commission on Intergovernmental Relations 1991) points to evidence that the taxation of workers, especially those with highly specialized skills and consequently high incomes, may influence their locational choices. Howard Chernick and I (1989) have demonstrated that the reductions in marginal tax rates mandated by the federal Tax Reform Act of 1986, combined with the elimination of state sales-tax deductibility, will lead to some degree of migration of high-income taxpayers living in low-income central cities to high-income homogeneous suburbs, especially if those suburbs are located in adjacent, lower-tax states.

Oates and Schwab suggest that although a system of competitive local government finance is efficient, it is unlikely to be equitable. This is not surprising, in light of the conclusion that the only local government taxes will be benefit taxes. The regressive nature of many benefit taxes is well documented. In some recent work, Chernick and I (1990) have tried to extend our knowledge of the distributional consequences of state and local government taxation by focusing on the impact of the overall tax system on the poor. We have found, for example, that in Massachusetts, whereas the average state and local tax burden is 9.2 percent, the burden on those below the poverty line is 11.5 percent. These burdens, which I regard as high burdens, come primarily from the local property tax, a tax considered by some economists to be fundamentally a benefits tax.

I would like to close with a question. To what extent are local governments following the prescription of the Oates-Schwab competitive model and relying only on benefit taxation? This is a difficult question to answer precisely. On the one hand, many governments actively compete for business firms by giving tax breaks, credits, and abatements to attract business. Further, Steven Gold (1988) has reported that 13 of the 40 states using broad-based income taxation reduced their top marginal tax rate in 1987. On the other hand, there are many examples of state and local governments financing redistributive social programs. However, there have been few attempts to measure the magnitude of these efforts across the states. An exception is a recent study of state-financed spending in Massachusetts, which found that 31 percent of total state-financed programs are for programs targeted to low-income individuals (Weinstein and Keough 1987). There have been widespread attempts to convert benefit taxes, at least partially, to ability-to-pay taxes. A number of states and local governments have adopted "circuit breakers" and various credits to reduce the burden of property taxation on low-income taxpayers. These observations suggest that there is a great deal of fluidity in the current state and local fiscal environment, with competition pushing some governments toward benefit taxation, while other governments resist such moves, presumably for reasons of tax equity.

Note

1. In a recent paper, Michael Wolkoff (1987) presented an interesting game-theoretic model of state and local governments' competition for business firms.

References

Chernick, Howard, and Andrew Reschovsky. 1990. "The Taxation of the Poor." *Journal of Human Resources* 25 (4, Fall): 712–35.

Gold, Steven D. 1988. "Recent Changes in State-Local Tax Levels." *Tax Notes*, March 21.

McClure, Charles E. 1986. "Tax Competition: Is What's Good for the Private Goose Also Good for the Public Gander?" *National Tax Journal* 39 (3, September): 341–48.

Reschovsky, Andrew and Howard Chernick. 1989. "Federal Tax Reform and the Taxation of Urban Residents." *Public Finance Quarterly* 17 (2, April): 123–57.

U.S. Advisory Commission on Intergovernmental Relations. 1991. *Interjurisdictional Tax and Policy Competition: Good or Bad for the Federal System?* Washington, D.C.: Author.

Weinstein, Deborah, and Robert Keough. 1987. *The Poor People's Budget: FY 1988.* Boston: Meredith & Associates.

Wolkoff, Michael J. 1987. "Economic Development as a Signaling Game." University of Rochester, Public Policy Analysis Programs, Rochester, New York, April. Photocopy.

Chapter Nine

FEDERAL AID TO STATES AND LOCALITIES AND THE APPROPRIATE COMPETITIVE FRAMEWORK

Therese J. McGuire

This chapter investigates whether interjurisdictional competition provides an untapped rationale for federal aid to states and localities. In most contexts, competition is viewed as a positive force for bringing about more efficient and more desirable resource allocations. However, when some jurisdictions are at an unfair disadvantage in this competition, or when key assumptions do not hold, the competitive outcome is less satisfactory. In these situations, intervention of the federal government may be justified, and the solution may involve intergovernmental grants.

In this chapter, I describe two models of competition among jurisdictions. I argue that the model of efficient competition is likely to apply to local governments, but that the model of destructive competition may apply to state governments. Because destructive competition results in the provision of inefficiently low levels of public goods and services, federal grants to state governments may be justified. To mitigate the incentives to engage in destructive competition, federal grants should be accompanied by federal restrictions on the structures of state taxes.

DEFINING COMPETITION

Consider two opposing economic views of interjurisdictional tax competition. In one view, which I will refer to as the Tiebout model,[1] jurisdictions compete for mobile residents by offering tax-expenditure bundles. Given enough latitude in the choice of tax instruments

Helen Ladd and Robert Rafuse provided useful discussions of an earlier version of this paper. I am grateful to Michael E. Bell, James Hines, Jr., Daphne Kenyon, and Robert Porter for very helpful comments and conversations.

and in the variety of bundles offered, allocative and productive efficiency are achieved. Allocative efficiency results when mobile residents, with heterogeneous tastes for local services, allocate themselves among jurisdictions to obtain their preferred bundles of goods and services at the lowest tax price. Productive efficiency results as jurisdictions competing for these mobile residents are constrained to produce public goods and services efficiently and to offer a set of services desired by some subset of these mobile consumers. The competitive equilibrium is characterized by jurisdictions composed of residents with like tastes (and typically, like resources) but by heterogeneity across jurisdictions, reflecting heterogeneity of tastes in the population.

The other view of tax competition among jurisdictions can be called destructive competition. The possibility of a competitive equilibrium resulting in inefficient outcomes for the players is supported by game-theoretic models of competition between firms in an industry. Whether such an outcome is plausible for competing jurisdictions depends on whether they face incentives similar to those faced by players in the noncooperative games of industrial organization.

Suppose, for example, that jurisdictions choose tax/expenditure bundles that are optimal for the nation as a whole. In defining this optimal allocation, a critical assumption is that individuals have preferences for redistribution and thus choose revenue systems that rely on ability-to-pay taxes. The optimal allocation is the set of taxes and expenditures that maximizes a social welfare function based on the preferences of individuals, subject to an aggregate resource constraint. The many optimal tax/expenditure systems chosen by the jurisdictions are devised without consideration for mobility.

Further suppose that the nation's population is heterogeneous in terms of income (or wealth) and mobility. Then, any one jurisdiction would have an incentive to cut taxes for relatively wealthy and mobile individuals (or corporations), if through these tax breaks, the jurisdiction could attract enough new wealthy residents that it could afford to cut taxes for its immobile residents or provide more public goods. However, all jurisdictions would have an incentive to provide these discriminatory tax breaks. In equilibrium, there would be no movement or little movement of relatively wealthy, mobile individuals. At the competitive equilibrium, because jurisdictions provide tax breaks to the mobile wealthy, they collect less revenue from mobile individuals and provide a lower level of public goods or charge higher taxes on immobile residents than those that result in the optimal allocation.

In this view, jurisdictions compete for relatively mobile, relatively wealthy residents by selectively granting tax breaks for these residents, or by shifting tax burdens to nonresidents, or by choosing tax bases and tax rates (a mix of tax instruments)[2] that result in relatively low tax burdens for relatively wealthy and mobile residents. In this view, taxes are not appropriately thought of as benefit taxes, but are related to ability to pay, to economic activity, and to mobility rather than to public goods and services received. This competition is sometimes described as a zero-sum game, but is more appropriately viewed as negative-sum because no new economic activity is generated in the aggregate,[3] and state and local revenues are lower, resulting in lower public goods and services. In this noncooperative solution, the competing jurisdictions are all worse off than if they could somehow cooperate and agree not to compete (an example of the prisoners' dilemma).

Both of these paradigms are too simplistic. Jurisdictions differ in more respects than tax/expenditure bundles. Thus, mobile workers, consumers, and firms trade off fiscal differences for differences in climate, wages, amenities, and the cost of living. Also, jurisdictions may choose or be constrained to use tax instruments that are imperfect benefit taxes. Still, the two models in their simple forms can lead to useful insights, the most important being an understanding of the basic assumptions distinguishing the two views.

In the Tiebout model, taxes are benefit taxes. The tax price paid by a new resident is the marginal cost associated with providing public goods and services to the resident. The incentives faced by mobile residents are correct in that a new resident will move in (or move out) only if he or she values the public goods at least as much as (or less than) the cost to the jurisdiction of providing the extra goods. No consumer can enjoy the benefits of the goods and services offered by a jurisdiction until he or she becomes a resident of the jurisdiction.

In the destructive competition model, it is assumed that people desire redistribution, and thus that taxes are divorced from benefits received. The value of the public goods and services received by any resident need not be related to the taxes paid by the resident. The ability of jurisdictions to break the link between taxes and expenditures is limited by the threat of relocation by highly mobile, relatively wealthy individuals. In an effort to attract these relocators, jurisdictions offer selective tax breaks or lower the overall burden or progressivity of broad-based taxes. This, then, cripples the ability of the jurisdictions to fund public goods and services through a tax system based on ability to pay. The outcome is inefficient because the resulting level of public goods and services is lower than desired (even than the level desired by the mobile wealthy); yet, no one has an incentive to change his or her behavior in a way that will correct for the underallocation.

The irony is that the desire of jurisdictions (and of all individuals) to raise taxes based on ability to pay[4] and to provide public goods and services (with both taxes and expenditures potentially on a redistributive basis) results in an inability to attain such a fiscal system. Mobile, relatively wealthy individuals have an incentive to move out of jurisdictions that attempt to break the link between taxes and benefits, and competing jurisdictions redesign their tax systems to be less redistributive in an effort to retain these fiscally desirable residents.[5]

Equilibrium in the Tiebout model is characterized by benefit taxes. In the destructive competition model, a fiscal system will be a mixture of benefit taxes and ability-to-pay taxes, where individuals of differing mobility and wealth are treated differentially. In the former case, the result is efficient, but in the latter, inefficiently low levels of the public goods are provided. The distinction between the two models is thus of more than theoretical interest. Competition in the destructive model is, by an efficiency criterion, undesirable.

NORMATIVE ANALYSIS OF COMPETITION AMONG GOVERNMENTS

It is reasonably clear that both productive and allocative efficiency result under the Tiebout model of competition. It is also reasonably clear that the assumptions required for the Tiebout model are not likely to occur in many real-world situations. In particular, the number of jurisdictions is not likely to be great enough to accommodate the diversity of tastes for public goods. Thus, we are unlikely to achieve allocative efficiency (the provision of desired levels and mixes of public goods and services) whether our operating model is Tiebout competition or destructive competition.

The situation for productive efficiency is, perhaps, different. So long as residents are mobile, under either model of competition, jurisdictions have an incentive to produce publicly provided goods and services at the lowest possible cost. Low-cost production enables one jurisdiction to compete with a like jurisdiction by levying the lowest possible taxes. Thus, *if* residents are mobile, competition among jurisdictions is likely to result in productive efficiency.

Competition among jurisdictions is likely to lead to both horizontal and vertical inequities. These inequities are only relevant in a world where the assumptions of the Tiebout model do not hold. In a perfect Tiebout world, all taxes are benefit taxes, and there is no issue of incidence or fairness. But in a world where at least some taxes are not benefit taxes and, particularly where the nature of the public goods and services provided is redistributive, both types of inequities are likely to result from the destructive competition that ensues. As jurisdictions compete for relatively mobile residents, those residents who are less mobile may face higher burdens. For example, tax breaks to newly locating firms result in horizontal inequity between old and new firms. Vertical inequities can occur if the more mobile individuals (and thus the individuals who are more capable of extracting tax deals) are also relatively wealthy. Then, despite a general desire for redistribution or progressive taxes, competition will result in lower taxes (or less high tax burdens) for relatively wealthy residents. Whatever the evidence on the relative mobility of the poor versus the rich, it is clear that many state and local policymakers are concerned about outmigration of the relatively rich and, therefore, they design tax systems that are perhaps more regressive than desired or than would result if the residents were immobile and there were no competition.

Thus far I have referred to generic jurisdictions. In the United States, states and localities (municipalities, counties, townships, special districts, and school districts) represent two distinct sets of jurisdictions. The nature of the environment in which states and localities compete, the nature of the goods and services provided publicly by the two, and the availability of tax and other revenue instruments, vary between the two sets of jurisdictions. In the next section I argue that, although the distinction is by no means clear-cut, the Tiebout model and its assumptions are more appropriate when evaluating competition among localities, whereas the destructive competition model and its assumptions are more appropriate for evaluating competition among states.

STATES VERSUS LOCALITIES

The primary distinction between the Tiebout model of competition and the destructive competition model is that the former is based on benefit taxation, whereas in the latter, it is assumed that there is little relationship between an individual's benefits and taxes. Goods and services provided by localities lend themselves more readily to benefit taxation financing than do the goods and services provided by states. Whether the financing instruments actually employed by localities are, in fact, benefit taxes is open to debate.[6] However, if we assume that localities provide goods and services whose benefits can be easily attributed to residents (either through user charges or because benefits are basically per capita and the population is homogeneous), then competition among localities for mobile residents may result in allocative and productive efficiency. In other words, competition among localities should be encouraged.

If state governments, on the other hand, provide goods and services that are primarily redistributive in nature, or that generate benefits that are either not fully appropriated by the residents or are difficult to attribute to heterogeneous residents, then the method of financing is unlikely to be benefit taxation. Assume further that ability-to-pay taxes are a primary source of revenue for state governments. Also, assume that, as a group, residents of states are more likely than residents of localities to be heterogeneous in terms of tastes, income, and mobility. In this situation, competition among jurisdictions is likely to be destructive and to result in inefficiently low levels of public goods and services, regressive tax systems, and horizontal inequities. It could be argued that cooperation, rather than competition, should be encouraged.

In fact, states do rely on income and sales taxes, which are not generally considered to be benefit taxes, whereas the primary source of locally raised revenue is property taxes, a tax often thought of as a benefit tax. State welfare programs are one of the larger expenditure categories, whereas local goverments rarely engage in explicit income redistribution. Thus, competition among local governments, which rely on benefit taxes, is likely to be beneficial, whereas competition among state governments, which do not rely on benefit taxes and which engage in redistribution, is likely to be destructive and inefficient.

I have attempted to justify a government role to either encourage or discourage competition. Clearly, in our federal system, that role could only be played by the federal government, using possibly several policy instruments at its disposal. The sections following consider whether federal intergovernmental grants could be used as an instrument for setting the competitive framework for state and local governments.

RATIONALES FOR FEDERAL AID

The economic theory of intergovernmental grants identifies two separate roles for aid from the federal government to states and localities.[7] The first role for intergovernmental grants is to correct for positive interjurisdictional spillovers. If the benefits of locally provided public goods and services are not completely appropriated by the residents of the jurisdiction providing the goods and services, then the jurisdiction will choose an inefficiently low level of public goods and services. When the externality is present at the margin (for incremental units of the public good or service), an appropriate solution is for the other affected jurisdictions, which possibly comprise the whole nation, to subsidize local provision at a rate equal to the marginal external benefit associated with the level of provision that equates total social marginal benefit with marginal cost. The form of grant often suggested is an open-ended matching categorical grant.

If we examine the nature of the goods and services provided by state and local governments, it is easy to identify a role for matching grants. Nonresidents of a given jurisdiction benefit from the transportation system provided and maintained by the jurisdiction. They also benefit from the education system (especially if people are highly mobile, but even when there is no interjurisdictional mobility, if education leads to higher participation in the political system and increased concern for the community and society, in general), from recreation facilities, from public welfare, and from publicly provided safety. Clearly, nonresidents benefit less than residents, but the marginal external benefit is likely to be large enough that, without outside support, the resulting level of goods and services would be significantly less than the efficient level.

The second primary role for intergovernmental grants is to facilitate fiscal equalization or to mitigate the impact on local jurisdictions and their residents of unequal fiscal resources and needs (fiscal disparities). The problem is that in a federal system, jurisdictions will vary in terms of their wealth (and needs); therefore, different tax rates will be necessary to provide equal expenditures (or equal levels of public service). Because individuals of equal income may live in different jurisdictions, horizontal inequities may be generated.

However, if lower tax rates are fully capitalized into the value of residential property, the full price of residency in any two jurisdictions containing people of equal income will be the same. This outcome will occur only if there is a sufficient number of individuals at each income level (relative to the number of jurisdictions) and sufficient mobility. Under this view, there are no horizontal inequities because housing prices reflect differences in tax rates; hence, two people of equal income living in jurisdictions with different tax rates will face the same tax-inclusive price of entry (i.e., the same tax-inclusive price for housing).

Individuals are not perfectly mobile, however, as indicated by studies that find less than 100 percent capitalization of fiscal differences into the price of housing.[8] Thus, it is likely that a federal system will lead to horizontal inequities because relatively wealthy jurisdictions can provide a given level of services at a lower tax rate and a lower overall price of admission (tax-inclusive price of housing) than less-wealthy jurisdictions.

A further consideration, which may lead to additional inequities or to inabilities on the part of less-wealthy jurisdictions to provide public services, is the desire of the federal government to impose a minimum standard or level of expenditures for certain categories of goods and services (e.g., primary education). Here the justification is not the positive spillover argument, but rather an equal opportunity argument that citizens, regardless of where they reside, should have equal access to certain goods and services.

Some observers would argue that because the federal government mandates these standards, it is only fair that the federal government pay for them. But fairness between governments is a vacuous concept. Fair treatment of individuals is the appropriate concern. A role for federal funding of programs with federally determined minimum standards can be found by reference to the horizontal equity argument. If the tax prices faced by individuals of equal income in different jurisdictions differ because one is less wealthy than another and if, in particular, less-wealthy jurisdictions find it prohibitively expensive to achieve a given minimum standard, then grants from the federal government to relatively poor jurisdictions can be justified.

Thus, there would appear to be a role for both matching grants and block grants in a federal system. The justification for matching grants is positive interjurisdictional spillovers. For block grants, the justification is the correction of horizontal inequities and the assurance of the fiscal ability of all jurisdictions to achieve given minimum standards.

Most current federal grants are matching rate grants, many of them closed-ended, where the matching rates vary with some measure of need or resources of the recipient jurisdictions.[9] Per-capita income is an imperfect, but readily available, measure of average need or resources of a jurisdiction. When per-capita income is compared to per-capita total federal grants to state and local governments by state, the inverse relationship between the two appears to be weak.[10] Federal grants would seem to be ineffective in alleviating wealth-induced horizontal inequities or fiscal inabilities to provide minimum standards.

This discussion of grants-in-aid has implicitly assumed that recipient jurisdictions act rationally and in the best interests of their residents. This may not be a good assumption and, contrary to the median-voter view of the world, there is evidence of an excessively large impact of grants on local government expenditures and budgets.[11] I mention this merely as a caution against blind faith in the ability of grants to accomplish any of the goals set out for them.

IMPACT OF CURRENT FEDERAL AID ON COMPETITIVE EFFICIENCY

In the previous discussion of the role of federal aid, there was no mention of competition among jurisdictions or of the possibilities for grants-in-aid to facilitate useful competition or inhibit destructive competition. This section briefly explores such possibilities for federal aid.

The current federal aid structure, which is a mix of matching and block grants of a slightly redistributive nature, facilitates interjurisdictional tax and expenditure competition if grant monies substitute for own-source tax revenues or if grant monies finance increases in public goods or services. Then, less-wealthy jurisdictions could offer lower tax rates and burdens to mobile residents without having to cut expenditures, or could provide more services without an increase in taxes. Thus, grants may finance enhanced competition among jurisdictions and may thus improve allocative efficiency.

Recall that one advantage of interjurisdictional competition is that local governments or bureaucracies are constrained in the extent to which they can waste public funds. This productive efficiency advantage of competition would appear to be present in either the Tiebout model or the destructive competition model. However, intergovernmental grants would appear to be a most inappropriate tool for attempting to facilitate competition that achieves cost-effectiveness. There is overwhelming evidence[12] that grants have a strong stimulative effect on expenditures, and it is not clear that the increased expenditures are reflected in increased quantity or quality of services or goods.

DESIGN OF AID PROGRAMS TO FACILITATE OR INHIBIT COMPETITION

Do models of competition provide new normative arguments for the federal government to intervene in the federal system through aid programs? I conclude that, except when there is destructive competition, there is no justification on *efficiency grounds* for the federal government to interfere with interjurisdictional competition. The old adage "if it ain't broke, don't fix it" would seem to apply.

But suppose destructive competition is the relevant model. This model is likely to be more relevant to states than localities, both because of the types of taxes employed by most states and because of the redistributive nature of some of the goods and services provided by states. The inefficiency that results from competition among states for relatively mobile and wealthy residents is that the overall level of state expenditures will be too low. Competition for the pool of relatively wealthy and mobile residents results in each state forgiving taxes on these individuals, thus leading to a paucity of resources to accomplish the state's expenditure goals.

Can a federal grant program be designed for states that would diminish the incentive to give tax breaks to relatively wealthy and mobile individuals and firms, while preserving the efficiency aspects of competition (i.e., the diversity across states in tax/expenditure bundles offered, and the constraints on bureaucratic waste)? Consider a program like the recently abandoned General Revenue Sharing program, which provided unrestricted funds to states and localities based on a formula that included population and per-capita income. Such a program provides an alternative source of revenues for state governments that enables them to be less sensitive to the loss of relatively wealthy residents, and thus, perhaps, less likely to engage in destructive competition for those residents. If there were no constraints on how the states spent the grant monies, we would expect to see diversity in the types and levels of public goods and services provided.

However, a federal grant program unaccompanied by restrictions on interstate competition is likely to be ineffective in inhibiting destructive competition. The incentive to compete with other states in a zero-sum or negative-sum game for wealthy residents remains, even though the incentive may be diminished by the availabilty of grant monies. Mobile, wealthy residents still provide fiscal dividends to those states that are able to attract them through the use of tax breaks or regressive tax systems.

It seems that another instrument, other than intergovernmental grants, is needed to prevent states from engaging in destructive competition (i.e., from competing with one another for wealthy, mobile residents). The most straightforward method is to take away the states' means of competition. This could be accomplished by limiting states to tax bases that are difficult to tailor to mobile, wealthy individuals, or by restricting the parameters available to states in designing tax stuctures. For example, most of the special breaks to mobile individuals and firms are implemented through state personal and corporate income taxes. Suppose states were restricted to the federal definition for the base of these taxes and to a federally defined taxpayer, and were not allowed to grant special exemptions but were free to set the rate structure only.[13] Then any preferential tax treatment would be applicable to mobile and immobile residents alike, and all residents would have a better understanding of the implications of chosen tax policies. State general sales taxes are an example of a tax base that is difficult to tailor to a specific set of taxpayers. They are, therefore, less often involved in interstate tax competition (except sometimes over the overall rate, which is applicable to all taxpayers).

One proposal, then, is for a federal intergovernmental grant program to state governments, financed with federal personal and corporate income taxes. It would be distributed by a formula based on population and per-capita income, and, if so desired, at a level high enough to enable all states to achieve a nationally determined minimum level for a select set of goods and services. The grant program also would be accompanied by restrictions on allowable state tax bases, restrictions that would limit tax base and taxpayer definitions to those of the federal government, while allowing tax rates to be set by state governments. The proposal includes a grant program because the identified inefficiency, resulting from destructive competition, is in the direction of too little being spent. The grant is redistributive in nature because low-income states have a greater need to compete for relatively wealthy, mobile residents. The additional constraints on the fiscal systems of the states are imposed because the grant by itself does nothing to address the underlying incentives that lead to the inefficiency.

States would still compete with one another, but would be less at the mercy of mobile, wealthy residents in setting tax policy. States would have a steady source of revenue in the revenue-sharing program, and competition among states would involve tax rates applicable to all residents. Tax competition would thus be less desirable because its revenue consequences would be more pronounced. The incentive to produce public goods efficiently would remain, because efficient production allows states to set tax rates as low as possible for any given level of expenditures. The idea is to diminish the incentive to compete for a select set of wealthy residents, while maintaining the incentive to compete for all (potentially mobile) residents.

CONCLUSION

I have attempted to determine here whether federal aid to states and localities has a role to play in setting the appropriate competitive framework. Competition among jurisdictions can be beneficial. Accordingly, the only role for grants is to provide monies to less-wealthy jurisdictions to enable them to provide minimum levels of public goods and services at more "competitive" tax rates.

When competition is destructive and inefficiently low levels of public goods and services result, intergovernmental grants may be justified. The justification for federal aid applies to state governments rather than local governments because destructive competition is more likely to ensue among states than among localities. This is the case because the taxes employed by states are generally not benefit taxes, the goods and services provided by states are often redistributive in nature, and state residents display greater diversity in tastes, income, and mobility. In addition to federal aid programs, federal restrictions on state tax structures may be called for to weaken the mechanisms for destructive tax competition among states.

Notes

1. See Tiebout (1956) and chapter 7, this volume.
2. For a discussion of the issues surrounding the choice of tax mix, see Ladd and Weist (1987).

3. One could argue that lower overall taxes might lead to an increase in overall economic activity. But this argument fails to account for the negative impact on economic activity of correspondingly lower expenditures on public goods and services.

4. By ability-to-pay taxes I mean taxes whose burdens increase with increases in income, wealth, or other measures of well-being. No degree of "gressivity" is assumed.

5. See Oates (1972), Pauly (1973), Ladd and Doolittle (1982), and Brown and Oates (1987) for discussions of interjurisdictional migration and redistribution in a federal system.

6. See Hamilton (1975) for a model in which property taxes are benefit taxes.

7. An early, and one of the best, treatments of the economic theory of intergovernmental grants is Oates (1972).

8. See Bloom, Ladd, and Yinger (1983) for a survey of empirical studies of the capitalization of taxes and expenditures into property values. Oates (1969) is the progenitor of this literature.

9. See Gramlich (1987) for a brief discussion of the level and nature of the current federal grant structure.

10. As an example, see U.S. Advisory Commission on Intergovernmental Relations (1987: tables 9, 74).

11. See Gramlich (1977) and Inman (1979) for surveys of the literature. Recent studies that find large positive effects on expenditures of intergovernmental grants include Bradbury et al. (1984) and Holtz-Eakin and McGuire (1988).

12. See references cited in note 11, as well as various articles in Mieszkowski and Oakland (1979).

13. Douglas Clark of the Department of Finance, Government of Canada, pointed out to me (March 1988) that provincial income taxes are structured this way in Canada, and that there appears to be less interprovincial tax competition in Canada than in the United States.

References

Bloom, Howard, Helen F. Ladd, and John Yinger. 1983. "Are Property Taxes Capitalized into House Values?" In *Local Provision of Public Services: The Tiebout Model after Twenty-Five Years*, edited by George R. Zodrow. New York: Academic Press.

Bradbury, K. L., H. F. Ladd, M. Perrault, A. Reschovsky, and J. Yinger. 1984. "State Aid to Offset Fiscal Disparities across Communities." *National Tax Journal* 37(2, June): 151–70.

Brown, Charles C., and Wallace E. Oates. 1987. "Assistance to the Poor in a Federal System." *Journal of Public Economics* 32(3): 307–30.

Gramlich, Edward M. 1977. "Intergovernmental Grants: A Review of the Empirical Literature." In *The Political Economy of Fiscal Federalism*, edited by Wallace E. Oates, Lexington, Mass.: Lexington Books.

_____. 1987. "Federalism and Federal Deficit Reduction." *National Tax Journal* 40(3, September): 299–313.

Hamilton, Bruce W. 1975. "Zoning and Property Taxation in a System of Local Governments." *Urban Studies* 12: 205–11.

Holtz-Eakin, Douglas, and Therese McGuire. 1988. "Will They Know Me When I'm Gone? An Epitaph for Federal General Revenue Sharing." Columbia University, Dept. of Economics, New York. Photocopy.

Inman, Robert P. 1979. "The Fiscal Performance of Local Governments: An Interpretative Review." In *Current Issues in Urban Economics*, edited by Peter Mieszkowski and Mahlon Straszheim. Baltimore: Johns Hopkins University Press.

Ladd, Helen F., and Fred C. Doolittle. 1982. "Which Level of Government Should Assist the Poor?" *National Tax Journal* 35(3, September): 323–36.

Ladd, Helen F., and Dana R. Weist. 1987. "State and Local Tax Systems: Balance among Taxes vs. Balance among Policy Goals." In *The Quest for Balance in State-Local Revenue Structures*, edited by Frederick D. Stocker. Cambridge, Mass.: Lincoln Institute of Land Policy.

Mieszkowski, Peter, and William H. Oakland. 1979. *Fiscal Federalism and Grants-in-Aid*. Washington, D.C.: Urban Institute.

Oates, Wallace E. 1969. "The Effects of Property Taxes and Local Public Spending on Property Values: An Empirical Study of Tax Capitalization and the Tiebout Hypothesis." *Journal of Political Economy* 77(6, November/December): 957–71.

_____. 1972. *Fiscal Federalism*. New York: Harcourt Brace Jovanovich.

Pauly, Mark V. 1973. "Income Redistribution as a Local Public Good." *Journal of Public Economics* 2(February): 33–58.

Tiebout, Charles M. 1956. "The Pure Theory of Local Expenditures." *Journal of Political Economy* 64(October): 416–24.

U.S. Advisory Commission on Intergovernmental Relations. 1987. *Significant Features of Fiscal Federalism, 1987*. Washington, D.C.: Author.

Chapter Ten

SOME OBSERVATIONS ON INTERJURISDICTIONAL COMPETITION AND FEDERAL GRANT POLICY

Robert W. Rafuse, Jr.

Therese J. McGuire, in chapter 9, has explored at length the extent to which grants-in-aid can be a solution to a problem—competition among governments—that, in my view, does not warrant intense concern. In this chapter, I include a few specific observations on interjurisdictional competition, but my primary focus is on federal grant policy.

INTERJURISDICTIONAL COMPETITION

Arguments that competition among state and local governments is somehow "destructive" rest on the premise that competition makes it difficult for those governments to pursue certain types of policies. To assess the seriousness of the problem, two things are needed: (1) a framework for evaluating the appropriateness of the policies that interjurisdictional competition is alleged to frustrate, and (2) the identities of these policies. McGuire and I agree that the most useful framework can be found in established normative theory concerning the agendas of governments in a federal system in which efficiency, equity, and accountability are paramount values.

The primary purpose of the state and local policies whose pursuit is most severely constrained by interjurisdictional competition is the redistribution of income. This greatly simplifies the assessment of the seriousness of the problem: the policies impaired by competition relate to a matter that should not be a major concern of the states and local governments. If redistribution is most appropriately a responsibility of the federal government, then most discussion that views competition among the states and localities with alarm is a waste of time.

Competition among subnational units of government is an inevitable feature of the U.S. federal system. That competition generally is healthy, in the sense that McGuire talks about productive as opposed to destructive competition. The competition is productive because it pressures state and local officials to perform more efficiently. They are impelled to deliver packages of public services that respond to the tastes and preferences of their residents, and to ensure that those services are produced at minimal cost.

From my personal experience in state and local finance and intergovernmental fiscal policy over the past decade, I can only conclude that the federal system is generally in excellent health. There are few manifestations of destructive competition that we ought to worry about. Indeed, most of us speaking at a 1988 conference on this subject[1] seemed to agree that, generally, competition among state and local governments is healthier, on balance, than it is, in any sense, destructive.

Real suburban-central city problems exist, for example, but most are considerably less acute than they were a decade or two ago. In fact, I would be hard-pressed to identify any such problems that are not well within the capacities of the state governments to solve—the states are, of course, largely responsibile for the problems in the first place. The difficulty—in a word—is less one of interjurisdictional competition, per se, than it is of the rules of the game defined by the states, which not infrequently stack the deck against central cities.

The performance of the national economy is the major imponderable for state and local governments in today's environment, where there is much more modest federal backstopping of state and local budgets than was the case a decade ago.[2] Overall, the record of the states and localities in coming to grips with the decline in real federal funding since the late 1970s is persuasive evidence of the overall fiscal health of the state-local sector.

OBSTACLES TO EFFECTIVE GRANT POLICY

I have no quarrel with McGuire's argument that the primary functions of federal grants are to deal with benefit externalities and with disparities in state and local fiscal capacities. However, I will focus the remainder of my comments on four obstacles to reliance on grant policy as a key element of intergovernmental fiscal relations. First, it is difficult to define the proper matching requirements for grant programs that are intended to improve the allocation of resources in the presence of service-benefit externalities.

Second, the possibility that local taxes and public-service benefits are capitalized into the value of residential property, raises questions about the need for equalization grants.

The third obstacle is the "flypaper effect"—that is, higher levels of outlays by grant recipients for aided services (in the case of categorical grants) or overall spending (in the case of general-purpose fiscal assistance) than theory suggests would result if the decision-making officials of recipient governments were perfectly responsive to the preferences of the proverbial median voter. This phenomenon calls into question our ability to design grant programs that accomplish national objectives efficiently.

The fourth obstacle is the challenge to the assumptions underlying the conventional wisdom on grant policy—as articulated, for example, in the 1985 U.S. Treasury report on federal-state-local fiscal relations—presented by the models of Leviathan and budget-maximizing bureaucracies. The behavior of grant recipients may be driven as much by the tactics of bureaucrats as by the median voter. From this perspective, one reason for the flypaper effect may be that state and local bureaucracies capture the federal funding to pad their budgets by successfully obstructing the efforts of elected officials to reallocate own-source funds to higher-priority uses by substituting the federal financing. Each of these obstacles is discussed in turn in the following subsections.

Identifying Proper Matching Ratios

It is, indeed, very difficult to define the right matching ratios for grant programs intended to internalize externalities. The literature is astonishingly thin when it comes to estimates of externality values, especially values at the margin. The academic community could make a real contribution to public policymaking if it were to devote more energy to empirical analysis of the benefits of public services.

It has long been clear to thoughtful analysts that the matching requirements of virtually all federal grant programs are much too low. That is, the proportion of outlays nominally financed by the federal government is far too high. The external benefits of the aided services could not possibly be as large proportions of the total benefits at the margin as the matching requirements imply.

Edward M. Gramlich (1985: 57–58) has suggested that a good start on reform would be to establish a statutory presumption that 20 percent of the benefits of an aided service at the margin spills over the boundaries of the jurisdiction providing the service. This implies a requirement that state and local governments match each $1 of a federal grant with $4 of their own-financed outlays on the aided service. (Gramlich estimates that current programs, on average, require recipients to spend 25 cents of their own funds for each $1 of federal grant received.) This requirement would be incorporated in all categorical programs, except where those who believe the federal government should be paying a higher share can sustain the burden of proof that significantly more than 20 percent of service benefits at the margin are externalities.

This is a very appealing strategy for grant reform. The problem is that program supporters and administrators are not likely to be happy with a rule that, to many of them, will appear to be "off the wall." Regrettably, the research community has not done much to arm those in the bureaucratic trenches with the estimates of externalities they need to focus the debate. It is very difficult to make a persuasive case for raising state-local matching requirements without solid evidence from sound empirical studies.

My second comment on the design of matching grants relates to the institutional position of the staff at the Office of Management and Budget (OMB) in the Executive Office of the President. My colleagues and I had animated discussions with some of these good people during the review of drafts of the 1985 Treasury report. Special attention was given to the argument for drastically raising state-local matching requirements while, at the same time, moving to open-ended federal funding. This would convert these programs from back-door revenue-sharing to policies with genuine prospects for increasing total spending on the aided services.

The response of the OMB staff was considerable distress. It appears that the experience with grants to the states for social services under the public assistance titles of the Social Security Act during the decade ending in 1972 traumatized a generation of custodians of the federal purse. That incredible program, enacted in 1962, offered federal reimbursement for 75 percent of the costs of a broadly defined range of eligible expenditures, with no ceiling on the federal outlay.

Logically enough, the states ran with it, although it took them a surprisingly long time to figure out the game. When they did, however, federal outlays exploded—from $354 million in fiscal year (FY) 1969 to $1.69 billion in FY 1972. Unfortunately, the response of Congress was to limit the damage by capping the funding at $2.5 billion (allocated among the states in proportion to population), rather than by slashing the proportion of eligible costs for which federal reimbursement would be paid.[3]

From this experience, the OMB staff concluded that open-ended programs are out of the question because of the risk that they will bankrupt the federal treasury, and because Congress will never permit another grant program to offer open-ended funding. (Congress has lived for many years with such funding for the Aid to Families with Dependent Children (AFDC) program and Medicaid, which are the only open-ended matching programs.)

The obvious answer to the anxiety about a runaway federal budgetary commitment is that it would not be a problem if matching requirements were defined properly. The response of OMB staff to this argument was, understandably, "How can we be sure—where's the evidence?" Where's the evidence on the external benefits of the government services that are the objects of federal grants? What are the right ratios? Well, we don't really know. What does the literature say? The literature says very little.

An additional consideration is that the state and local officials who understand the game being played with the grant system (that most—but a declining proportion of—federal aid is really back-door revenue sharing) could be expected not to be terribly happy if the system were reformed to work the way it is supposed to. If I were a state or local official under the current system, I would be content to attend to the modest paperwork necessary to enable me to treat the "revenue-sharing" funds as though they were revenues from my own sources, and to go on about my duties. So long as members of Congress believe they are "doing something" about a problem, even though they really are not, then, why should I care? Why look a gift horse in the mouth? Things would be very different if programs were open-ended, with matching requirements that actually impelled us to increase spending on the specific services for which aid is available.

Capitalization

It is useful to be reminded by McGuire (chapter 9) that apparent differences in fiscal capacities may not represent horizontal inequities among individuals to the extent that state-local taxes and service benefits are capitalized in local real estate values. The true extent of capitalization should not be exaggerated, however. The inadequacies of the fiscal capacities of some states, most of them southern and border states, do pose serious problems, although disparities are generally smaller than they were before World War II.[4]

Moreover, a substantial (but probably not huge) number of towns, cities, and counties with poor fiscal capacities are not well treated by their state governments. Their circumstances may be serious enough to warrant a response—albeit a temporary, or transitional, one—from the national government. The Texas border counties are a striking example. The state government is notoriously unresponsive to the disparities in local fiscal capacities within Texas. As a consequence, the governments serving the border area are not in a position to deliver, at tax rates that would not compound their problems, what most Americans would probably agree are minimally acceptable levels of essential public services. It is difficult to take issue with those who argue that the federal government ought to do something in such cases. Some good research and policy analysis are being done in this area.[5]

The Flypaper Effect

The flypaper effect is more than an econometric aberration. However, I do not share some analysts' concern that it may be a serious challenge to the established theory underpinning the approach to intergovernmental fiscal relations that offers the most promise of equitable and efficient grant policy. For the most part, certain illusions, or even naiveté, in the local decision-making process are more responsible for the behavior that results in observations of a flypaper effect than are the machinations of self-interested bureaucrats.

Leviathan and Bureaucracies

I have no profound observations to offer about Leviathan or various other models of bureaucratic behavior. I prefer to assume that government officials in the U.S. are, for the most part, both responsive to their constituents and rational—in the way economists usually define those terms. Consequently, one can conceptualize demand curves for public services and proceed on the premise that, if provision is made for the right matching requirements for grant programs, those requirements will induce responses by state and local officals that improve the allocation of resources.

One can certainly observe an abundance of self-aggrandizing behavior by bureaucrats. However, it is naive (although, perhaps, not imprudent for a conservative) to postulate such behavior as a central attribute of the operation of governments. We must be alert to the potential for such behavior, and act to prevent, counteract, or harness it where necessary.

PROSPECTS FOR GRANT REFORM

Given the foregoing assessments of the obstacles to effective grant policy, what can one conclude about the prospects for improving the efficiency and equity of the grant system? I am cautiously optimistic that, with the help of the analytical talents of public finance specialists and economists in developing credible externality estimates and resolving other difficult design issues in grant policy, real progress can be achieved.

The budgetary grease necessary for rapid progress will certainly not be there. Nonetheless, the pressure to make programs more efficiet will not diminish. We know enough—even with the gaps I have mentioned in some types of important information—to design programs that are vastly more efficient than those currently in effect. The real issue is the politics of the necessary changes (increases in state-local matching requirements, for example). The central challenge for today's policy analysts is to craft reform proposals with political appeal as well as technical merit, and to devise the necessary strategies to get these proposals enacted into law.

Notes

1. The conference, entitled "Interjurisdictional Tax and Policy Competition: Good or Bad for the Federal System?" was held March 23–24, 1988, at The Urban Institute. It was cosponsored by the U.S. Advisory Commission on Intergovernmental Relations and the State Policy Center of The Urban Institute.

2. A decade ago, federal grants accounted for more than 23 percent of the total receipts of state and local governments in the national income accounts (*Economic Report of the President, 1989* [1989: 404]). By mid-1990, that ratio had plunged to 16 percent (*Survey of Current Business 70*, no. 12 [December 1990, table 3.3]).

3. Ironically, but more than coincidentally, the cap was imposed by Title III of the State and Local Fiscal Assistance Act of 1972 (PL 95–512), the law that initiated Revenue Sharing, the centerpiece of the Nixon administration's New Federalism. For a fascinating review of the experience with the social services grants, see Derthick (1975).

4. By virtually any measure of revenue-raising ability, adjusting for the relative cost of service responsibilities ("needs"), the fiscal capacities of 10 states are below 80 percent of the U.S. average. The states are Alabama, Arkansas, Idaho, Kentucky, Mississippi, South Carolina, South Dakota, Tennessee, Utah, and West Virginia. See Rafuse (1986).

5. See, for example, Fastrup (1988a, b).

References

Derthick, Martha. 1975. *Uncontrollable Spending for Social Services Grants.* Washington, D.C.: Brookings Institution.

Executive Office of the President. 1989. *Economic Report of the President.* Washington, D.C.: U.S. Government Printing Office.

Fastrup, Jerry C. 1988a. "Models of Fiscal Equalization, Inplications for Targeting Grants, and Methodology for Evaluating the Distribution of Federal and State Aid to General-Purpose Local Governments." Washington, D.C.: U.S. General Accounting Office, April 5. Draft.

————. 1988b. "Targeting Efficiency and Equity in Achieving Fiscal Equalization: A Comparison of Federal and State Aid to Massachusetts Cities and Towns." Paper presented at the annual meeting of the Midwest Political Science Association, April.

Gramlich, Edward M. 1985. "Reforming U.S. Federal Fiscal Arrangements." In *American Domestic Priorities: An Economic Appraisal,* edited by John M. Quigley and Daniel L. Rubinfeld. Berkeley: University of California Press.

Rafuse, Robert W., Jr. 1986. "A Representative-Expenditure Approach to the Measurement of the Cost of the Service Responsibilities of States." In *Federal-State-Local Fiscal Relations: Technical Papers,* vol. 1, p. 168. U.S. Department of the Treasury, Office of State and Local Finance. Washington, D.C.: U.S. Government Printing Office.

U.S. Department of the Treasury, Office of State and Local Finance. 1985. *Federal-State-Local Fiscal Relations: Report to the President and the Congress.* Washington, D.C.: U.S. Government Printing Office.

Part Three

INTERSTATE COMPETITION AND TAX POLICY

Chapter Eleven

THE U.S. TAX REFORM ACT OF 1986 AND STATE TAX COMPETITIVENESS

Robert Tannenwald

Five years after passage of the Tax Reform Act (TRA) of 1986, state policymakers are still debating its effects on the lucrativeness, equity, simplicity, and competitiveness of their tax systems. Perhaps the most salient state tax issue of 1987 and 1988 was how to respond to these effects. Although some states let these effects stand, others attempted to offset them by changing their tax rates, exemption levels, and/or definitions of taxable income. A few states used federal tax reform as an opportunity to revamp their income taxes entirely.[1]

This chapter gauges the pressure exerted on states by the TRA—in the five years following its enactment—to enhance their tax competitiveness, that is, the relative attractiveness of their tax system to employers and mobile workers. I assume that, unless deterred by other considerations, states attempt to restore the competitive position of their tax system when they perceive that it has deteriorated. I also assume that, in evaluating their competitive position, states rely heavily on two indicators: (1) the effective burden imposed by their highest statutory tax rate on individual income and (2) the effective burden imposed by their state and local taxes, fees, and charges as a whole. Furthermore, I assume that, in evaluating these two burdens, states take into account the mitigating effects of the "federal offset"—the deductibility of state and local taxes from federal taxable income.

This discussion finds that, by collapsing the structure of federal income tax rates, the TRA increased both the level and dispersion of the net burden of top statutory income-tax rates among states. As a result, states with high top rates prior to the act found the net

I wish to thank Daphne A. Kenyon for her helpful comments on an earlier draft of this paper and Natalie Inman for her research assistance. The views presented here do not necessarily reflect the position of either the Federal Reserve Bank of Boston or the Board of Governors of the Federal Reserve System.

burden of those rates to be further out of line with those of their competitors after the TRA. This reduction in competitive standing may have contributed to the decision of many states to lower their top rates in 1987 and 1988. However, other considerations, such as a desire to offset the act's distributional effects, may have been more important.

Although the act increased the net burden of total own-source revenues in every state, it had little effect on interstate variation in this burden, and changed states' rankings by more than two places in only a few instances. Thus, according to this indicator, the TRA had no significant impact on states' competitive standing. These results imply that, according to evaluative criteria widely used by policymakers, states did not have to alter their revenue systems dramatically to offset possible erosion of their competitive standing induced by the Tax Reform Act of 1986. State tax reform in 1987 and 1988 appears to have been motivated largely by other concerns.

Some economists will question the usefulness of this discussion because empirical investigators have yet to demonstrate that interstate tax differentials significantly affect business location. Why, then, lend credence to the myth that such differentials "matter" by attempting to quantify them? Other critics, although believing that tax differentials matter, will point out that firms and households do not necessarily evaluate a state's tax competitiveness the way state policymakers do.[2] Why, then, encourage the spread of policymakers' misperceptions by viewing the impact of the TRA through their eyes? Regardless of what academics say, many state policymakers believe that taxes do matter, and they continually monitor the competitiveness of their tax system according to the indicators they deem appropriate. Consequently, policy analysts should assume the perspective of state policymakers in order to understand and, perhaps, influence their competitive behavior.

Many potential effects of the TRA on interjurisdictional competition are not discussed here. For example, I do not analyze the act's impact on the relative attractiveness of alternative instruments used by state and local governments to enhance their tax competitiveness. Nevertheless, the TRA's tightening of the tax exemption for interest on industrial revenue bonds discourages projects financed by such bonds and motivates states and municipalities to seek other means of attracting businesses.[3] Nor do I discuss the act's implications for the intensity of competition among municipal governments and levels of government.[4]

TWO INDICATORS OF TAX COMPETITIVENESS

The way in which states should evaluate the attractiveness of their tax system is a contentious issue in public finance. Many analysts have concluded that this issue is a red herring because empirical studies have yet to detect a strong link between interstate tax differentials and business's locational choices.[5] Other analysts disagree over what characteristics of a state and local tax system are of greatest concern to businesses and households and, therefore, over which indicators of tax competitiveness should be monitored by policymakers.

Marginal Tax Rate on High-Income Households

Regardless of what experts recommend, states often evaluate the competitive standing of their tax system by comparing their highest statutory marginal tax rate on personal income with those of their economic rivals. Proponents of this indicator argue that employers often encounter stiff interstate competition when recruiting managers and other skilled professionals. Because these geographically mobile employees are highly paid, many of them fall within each state's highest income-tax bracket. Managers responsible for the locational decisions of firms generally fall into this tax bracket as well. Consequently, many policymakers believe that they must keep their highest marginal personal income-tax rate "in line" with those of rival states to compete for employers and skilled labor. The highest statutory marginal personal income-tax rate levied by each state prior to the TRA is presented in table 11.1, column 1.

Any competitive disadvantage that may result from imposing relatively high marginal statutory tax rates on high-income taxpayers is partially mitigated by the federal offset, which reduces the burden on a taxpayer of each dollar of state or local tax by a dollar times the taxpayer's marginal federal income-tax rate. Prior to the TRA, the highest federal statutory marginal tax rate was 50 percent. Consequently, if a household in the top federal income-tax bracket faced a state statutory marginal tax rate of 10 percent, its "net" marginal tax rate was 5 percent.[6]

Net state marginal tax rates on high-income households vary considerably less than those of their nominal counterparts. Although nominal rates in 1986 ranged from 2.16 percent to 13.5 percent, with a standard deviation of 2.9 percentage points, effective rates ranged

Table 11.1 HIGHEST NOMINAL AND EFFECTIVE STATUTORY PERSONAL INCOME-TAX RATE, BY STATE

	Highest Statutory Tax Rate, 1986 (%) (1)	Highest Effective Statutory Tax Rate, 1986, Given Federal Income-Tax Rates Prior to Tax Reform Act of 1986 (.5 of col. 1) (%) (2)	Highest Effective Statutory Tax Rate, 1986, Given Federal Income-Tax Rates Enacted under Tax Reform Act of 1986 (.72 of col. 1)[a] (%) (3)	Highest Statutory Tax Rate, 1988 (%) (4)	Change in Highest Statutory Tax Rate, 1986–88 (percentage points) (5)
Alabama	5.0	2.5	3.35	5.0	0
Alaska	No income tax	--	--	--	--
Arizona	8.0	4.0	5.36	8.0	0
Arkansas	7.0	3.5	4.69	7.0	0
California	11.0	5.5	7.37	9.3	-1.7
Colorado	8.0	4.0	5.36	5.0	-3.0
Connecticut	Income tax applies to interest and dividend income only	--	--	--	--
Delaware	8.8	4.4	5.90	7.7	-1.1
District of Columbia	11.0	5.5	7.37	9.5	-1.5
Florida	No income tax	--	--	--	--
Georgia	6.0	3.0	4.02	6.0	0.0
Hawaii	11.0	5.5	7.37	10.0	-1.0
Idaho	7.5	3.75	5.03	8.2	+0.7
Illinois	2.5	1.25	1.68	2.5	0
Indiana	3.0	1.5	2.01	3.4	+0.4
Iowa	13.0	6.5	8.71	9.98	-3.02
Kansas	9.0	4.5	6.03	6.1	-2.9

State					
Kentucky	6.0	3.0	4.02	6.0	0
Louisiana	6.0	3.0	4.02	6.0	0
Maine	10.0	5.0	6.7	8.0	-2.0
Maryland	5.0	2.5	3.35	5.0	0
Massachusetts	5.0	2.5	3.35	5.0	0
Michigan	4.6	2.3	3.08	4.6	0
Minnesota	9.9	4.45	6.63	8.0	-1.9
Mississippi	5.0	2.5	3.35	5.0	0
Missouri	6.0	3.0	4.02	6.0	0
Montana	11.0	5.5	7.37	11.0	0
Nebraska	Piggyback tax	--	--	5.9	--
Nevada	No income tax	--	--	--	--
New Hampshire	Income tax applies to interest and dividend income only	--	--	--	--
New Jersey	3.5	1.75	2.35	3.5	0
New Mexico	8.5	4.75	5.70	8.5	0
New York	13.5	6.75	9.05	8.375	-5.125
North Carolina	7.0	3.50	4.69	7.0	0
North Dakota	9.0	4.5	6.03	12.0	+3.0
Ohio	8.55	4.28	5.73	6.9	-1.65
Oklahoma	6.0	3.0	4.02	6.0	0
Oregon	10.0	5.0	6.70	9.0	-1.0
Pennsylvania	2.16	1.08	1.45	2.1	-0.06
Rhode Island	Piggyback tax	--	--	--	--
South Carolina	7.0	3.5	4.69	7.0	0
South Dakota	No income tax	--	--	--	--

continued

Table 11.1 HIGHEST NOMINAL AND EFFECTIVE STATUTORY PERSONAL INCOME-TAX RATE, BY STATE (continued)

	Highest Statutory Tax Rate, 1986 (%) (1)	Highest Effective Statutory Tax Rate, 1986, Given Federal Income-Tax Rates Prior to Tax Reform Act of 1986 (.5 of col. 1) (%) (2)	Highest Effective Statutory Tax Rate, 1986, Given Federal Income-Tax Rates Enacted under Tax Reform Act of 1986 (.72 of col. 1) (%)[a] (3)	Highest Statutory Tax Rate, 1988 (%) (4)	Change in Highest Statutory Tax Rate, 1986–88 (percentage points) (5)
Tennessee	Income tax on certain interest or dividends only	---	---	---	---
Texas	No income tax				
Utah	.75	3.88	5.19	7.75	0
Vermont	Piggyback tax	---	---	---	---
Virginia	5.75	2.88	3.85	5.75	0
Washington	No income tax				
West Virginia	13.0	6.5	8.71	6.5	-6.5
Wisconsin	7.9	3.95	5.29	6.93	-0.97
Wyoming	No income tax				
U.S. average	7.6	3.8	5.09	6.81	-.77
Standard deviation	2.86	1.43	1.92	2.19	1.64

a. Starting in taxable year 1988, a 5 percent surcharge was imposed on taxable income between $71,900 and $149,250 for joint filers and between $43,150 and $89,560 for single filers. For taxpayers falling between these ranges, the surcharge produces an effective marginal tax rate of 33 percent. If 33 percent is considered the top federal rate, then column 1 should be multiplied by .67 instead of .72.

Notes: All rates are for individual filers. Rates in column 1 are as of October 1986; rates in column 4 are as of June 1988.

Sources: U.S. Advisory Commission on Intergovernmental Relations, 1987, Significant Features of Fiscal Federalism, 1987 (Washington, D.C.: Author), 68–73; Commerce Clearing House. 1987. "Personal Income Taxes—Table of Rates." In State Tax Guide. Chicago: Commerce Clearing House.

from 1.08 percent to 6.75 percent, with a standard deviation of 1.4 percentage points (see table 11.1, column 2). Thus, deductibility lowers the competitive risk to a state of taxing upper-income tax-payers at a relatively high statutory marginal rate.

Revenue Burden

Revenue burden, perhaps the most closely monitored indicator of state tax competitiveness, is the ratio of total state and local taxes, fees, and charges to statewide personal income. Policymakers monitor revenue burden closely because it is simple and readily available. It is the most comprehensive measure of the revenues collected by a state and its subdivisions relative to residents' ability to pay. The revenue burden of each state in fiscal year 1986, gross of the federal offset, is presented in table 11.2, column 1a.

Just as the federal offset reduces the net burden imposed by a state's highest statutory marginal tax rate, it also reduces the net burden of all deductible state and local tax dollars. How much the federal offset mitigates the burden of deductible taxes on a given household depends partly on whether the household itemizes its federal deductions. If it does not itemize, it cannot benefit from the federal offset. If it does itemize, as noted earlier, the net burden imposed on it by each deductible tax dollar is $(1 - i) \times (100$ cents), where i is the household's federal statutory marginal income-tax rate. Similarly, the net burden imposed on a business by a deductible state or local tax dollar is $(1 - c) \times (100$ cents), where c equals the business's marginal federal statutory income-tax rate. (Businesses may deduct state and local taxes, fees, and charges as costs of earning income.)

The propensity of households in a given state to itemize, and the average marginal statutory federal income-tax rate that itemizers face (AMSTAR), depend in part on the level and distribution of their income. Major deductible items, such as home-mortgage interest, deductible state and local taxes, and charitable contributions, rise with income. Furthermore, federal personal income-tax rates are progressive. Consequently, the higher a state's average income per household and the more skewed its income distribution toward the upper end of the income scale, the greater the proportion of its households that itemize and the higher its households' average marginal statutory income-tax rate (Clotfelter and Feenberg 1988; Kenyon 1986; Noto and Zimmerman 1984).

The propensity of households in a particular state to itemize also

Table 11.2 NOMINAL AND NET REVENUE BURDEN, BY STATE, BEFORE AND AFTER THE TAX REFORM ACT OF 1986

| | Nominal Revenue Burden | | Net Revenue Burden, Pre–Tax Reform | | Net Revenue Burden, Post–Tax Reform | | Difference in Net Revenue Burden, Pre–Tax Reform and Post–Tax Reform |
	Value and Rank (1a)	Percentage of Mean (1b)	Value[a] and Rank (2a)	Percentage of Mean (2b)	Value[b] and Rank (3a)	Percentage of Mean (3b)	(col. 3a – col. 2a) (4)
Alabama	$157.86 (25)	91.01	$132.95 (24)	91.00	$139.04 (24)	90.79	$ 6.19
Alaska	651.86 (1)	375.82	592.70 (1)	405.99	602.26 (1)	393.26	9.56
Arizona	177.74 (11)	102.47	143.65 (14)	98.34	153.33 (13)	100.12	9.68
Arkansas	139.06 (45)	80.17	117.83 (42)	80.71	122.96 (42)	80.29	5.13
California	156.30 (29)	90.11	126.74 (33)	86.82	134.66 (32)	87.93	7.92
Colorado	153.78 (31)	88.66	131.35 (27)	89.97	140.32 (22)	91.62	8.96
Connecticut	139.58 (44)	80.47	110.23 (47)	75.51	116.91 (47)	76.34	6.68
Delaware	182.25 (8)	105.07	148.78 (10)	101.91	155.97 (10)	101.85	7.20
Florida	142.43 (43)	82.12	116.95 (43)	80.11	121.97 (44)	79.64	5.02
Georgia	157.30 (26)	90.69	128.01 (32)	87.68	136.53 (30)	89.15	8.52
Hawaii	173.63 (15)	100.10	140.40 (16)	96.17	151.67 (15)	99.03	11.27
Idaho	137.94 (47)	79.53	123.55 (36)	84.63	128.07 (37)	83.63	4.52
Illinois	138.19 (46)	79.67	112.90 (46)	77.33	119.84 (46)	78.25	6.94
Indiana	142.92 (41)	82.40	119.45 (40)	81.82	126.09 (40)	82.33	6.64
Iowa	162.30 (21)	93.57	138.26 (14)	94.71	147.16 (19)	96.09	8.89
Kansas	152.54 (32)	87.94	126.08 (34)	86.36	134.61 (33)	87.90	8.53
Kentucky	152.24 (33)	87.77	130.89 (28)	89.66	138.99 (25)	90.76	8.10
Louisiana	179.00 (9)	103.20	161.22 (6)	110.43	169.24 (6)	110.51	8.02
Maine	156.99 (27)	90.51	129.26 (30)	88.54	137.53 (28)	89.80	8.27
Maryland	149.32 (35)	86.09	123.12 (37)	84.33	129.59 (36)	84.62	6.47
Massachusetts	150.56 (34)	86.80	119.97 (39)	82.18	126.64 (39)	82.69	6.67
Michigan	174.65 (14)	100.69	137.74 (19)	94.35	147.21 (18)	96.12	9.47
Minnesota	187.35 (7)	108.01	154.80 (9)	106.04	164.88 (8)	107.66	10.08

Mississippi	167.10 (18)	96.34	141.66 (15)	97.03	148.30 (17)	96.84	6.64
Missouri	125.20 (49)	72.18	105.00 (49)	71.92	112.99 (49)	73.88	7.99
Montana	191.58 (6)	110.45	160.50 (7)	109.94	165.61 (7)	108.14	5.11
Nebraska	155.44 (30)	89.62	137.74 (20)	94.35	141.49 (20)	92.39	3.75
Nevada	162.34 (20)	93.59	134.31 (23)	92.00	139.79 (23)	91.28	5.48
New Hampshire	118.81 (50)	68.50	96.03 (50)	65.79	99.37 (50)	64.89	3.34
New Jersey	146.63 (39)	84.54	114.12 (45)	78.17	120.03 (45)	78.38	5.90
New Mexico	231.48 (3)	133.46	198.28 (3)	135.82	206.43 (3)	134.79	8.15
New York	202.46 (4)	116.73	162.87 (5)	111.56	174.60 (5)	114.01	11.73
North Carolina	145.81 (40)	84.06	118.62 (41)	81.25	124.11 (41)	81.04	5.49
North Dakota	177.95 (10)	102.59	155.47 (8)	106.49	160.22 (9)	104.62	4.75
Ohio	148.74 (36)	85.75	123.68 (35)	84.72	131.52 (35)	85.88	7.84
Oklahoma	158.22 (23)	91.22	140.06 (17)	95.94	148.82 (16)	97.08	8.77
Oregon	175.80 (13)	101.35	147.12 (11)	100.77	153.93 (11)	100.51	6.81
Pennsylvania	147.30 (37)	84.92	120.98 (38)	82.87	127.01 (38)	82.93	6.03
Rhode Island	157.90 (24)	91.03	132.02 (26)	90.43	136.49 (31)	89.13	4.47
South Carolina	159.66 (22)	92.05	132.41 (25)	90.70	138.76 (26)	90.61	6.35
South Dakota	156.81 (28)	90.41	136.88 (21)	93.76	141.43 (21)	92.35	4.55
Tennessee	140.39 (42)	80.94	116.55 (44)	79.83	122.66 (43)	80.09	6.11
Texas	148.13 (38)	85.90	128.67 (31)	88.14	133.64 (34)	87.27	4.97
Utah	195.02 (5)	112.44	164.22 (4)	112.49	175.27 (4)	114.45	11.05
Vermont	170.88 (16)	98.52	134.40 (22)	92.06	138.25 (27)	90.27	3.85
Virginia	132.08 (48)	76.15	106.38 (48)	72.87	113.46 (48)	74.08	7.08
Washington	162.40 (19)	93.63	130.25 (29)	89.22	137.38 (29)	89.71	7.14
West Virginia	168.99 (17)	97.43	144.35 (13)	98.88	151.70 (14)	99.06	7.36
Wisconsin	176.05 (12)	101.50	145.16 (12)	99.44	153.80 (12)	100.42	8.63
Wyoming	333.38 (2)	192.21	305.02 (2)	208.93	314.79 (2)	205.55	9.77

Note: For further methodological details, see technical appendix, available from author on request.
a. Estimated according to equation 11.1 in text.
b. Estimated according to equation 11.2 in text.
Sources: Author's calculations and unpublished data from National Bureau of Economic Research's TAXSIM model.

depends on the amount they spend on deductible items at each level of income. For example, in states where housing is expensive, households at each level of income spend relatively large amounts on home-mortgage interest. In Utah, where Mormonism encourages tithing, proportions of household budgets allocated to charitable contributions are high. Households residing in a state with a large state-and-local public sector spend a large proportion of their income on state and local taxes. The larger the proportion of household income spent on such deductible items at each income level, the greater the propensity of households to itemize (Clotfelter and Feenberg 1988).

A business's marginal federal statutory income-tax rate depends on such factors as its organizational form, current profitability, profitability in recent years (a determinant of the availability of loss carryovers), technology, asset mix, and financial structure. Many of these characteristics are correlated with a firm's industrial classification. Dobbins et al. (1987) estimated that, at the one-digit Standard Industrial Classification (S.I.C.) level, the average marginal corporate statutory tax rate varied in 1983 from highs of 39.7 percent in communications, 30.8 percent in wholesale and retail trade, and 28.2 percent in manufacturing to lows of 16 percent in mining and 17.6 percent in agriculture.

One can crudely estimate the average marginal statutory tax rate on corporate income in each state by analyzing the extent to which the state's economy depends on industrial sectors with high nationwide average marginal tax rates. Such estimates, based on 1983 tax law, are presented in table 11.3, column 1. Rates varied from a low of 23.9 percent in Wyoming, where mining accounts for about 25 percent of the state's payroll, to 27.5 percent in North Carolina, whose economy relies relatively heavily on manufacturing.[7]

The impact of the federal offset on a state's net revenue burden also varies directly with the importance of deductible taxes, fees, and charges in its revenue mix. Prior to the TRA, households could deduct all state and local income taxes, real estate taxes, personal property taxes, and general sales taxes. Firms have always been able to deduct virtually all of their state and local taxes as costs of doing business. Prior to the TRA, estimated deductible revenues (including business taxes) as a percentage of total own-source revenues ranged from a high of 88 percent in Alaska to a low of 58 percent in Nevada.

Not all deductible state and local tax dollars paid by individuals are actually deducted. The percentage deducted by households in a given state depends on their propensity to itemize and on the average amount of deductible taxes paid by an itemizer relative to a non-

Table 11.3 AVERAGE NET FEDERAL STATUTORY MARGINAL CORPORATE INCOME-TAX BURDEN AND AVERAGE NET BURDEN OF STATE AND LOCAL TAX DOLLAR PAID BY BUSINESS, BEFORE AND AFTER FEDERAL TAX REFORM ACT OF 1986, BY STATE

| | Average Net Federal Statutory Corporate Income-Tax Burden | | Average Net Burden of State and Local Tax Dollar Paid by Business | | Difference in Average Net Burden of Business Taxes |
	Pre-Tax Reform (1)	Post-Tax Reform (2)	Pre-Tax Reform ($1.00 − col. 1) (3)	Post-Tax Reform ($1.00 − col. 2) (4)	(col. 4 − col. 3) (5)
Alabama	$0.269	$0.226	$.731	$.774	$.043
Alaska	0.245	0.212	.755	.788	.033
Arizona	0.262	0.225	.738	.775	.037
Arkansas	0.270	0.226	.730	.774	.034
California	0.264	0.224	.736	.776	.040
Colorado	0.263	0.223	.737	.777	.040
Connecticut	0.267	0.225	.733	.775	.042
Delaware	0.267	0.224	.733	.776	.043
District of Columbia	0.252	0.218			
Florida	0.264	0.227	.736	.773	.037
Georgia	0.270	0.228	.730	.772	.042
Hawaii	0.259	0.225	.741	.775	.034
Idaho	0.265	0.226	.735	.774	.039
Illinois	0.266	0.225	.734	.775	.041
Indiana	0.271	0.226	.729	.774	.045
Iowa	0.270	0.227	.730	.773	.043
Kansas	0.268	0.226	.732	.774	.042
Kentucky	0.262	0.221	.738	.779	.041
Louisiana	0.257	0.220	.743	.780	.037
Maine	0.270	0.228	.730	.772	.042

continued

Table 11.3 AVERAGE NET FEDERAL STATUTORY MARGINAL CORPORATE INCOME-TAX BURDEN AND AVERAGE NET BURDEN OF STATE AND LOCAL TAX DOLLAR PAID BY BUSINESS, BEFORE AND AFTER FEDERAL TAX REFORM ACT OF 1986, BY STATE (continued)

| | Average Net Federal Statutory Corporate Income-Tax Burden | | Average Net Burden of State and Local Tax Dollar Paid by Business | | Difference in Average Net Burden of Business Taxes |
	Pre–Tax Reform (1)	Post–Tax Reform (2)	Pre–Tax Reform ($1.00 − col. 1) (3)	Post–Tax Reform ($1.00 − col. 2) (4)	(col. 4 − col. 3) (5)
Maryland	0.264	0.227	.736	.773	.037
Massachusetts	0.265	0.225	.735	.775	.040
Michigan	0.271	0.225	.729	.775	.046
Minnesota	0.267	0.226	.733	.774	.041
Mississippi	0.270	0.226	.730	.774	.044
Missouri	0.269	0.227	.731	.773	.042
Montana	0.262	0.225	.738	.775	.037
Nebraska	0.268	0.227	.732	.773	.041
Nevada	0.251	0.221	.749	.779	.033
New Hampshire	0.269	0.228	.731	.772	.041
New Jersey	0.269	0.227	.731	.773	.042
New Mexico	0.252	0.219	.748	.781	.033
New York	0.261	0.222	.739	.778	.039
North Carolina	0.275	0.230	.725	.770	.045
North Dakota	0.264	0.228	.736	.772	.036
Ohio	0.270	0.225	.730	.775	.045
Oklahoma	0.259	0.219	.741	.781	.040
Oregon	0.269	0.227	.731	.773	.042
Pennsylvania	0.266	0.224	.734	.776	.042
Rhode Island	0.267	0.225	.733	.775	.042

South Carolina	0.272	.728	.044
South Dakota	0.264	.736	.038
Tennessee	0.269	.731	.043
Texas	0.261	.739	.039
Utah	0.266	.734	.040
Vermont	0.265	.735	.041
Virginia	0.266	.734	.040
Washington	0.268	.732	.042
West Virginia	0.254	.746	.039
Wisconsin	0.270	.781	.043
Wyoming	0.239	.761	.031
U.S. average	.264	.736	.40
Standard deviation	.007	.004	

Source: Author's calculations. For methodological details, see technical appendix, available from author on request.

itemizer. Suppose that the households of two states have the same propensity to itemize. In State A, the average amounts of deductible taxes paid by itemizers and nonitemizers are $4,000 and $2,500, respectively. In State B, the comparable amounts are $5,000 and $2,500. A larger percentage of potentially deductible individual taxes will be paid by itemizers, and therefore will actually be deducted, in State B than in State A.[8] The various components of a state's effective revenue burden prior to the TRA are summarized in the following formula:

$$B^s = \underbrace{\frac{C^s(1-c^s)}{Y^s}}_{1} + \underbrace{\frac{N^s}{Y^s}}_{2} + \underbrace{\frac{D^s P^s(1-i^s)}{Y^s}}_{3} + \underbrace{\frac{D^s(1-P^s)}{Y^s}}_{4} \qquad (11.1)$$

$$= [C^s(1-c^s) + N^s + D^s(1-P^s i^s)]/Y^s,$$

where:

B^s = the effective revenue burden of State s;
C^s = own-source revenues collected by State s from businesses;
N^s = own-source revenues collected by State s from individuals not deductible from federal taxable income;
D^s = own-source revenues collected by State s from individuals that are deductible from federal taxable income;
P^s = the percentage of D^s for which itemizers are liable;
Y^s = the total personal income of the residents of State s;
i^s = the average federal marginal statutory personal income-tax rate faced by itemizers in State s; and
c^s = the average federal marginal statutory corporate income-tax rate faced by corporations in State s.

The formula is divided into four terms and labeled from above. The first term equals the net burden of state and local taxes, fees, and charges collected from businesses. The second term equals the net burden of nondeductible taxes, fees, and charges collected from individuals. The third term equals the net burden of deductible taxes, fees, and charges that individuals are legally liable for and that are actually deducted. The fourth term equals the burden of deductible taxes, fees, and charges that individuals are legally liable for but that are not deducted because they are collected from nonitemizers.

Estimates of each state's revenue burden—net of the federal offset and the deductibility of state and local taxes, fees, and charges on business—are presented in table 11.2, column 2a. Taking the federal offset into account has a dramatic impact on the rankings of several states. For example, gross of the federal offset, the net revenue burden of Idaho ranks 47th; net of the offset, it ranks 36th. Gross of the offset, Nebraska ranks 30th; net of offset it ranks 20th. In each instance, the low propensity to itemize and the low AMSTAR of the state's households restrict the degree to which the federal offset mitigates the state's revenue burden. On the other hand, the offset dramatically improves the competitive standing of such states as Massachusetts, Michigan, and New Jersey, all of which rely heavily on deductible revenue sources and whose households have high propensities to itemize and high AMSTARs.

TAX REFORM ACT'S IMPACT ON TAX COMPETITIVENESS: THEORY

The TRA reduced the net burden of each state's highest statutory marginal tax rate and the net burden of each state's own-source revenues.

Impact on Net Burden of Highest Marginal Tax Rate

The TRA collapsed the rate structure of the federal personal income tax into two brackets with statutory rates of 15 percent and 28 percent, respectively. As a result, the top federal marginal rate fell from 50 percent to 28 percent. The net burden of a state's top marginal income tax rate, m, rose from $m(1 - .50)$ to $m(1 - .28)$, or from $.5m$ to $.72m$.[9] The dispersion of the net burdens of states' top rates increased correspondingly, causing the competitive standing of states with relatively high top rates to deteriorate.

Impact on Net Burden of Own-Source Revenues

WINDFALL REVENUE GAINS FROM FEDERAL BASE-BROADENING

The TRA indirectly broadened the bases of many state and local individual income taxes by broadening the bases of their federal counterparts. Most states conform to some degree to the federal definitions of individual and corporate taxable income. Those states that conform automatically to changes in these definitions could have enjoyed a revenue gain without passing a single piece of legislation, although many elected to return some or all of their windfalls to their taxpayers. States that customarily adopt such changes within a year or two received an opportunity to expand their revenues by routinely updating their references to the Internal Revenue Code. Many of these states passed up this opportunity (Gold 1988; Tannenwald 1987a).

The potential revenue gain provided to a state by the broadening of the base of the federal individual income tax depended primarily on the point at which the state "decoupled" from the procedure for computing this tax when the TRA went into effect. This procedure consists of six steps. Federal individual income-tax filers (1) calculate their gross income by adding up their wages, salaries, interest, dividends, rents, royalties, and other includable items; (2) subtract certain costs of earning income and make other "adjustments" to arrive at their "adjusted gross income;" (3) subtract either a standard deduction or itemized deductions; (4) subtract personal exemptions to arrive at their "taxable income;" (5) apply a set of rates to their taxable income to determine their tax liability gross of credits; and (6) subtract tax credits for which they are eligible to determine how much income tax they actually owe.

The TRA affected every stage of this procedure. It generally augmented the array of income sources includable in gross income, limited the adjustments taxpayers can make to reduce their adjusted gross income, eliminated or curtailed deductions they can take to reduce their taxable income, expanded the personal exemption and the standard deduction, and generally lowered personal income-tax rates. It increased the value of some tax credits and eliminated others. Consequently, states with broad-based income taxes that tracked the federal procedure through step 3 (the calculation of taxable income before personal exemptions), but set their standard deductions independently, enjoyed the largest percentage individual income-tax increases from the TRA.

Four states—Nebraska, North Dakota, Rhode Island, and Vermont—would have suffered revenue losses from the TRA (had they not offset them with tax increases) because, when the act went into effect, they followed every step of the federal tax computation procedure. They set individual taxpayers' state income-tax liabilities equal to a stipulated, uniform percentage of their federal income-tax liabilities. In effect, these states would have automatically adopted the changes to both federal individual income-tax rates and the federal individual income-tax base. They would have lost revenue because, according to federal estimates, the revenue losses from the act's reductions in personal income-tax rates outweigh the revenue gains from its base changes.

The impact of these revenue windfalls on a state's revenue burden depended not only on the magnitude of these windfalls but also on the importance of the personal income tax in its revenue mix. Several of the states enjoying relatively large personal income-tax windfalls rely relatively lightly on personal income taxes (e.g., New Mexico and Louisiana). On the other hand, many states relying heavily on the income tax, such as Idaho, Massachusetts, North Carolina, and Wisconsin, experienced relatively small windfalls.

The TRA's potential effect on a state's corporate income-tax revenue raises a tricky issue. During and immediately after federal tax reform, analysts and policymakers were busy attempting to determine the magnitude of the corporate windfall, just as they worked on estimates of the so-called personal income-tax windfall. However, several years after the TRA, it turned out that there was little, if any, actual corporate windfall (Aten and Gold 1989). Since this chapter attempts to estimate the impact of the TRA on state tax competitiveness as viewed by policymakers immediately after the act's passage, the fact that a corporate windfall never materialized is irrelevant. Therefore, estimates of a potential corporate windfall, using the best information available to policymakers at the time, are taken into account.

Like its potential effect on a state's personal income-tax revenue, the TRA's potential effect on a state's corporate income-tax revenue depended in part on the degree to which its corporate income-tax base conformed to its federal counterpart. State corporate income-tax bases tend to conform more closely to their federal counterpart than to state personal income-tax bases and tend to vary less in their degree of conformity.

This pattern is evident in estimates made by the Council of State Chambers of Commerce (1987) of the extent to which each state conformed to the federal corporate tax base as of 1986. The council derived its estimates in the following manner. First, it estimated the consequences for federal revenue of all the provisions of the TRA that altered the base of the federal corporate income tax. It then identified which of these provisions would be adopted by each state either automatically or if the state updated its references to the Internal Revenue Code. The council then compared the revenue consequences of the adopted base changes with the revenue consequences of all base changes. By taking the ratio of the former to the latter, one obtains an index for comparing each state's degree of conformity. California and Wisconsin, each with an index value of 49 percent, exhibited the least degree of conformity. Twenty-six states had index values exceeding 99 percent.[10]

The extent to which each state's potential gain in corporate income-tax revenue attributable to federal base-broadening affected its potential overall revenue burden depends not only on the magnitude of this potential gain but also on the importance of the corporation income tax in its revenue mix.[11] In fiscal year 1986, corporate income taxes accounted for only 3.0 percent of nationwide state and local own-source revenues. Corporate income-tax revenue exceeded 4 percent of total own-source revenues in only eight states—California, Connecticut, Delaware, Massachusetts, Michigan,[12] New Hampshire, New Jersey, and New York. Of these, California and New Jersey do not conform closely to the federal definition of taxable corporate income.

SHORT-RUN BEHAVIORAL EFFECTS

The TRA induced many taxpayers to alter the intertemporal pattern of their transactions to minimize their exposure to tax increases introduced by the act. For example, many investors accelerated their realizations of long-term capital gains in 1986 to take advantage of more favorable capital gains taxation under prior law. Similarly, many consumers purchased "big-ticket" items, such as automobiles, stoves, and refrigerators, in calendar year 1986, before the elimination of the general sales tax deduction. Such behavior bolstered state and local income- and sales-tax revenues in state fiscal years 1986 and 1987.

However, much of the acceleration in consumption and capital gains realizations in these two fiscal years displaced such transactions in fiscal year 1988. Partially as a result, in fiscal year 1988, state and local revenues fell sharply relative to personal income in several states, most notably California, Massachusetts, and New York (Fiordalisi 1988).[13]

REDUCTION IN PERCENTAGE OF FEDERAL INCOME TAXPAYERS ITEMIZING RETURNS

The TRA reduced the value of itemizing by substantially increasing the level of the standard deduction and eliminating or curtailing itemized deductions. As a result, according to the U.S. Department of the Treasury, the proportion of federal taxpayers itemizing fell from 37 percent in 1983 to an estimated 30 percent in 1988 (Nunns

1987). Because of the lower propensity to itemize, a smaller fraction of state and local taxes legally deductible from federal taxable income were actually deducted. The net burden of taxes that would otherwise have been deducted therefore increased, as did each state's net total revenue burden.

ELIMINATION OF DEDUCTIBILITY OF SALES TAXES

By eliminating the deductibility of state and local general sales taxes paid by households, the TRA sharply increased the net burden of a sales tax dollar. Prior to the act's passage, the average net burden of each dollar of sales tax collected from households by a state was $[P(1-i) + 1 - P] \times 100$ cents, where P is the proportion of the state's general sales tax revenues collected from individuals that are paid by itemizers, and i is the state's AMSTAR. For example, if P were .50 and i were .25, prior to the TRA, the average net of each dollar of sales tax collected by the state from households would have equaled $\{1 - [.5 (1 - .3)] + .5\} \times 100$ cents, or 85 cents.[14] Under the TRA, the average net burden of each of these sales tax dollars was one dollar.

REDUCTION IN AVERAGE MARGINAL FEDERAL INCOME-TAX RATE OF ITEMIZERS

By collapsing the federal rate structure, the TRA reduced AMSTARs in all states. According to the Department of the Treasury, because of the act, the nationwide AMSTAR dropped from 29 percent in 1985 to 23 percent in 1988.[15] The average net burden of a state and local tax dollar paid by itemizers therefore rose from $(1 - .29)$ dollars, or 71 cents, to $(1 - .23)$ dollars, or 77 cents.[16]

Unfortunately, the Treasury Department has not made estimates of the act's effect on the AMSTAR in each state. State-by-state estimates of this effect were derived instead from the TAXSIM model of the National Bureau of Economic Research (NBER). The NBER's sample consists of 75,960 records of federal tax filers, all with annual adjusted incomes below $200,000 (Clotfelter and Feenberg 1988). (To preserve confidentiality, The Treasury Department does not provide state-by-state breakdowns of the records of tax filers with higher incomes. According to Treasury data, these high-income filers accounted for 6.8 percent of nationwide adjusted gross income in 1983 (Nunns 1987). Although the omission of these filers potentially biases the estimates presented later in this chapter of the Tax Reform Act's impact on states' effective revenue burdens, the direction of this potential bias is unclear.[17])

The TRA partially offset the federal revenue consequences of its corporate base-broadening provisions by reducing the top federal statutory marginal corporate income-tax rate from 46 percent to 34 percent. According to Dobbins et al. (1987), the TRA reduced the average federal statutory marginal corporate tax rate from 26.7 percent in 1983 to an estimated 22 percent in 1988. As a result, the act increased the nationwide average effective burden of a dollar of state or local business tax from 73.3 cents to 78 cents.

Column 5 of table 11.3 shows for each state the increase in the average effective burden of a state and local business tax dollar attributable to the TRA. Differences among states are small, ranging from 3.1 cents in Wyoming to 4.6 cents in Michigan. These differences reflect differences in industrial mix. For example, the increase in the burden of business taxes is relatively large in Michigan because its economy relies relatively heavily on manufacturing, a sector experiencing a relatively large decrease in its average federal statutory marginal income-tax rate.

Formula Summarizing Components of Net Revenue Burden after TRA

If all the TRA's provisions had been fully effective in 1986, each state's net revenue burden would have equaled:

$$B^{*s} = \underbrace{\frac{C^s(1-c^{*s})}{Y^s}}_{1} + \underbrace{\frac{C^s(1-c^{*s})}{Y^s}}_{2} + \underbrace{\frac{N^{*s}}{Y^s}}_{3} + \underbrace{\frac{D^{*s}P^{*s}(1-i^{*s})}{Y^s}}_{4}$$

$$+ \underbrace{\frac{D^{*s}(1-P^{*s})}{Y^s}}_{5} + \underbrace{\frac{D^{*s}(1-i^{*s})}{Y^s}}_{6} \qquad (11.2)$$

$$= \{(C^s + C^s)(1-c^{*s}) + N^{*s} + D^{*s}[p^{*s}(1-i^{*s})$$

$$+ 1 - P^{*s}] + D^{*s}(1-i^{*s})\}/Y^s,$$

where:

* indicates that the variable takes on its posttax reform value;

C^s is the estimated change in state corporate tax revenues attributable to the TRA; and

D^{*s} is the estimated change in state individual income-tax revenues attributable to the TRA.

Equation 11.2 contains two terms, numbered 2 and 6, respectively, not included in equation 11.1 Term 2 is the net burden of the increase in state and local corporate income-tax revenues induced by the TRA. Term 6 is the net burden of the comparable changes in state and local personal income-tax revenues. Implicit in term 6 is the assumption that all increases (decreases) in personal income-tax revenues induced by federal tax reform are borne (enjoyed) by itemizers.

EMPIRICAL RESULTS

Table 11.1, column 3, presents estimates of the impact of the TRA on the highest effective statutory income-tax rate imposed by each state. The act exerts a large effect on both the level and dispersion of these effective rates. The mean effective rate has increased from 3.8 percent to 5.1 percent, and the standard deviation of the distribution of rates has risen from 1.43 to 1.92, an increase of 37 percent. States with the highest marginal statutory tax rates prior to the TRA experienced palpable increases in their deviation from the mean.

These effects could have contributed to the decisions of several states to cut their top statutory rates in 1987–88. Those states, all with higher-than-average top rates in 1986, included California, Colorado, Delaware, Hawaii, Iowa, Kansas, Maine, Minnesota, New Mexico, Ohio, Oregon, and West Virginia (table 11.1, columns 4 and 5). However, a desire to offset the distributional effects of the TRA might have been a more significant motivation.[18]

Table 11.2, column 4, presents estimates of the impact of the TRA on each state's effective revenue burden. The act has increased the effective revenue burden of all states by an average of $7.16 per $1,000 of income. Increases range from $3.75 per $1,000 of income in Nebraska to $11.73 per $1,000 of income in New York.

Because the TRA would have significantly depressed the personal income-tax revenues of the four "piggyback" states (in the absence of offsetting tax increases), all of them have among the lowest increases in effective revenue burden. Three of the four states without a general sales and use tax—New Hampshire, Oregon, and Montana—exhibit relatively small increases, mainly because they do not experience the increase in the revenue burden of sales taxes resulting from the elimination of their deductibility. Idaho's relatively small increase in revenue burden is attributable largely to its relatively small windfall and its relatively small decline in the proportion of its tax filers who itemize. Florida's relatively small increase in revenue burden is due primarily to its small windfall, in turn a result of its lack of a personal income tax. The relatively small effects on Florida, Idaho, and New Hampshire also reflect their relatively small nominal pre–tax-reform revenue burdens. A state's nominal burden affects the impact on its effective revenue burden of a change in the AMSTAR, propensity to itemize, or windfall revenue.

In general, the states exhibiting the largest increases in effective revenue burden had high nominal revenue burdens prior to federal tax reform. Colorado, Hawaii, Minnesota, New York, and Utah have experienced relatively large burden increases in part because of their relatively large windfalls. Alaska's and Wyoming's relatively large increases in burden reflect primarily their heavy reliance on taxes with an initial impact on business. As a result, they have been hit especially hard by the decrease in the average marginal tax rate on business income attributable to the TRA. Because Arizona, Hawaii, and New York rely heavily on the sales and use tax, their effective revenue burdens are especially sensitive to the elimination of the sales tax deduction.

Although the TRA has a fairly large impact on effective state revenue burdens in the aggregate, it does not significantly alter the relative effective revenue burden of any state. The standard deviations of effective revenue burdens before and after federal tax reform are practically identical. The act's effects produce changes in ranking greater than two places in only five instances: Colorado, Kentucky, Rhode Island, Texas, and Vermont. Rhode Island's fall in the rankings (from 26th to 31st), as well as Vermont's (from 22nd to 27th), is attributable to negative windfalls. Yet, neither state hesitated to sacrifice the resulting competitive advantage by raising its statutory tax rate to recoup its revenue loss. The declines in relative burden experienced by Kentucky and Colorado reflect their proximity in the pre–tax-reform standings to Rhode Island and Vermont. Texas's fall from 31st to 34th reflects primarily the absence of any windfall due to its lack of income taxes.

SUMMARY AND POLICY IMPLICATIONS

Whether they should or not, states often evaluate the relative attractiveness of their revenue systems by comparing themselves with their competitors in terms of the burden of their highest statutory tax rate on personal income and the burden of their own-source revenues as a whole. With varying degrees of precision, they evaluate these burdens net of the federal offset; that is, they take into account the tax relief provided by the deductibility of certain state and local taxes from federal taxable income.

By collapsing the structure of federal income-tax rates, the TRA increased both the level and dispersion of the net burden of top statutory income-tax rates among states. Consequently, states with high top rates prior to the TRA found the net burden of those rates to be further out of line with those of their competitors after federal tax reform. This reduction in competitive standing may have contributed to the decision of many states to lower their top rates in 1987 and 1988. However, other considerations, such as a desire to offset the act's distributional effects, may have been more important.

Although the act increased the net burden of total own-source revenues in every state, it had little effect on interstate variation in this burden, and changed states' rankings by more than two places in only a few instances. In other words, according to this indicator, the TRA had no significant impact on states' competitive standing.

Thus, even if relative revenue burden is a valid indicator of tax competitiveness, states need not reduce their revenue burden to restore their competitive standing in the wake of the TRA. True, the TRA may have dampened public enthusiasm for expansion of the state and local sector by raising the net burden of state and local taxes in all states; however, the constraining effects of this across-the-board increase should not be confused with competitive pressure generated by changes in relative burdens. Policymakers should not conclude that growing resistance to tax increases since passage of the TRA implies that the act has damaged their state's competitive position.

Notes

1. For descriptions and analyses of state responses to federal tax reform, see Gold (1988) and Tannenwald (1987a).

2. See Tannenwald (1987b) for an evaluation of commonly used indicators of tax competitiveness.

3. See Kenyon (1987, 1989), Shafroth (1987), and Zimmerman (1987b) for discussions of the implications for the states of these provisions of TRA.

4. Articles dealing with the potential impact of federal tax reform on interlocal competition include Bahl (1987), Chernick and Reschovsky (1986, 1987), and Gramlich (1985).

5. This is the conclusion of the literature review presented by the New York State Legislative Commission on the Modernization and Simplification of Tax Administration and the Tax Law (1984). Netzer (1986) and Wasylenko and McGuire (1985) found the evidence less conclusive.

6. A complete analysis of interstate differences in tax burdens on households at the top of the income scale should also take into account the fact that some states permit their taxpayers to deduct their federal income-tax liability from their state taxable income.

7. The estimate for North Carolina is biased upward by the lack of available statistics on the payroll of the state's finance, insurance, and real estate sector. Prior to federal tax reform, the nationwide average marginal federal statutory corporate income-tax rate in this sector was lower than that for all industries. See Dobbins et al. (1988).

8. A state's effective revenue burden also depends in part on the extent to which it can export the burden of its taxes, fees, and charges to nonresidents through what Phares calls "price/migration" effects. He describes three channels through which these effects are exerted: (1) the interstate movement of taxed commodities, (2) the migration of people among political jurisdictions, and (3) the ownership by nonresidents of factors of production (Phares 1980). An example of the first channel is the payment of sales taxes on commodities purchased by tourists. An example of the second channel is the payment of income taxes by workers to their state of employment when they reside in a bordering state. An example of the third channel is the payment of taxes by residents of one state on property they own in another state. Residents "import" tax burdens through the same channels. The estimates presented in this chapter do not take price/migration effects into account.

9. Starting in taxable year 1988, a 5 percent surcharge was imposed on taxable income between $71,900 and $149,250 for joint filers and between $43,150 and $89,560 for single filers. For taxpayers falling between these ranges, the surcharge produces an effective marginal tax rate of 33 percent. Consequently, the net burden imposed on them by the top tax rate of a state is .67m.

10. For other estimates and discussion of the impact of the TRA on revenues from state corporate income taxes, see Aten (1987), Strauss (1987), and Vlaisavljevich (1988).

11. Corporation income taxes are defined by the Census Bureau as "taxes on net income of corporations and unincorporated businesses (when taxed separately from individual income)." They include distinctively imposed net income taxes on special kinds of corporations (e.g., financial institutions) (U.S. Bureau of the Census (1986a: 58, 1986b).

12. Michigan has a business activities tax that, for these calculations, is considered a corporate income tax.

13. The projections of individual income-tax windfalls used here attempt to take into account such behavioral effects. However, these projections assume too little intertemporal distortion of consumption and investment behavior, in light of the substantial distortion that has actually been observed in several states.

14. Zimmerman (1987a: 326) estimated that prior to federal tax reform, the average net burden of a state and local sales tax dollar was 88.4 cents.

15. Data from telephone interview I conducted with David Joulfaian, economist, U.S. Department of the Treasury, Office of Tax Analysis, July 12, 1988.

16. Several economists have analyzed the factors that determine each state's

AMSTAR, as well as propensity to itemize and the importance of deductible taxes in the state's revenue mix. Most of them have done so in the course of analyzing the effects of the deductibility of state and local taxes on state and local spending and revenue-raising behavior. Examples include Clotfelter and Feenberg (1988), Courant and Rubinfeld (1987), Feldstein and Metcalf (1987), Gramlich (1985), Huckins (1986), Inman (1986), Kenyon (1986, 1987, 1988, 1989), Noto and Zimmerman (1983), Oakland (1986), and Zimmerman (1987a).

17. The reason why the direction of this potential bias is ambiguous is presented in an unpublished appendix, available from me on request.

18. State-by-state estimates of the impact of the TRA on the distribution among income classes of both federal and state personal income-tax revenues are presented in U.S. Advisory Commission on Intergovernmental Relations (1988).

References

Aten, Robert H. 1987. "The Magnitude of the Additional State Corporate Income Taxes Resulting from Federal Tax Reform." *Tax Notes* 36(August): 529–34.

Aten, Robert H., and Steven D. Gold. 1989. "Where's the Corporate Tax Windfall?" *Tax Notes* 45(Oct. 2): 107–14.

Bahl, Roy. 1987. "Urban Government Finance and Federal Income Tax Reform." *National Tax Journal* 40(March): 1–18.

Chernick, Howard, and Andrew Reschovsky. 1986. "Federal Tax Reform and the Financing of State and Local Governments." *Journal of Policy Analysis and Management* 5(June): 683–706.

———. 1987. "Comment on the Deductibility of State and Local Taxes." *National Tax Journal* 40(March): 96–102.

Clotfelter, Charles T., and Dan Feenberg. 1988. *Is There a Regional Bias in Federal Tax Subsidy Rates for Giving?* Working Paper 2564. Cambridge, Mass.: National Bureau of Economic Research, April.

Council of State Chambers of Commerce. 1987. "State Income Tax Impact of Federal Tax Reform." Council of State Chambers of Commerce, Washington, D.C., January. Photocopy.

Courant, Paul N., and Daniel L. Rubinfeld. 1987. "Tax Reform: Implications for the State-Local Public Sector." *Journal of Economic Perspectives* 1(Summer): 87–100.

Dobbins, Paul, Lowell Dworin, Thomas Neubig, and George Plesko. 1987. "The Treasury Corporate Tax Model and Micro-Simulation Applications." Paper presented at the Fourteenth Annual Convention of the Eastern Economic Association, Boston, Mar. 10–12, 1988.

Feldstein, Martin, and Gilbert Metcalf. 1987. "The Effect of Federal Tax Deductibility on State and Local Taxes and Spending." *Journal of Political Economy* 95(August): 710–36.

Fessler, Pamela. 1987. "Tax Reform Was an Easy Act to Follow." *Governing* (November): 60–62.

Fiordalisi, Georgina. 1988. "States Hit by Sudden Shortfalls." *City and State* (May 23): 1, 6.

Gold, Steven D. 1988. "The Budding Revolution in State Income Taxes." In *Proceedings of the Eightieth Annual Conference: 1987*. Columbus, Ohio: National Tax Association–Tax Institute of America.

Gramlich, Edward M. 1985. "The Deductibility of State and Local Taxes." *National Tax Journal* 38(December): 447–65.

Huckins, Larry E. 1986. "Deductibility of State-Local Taxes and the Effect of State-Local Revenues and Spending Practices." In *Federal-State-Local Fiscal Relations—Technical Papers*, vol. 1. U.S. Department of the Treasury, Office of State and Local Public Finance. Washington, D.C.: U.S. Government Printing Office.

Inman, Robert P. 1986. "Does Deductibility Influence Local Taxation?" In *Federal-State-Local Fiscal Relations—Technical Papers*, vol. 1. U.S. Department of the Treasury, Office of State and Local Public Finance. Washington, D.C.: U.S. Government Printing Office.

Kenyon, Daphne A. 1986. "Federal Tax Deductibiliy of State and Local Taxes." In *Federal-State-Local Fiscal Relations—Technical Papers*, vol. 1. U. S. Department of Treasury, Office of State and Local Public Finance. Washington, D.C.: U.S. Government Printing Office.

Myers, Will S. 1981. *Interstate Tax Competition*. Washington, D.C.: U.S. ACIR.

————. 1987. "Recent Developments in Federal-State-Local Fiscal Relations." *Hamline Journal of Public Law and Policy* 8(Spring): 146.

————. 1988. "Implicit Aid to State and Local Governments through Federal Tax Deductibility." In *State and Local Finance in an Era of New Federalism*, edited by Michael E. Bell. Greenwich, Conn.: JAI Press.

————. 1989. "The Effects of the Tax Reform Act of 1986 on Texas State and Local Governments." In *Rethinking Texas Taxes: Final Report of the Committee on Tax Equity*. Vol. 2 of *Analysis of the Tax System*, edited by Billy Hamilton. Austin: State of Texas.

Netzer, Dick. 1986. "State Tax Policy and Economic Development: What Should Governors Do when Economists Tell Them Nothing Works?" *New York Affairs* 9(3): 19–36.

New York Legislative Commission on the Modernization and Simplification of Tax Administration and the Tax Law. 1984. *Interstate Business Location Decisions and the Effect of the State's Tax Structure on After-Tax Rates of Return of Manufacturing Firms*. New York Legislative Commission . . . , Albany, N.Y. December. Photocopy.

Noto, Nonna A., and Dennis Zimmerman. 1983. *Limiting State-Local Tax Deductibility in Exchange for Increased General Revenue Sharing: An Analysis of the Economic Effects*. Report prepared for the Senate Committee on Governmental Affairs, 98th Cong., 1st Sess. Com-

mittee Print 98-77. Washington, D.C.: U.S. Government Printing
Office.
_____. 1984. "Evaluating Proposals to Limit State-Local Tax Deductibil-
ity: Effects among the States." *National Tax Journal* 37(December):
539–49.
Nunns, James R. 1987. "Tabulations from the Treasury Tax Reform Data
Base." In *Compendium of Tax Research 1987*. U.S. Department of
the Treasury, Office of Tax Analysis. Washington, D.C.: U.S. Gov-
ernment Printing Office.
Oakland, William H. 1986. "Consequences of the Repeal of State and Local
Tax Deductibility under the U.S. Personal Income Tax." In *Federal-
State-Local Fiscal Relations—Technical Papers*, vol. 1. U.S. De-
partment of the Treasury, Office of State and Local Public Finance.
Washington, D.C.: U.S. Government Printing Office.
Phares, Donald. 1980. *Who Pays State and Local Taxes?* Cambridge, Mass.:
Oelgeschlager, Gunn & Hain.
Reschovsky, Andrew, Gregory Topakian, Françoise Carré, Randall Crane,
Peter Miller, and Paul Smoke. 1983. *State Tax Policy: Evaluating
the Issues*. Cambridge, Mass.: Joint Center for Urban Studies of
Massachusetts Institute of Technology and Harvard University.
Shafroth, Frank H. 1987. "Congressional and Administrative Actions Af-
fecting Municipalities." In *The Municipal Year Book 1987*. Wash-
ington, D.C.: International City Management Association.
Strauss, Robert. 1988. "Federal Tax Reform and State Corporate Income
Taxes: Greater Revenues or Greater Uncertainty?" In *Proceedings
of the Eightieth Annual Meeting of the National Tax Association–
Tax Institute of America, Pittsburg, Pennsylvania, November 10-
12*, edited by Frederick D. Stocker. Columbus, Ohio.
Tannenwald, Robert. 1987a. "State Response in New England to Federal
Tax Reform." *New England Economic Review* (September/October):
25–44.
_____. 1987b. "Rating Massachusetts' Tax Competitiveness." *New En-
gland Economic Review* (November/December): 33–45.
_____. 1989. "The Changing Level and Mix of Federal Aid to State and
Local Governments." *New England Economic Review* (May/June):
41–55.
U.S. ACIR. 1988. *The Tax Reform Act of 1986—Its Effect on Both Federal and
State Personal Income Tax Liabilities*. Washington, D.C.: Author.
U.S. Bureau of the Census. 1986a. *Government Finances, 1985–1986*. Washington, D.C.: U.S. Government Printing Office.
_____. 1986b. *State Government Finances, 1986*. Washington, D.C.: U.S.
Government Printing Office.
U.S. Bureau of Labor Statistics. 1987. *Employment and Wages: Annual Av-
erages, 1986*. Washington, D.C.: U.S. Government Printing Office,
December.

Vlaisavljevich, Michael. 1987. "Federal Impacts on State Business Taxes: How Can States Handle Them?" In The *Unfinished Agenda for State Tax Reform*, edited by Steven D. Gold (Denver, Colo.: National Conference of State Legislatures): 177–196.

Wasylenko, Michael, and Therese McGuire. 1985. "Jobs and Taxes: The Effect of Business Climate on States' Employment Growth Rates." *National Tax Journal* 38(December): 497–512.

Zimmerman, Dennis. 1987a. "Federal Tax Reform and State Use of the Sales Tax." In *Proceedings of the Seventy-Ninth Annual Conference of the National Tax Association–Tax Institute of America*, edited by Stanley Bowers. Columbus, Ohio.

_____. 1987b. *Tax-Exempt Bonds and 20 Years of Tax Reform: Controlling Public Subsidy of Private Activities*. Multilith 87-922E. Washington, D.C.: Congressional Research Service, November.

Chapter Twelve

INTERSTATE COMPETITION AND STATE PERSONAL INCOME-TAX POLICY IN THE 1980S

Steven D. Gold

Some analysts have suggested that interstate competition has three important effects on state income-tax policy:[1]

□ Competition causes states to reduce reliance on the income tax relative to other taxes.

⊓ Competition leads to a reduction in top marginal tax rates in states with relatively high tax rates.

□ Competition causes income taxes to become less progressive.

Two rationales for these effects are that income taxes are believed to have a more negative influence on economic development prospects than other taxes[2] and that high-income households are especially sensitive to the top tax rate. Other things being equal, all three of these effects would tend to reduce the progressivity (or increase the regressivity) of state-local tax systems, because the first two effects tend to increase the proportion of revenue from taxes that are not as progressive as the income tax.

The 1980s is a good period in which to examine these three postulated effects because it was a time of heightened interstate tax competition. First, the severe recessions of 1980 82 and the increased openness of the economy to international competition made state policymakers more sensitive to economic development concerns. Tax competition is one of the principal manifestations of economic development competition. Second, federal tax rates were sharply reduced, first from as high as 70 percent prior to 1981, to 50 percent as a result of the 1981 tax cut, and then to 33 percent as a result of

I appreciate comments on earlier versions of this paper by Daphne A. Kenyon and Ronald Snell. Research for this note was conducted as part of the National Conference of State Legislatures' (NCSL) Fiscal Federalism Project, funded by a grant from the Ford Foundation. The views expressed are mine and should not be attributed to the Ford Foundation or the NCSL.

the Tax Reform Act of 1986. Federal tax-rate reductions increased competition by raising the burden of paying deductible state and local taxes. In 1980, a taxpayer might have borne as little as 30 cents of tax burden for each dollar paid to a state, once federal taxes were taken into account. In 1988, that taxpayer would bear a cost of at least 67 cents for each dollar of state tax paid.

Before examining the record to see what it shows about the three postulated effects of interstate competition, one should note that three waves of change involving the state personal income tax occurred in the 1980s. First, in 1982 and 1983, there were widespread tax rate increases in response to depressed state fiscal conditions. At least 17 of the 40 states with broad-based income taxes increased their income tax in those years.[3] Second, once states began to recover, most of these tax increases were either repealed or partially rolled back, primarily in 1984 and 1985 (Gold 1987). Third, the final major wave of income-tax activity occurred in response to federal tax reform, mostly in 1987. Most states made significant changes in their income-tax structures; at least half the states increased the personal exemption and/or standard deduction, and 15 states reduced tax rates. These adjustments meant that states passed up most of the additional revenue they could have obtained from the broader tax base, retaining perhaps 20 percent of the potential $6.2 billion "windfall."[4]

The changing role of the personal income tax is not well understood because numerous crosscurrents influenced it in the 1980s. There are at least six sources of confusion. Robert Tannenwald, in chapter 11, has adjusted for one confusion by showing how the highest marginal tax rate in each state is reduced because income taxes are deductible for federal income-tax purposes. Because Tannenwald has analyzed this effect, it is not considered here; there are enough complicated factors to consider without making an adjustment for the fact that state income taxes are deductible on federal tax returns. The other five important sources of confusion are as follows:[5]

1. Some state tax-rate changes have been responses to earlier moves in the opposite direction. For example, many tax cuts in 1984 and 1985 offset tax increases in the two previous years when states were battling to avoid deficits (Gold 1987). If one considers only the 1984–85 cuts, one obtains a false impression of where state income taxes have been heading. A longer-term perspective is required.

2. Some tax reductions simply offset revenue increases that occurred because of "bracket creep," namely, the movement of taxpayers into higher tax brackets over time. For example, Delaware had a series of nominal tax cuts, but its effective tax rate remained relatively high.
3. Because it broadened the tax base, the federal Tax Reform Act of 1986 gave most states[6] the opportunity (which many, but not the majority, availed themselves of) to reduce nominal tax rates without lowering effective tax rates. Many nominal tax reductions should be viewed as avoidance of tax increases that would have occurred otherwise.
4. Because federal tax reform broadened the tax base the most at high levels, state income taxes tended to become more progressive in terms of effective tax rates, even when states did not change the progressivity of their nominal tax-rate schedules (and, in some cases, even when they reduced nominal tax-rate progressivity).
5. States that allow federal income taxes to be deducted in calculating state taxable income have considerably lower marginal tax rates than nominal tax rates imply. When the top federal tax rate was 50 percent, a state with a top nominal state rate of 10 percent really had a top rate of 5 percent if it allowed federal deductibility. (Of course, the deductibility of state income taxes for federal purposes reduces the marginal state tax rate even further, as Tannenwald has emphasized.)

As this chapter demonstrates, only one of the three effects of interstate competition is unambiguously true—that top marginal tax rates have been cut in states with relatively high tax rates. On balance, states have increased their reliance on the income tax relative to other taxes, and most income taxes became more progressive in the wake of federal tax reform.

Reliance on Income Tax

Contrary to expectations, income-tax revenue has continued to grow faster than total state tax revenue and personal income. As table 12.1 shows, income-tax revenue was steady at about 1.82 percent of personal income from 1978 to 1982. It then shot up in fiscal year (FY) 1984 to 2.09 percent of personal income because of increases enacted during the winter and spring of 1983, it fell slightly the following two years as temporary increases expired, it jumped to 2.16 percent in FY 1987, and then reached an all-time high of 2.20 percent in FY

Table 12.1 STATE PERSONAL INCOME-TAX REVENUE AS PERCENTAGE OF
PERSONAL INCOME

Fiscal Year	Level (%)
1989	2.20
1988	2.13
1987	2.16
1986	2.04
1985	2.06
1984	2.09
1983	1.88
1982	1.82
1981	1.82
1980	1.84
1979	1.81
1978	1.82
1977	1.77
1976	1.65
1975	1.57
1974	1.57
1973	1.60
1972	1.47
1971	1.24
1970	1.20

Sources: For tax revenue, U.S. Bureau of the Census, various years, *State Government Finances* (Washington, D.C.: U.S. Government Printing Office). For personal income, U.S. Department of Commerce, 1987, *Survey of Current Business* 67 (August): 44; U.S. Department of Commerce, 1988, *Survey of Current Business* 68 (August): 30.

1989.[7] Income-tax revenue was 31.3 percent of state tax collections in 1989, the highest ever, a significant increase from the 25.6 percent in 1978 on the eve of the tax revolt.[8]

Several factors account for the growth of the income tax, the most important being its relatively high elasticity, that is, the tendency for revenue to grow faster than personal income because (1) marginal tax rates usually rise as taxable income increases and (2) taxable income tends to grow faster than personal income because personal exemptions and standard deductions are usually fixed in value. These two forces more than offset the tendency for exempt income (e.g., for retirement) to grow faster than personal income.[9]

CHANGES IN MARGINAL TAX RATES

The popular perception that marginal tax rates have been falling is correct, provided one concentrates on the states with above-average tax rates. This trend did not originate in 1987; it has been in effect since the latter 1970s, when Delaware, Minnesota, New York, and Wisconsin—four of the states with the highest rates at that time (Council of State Governments 1976)—began lowering them. The same four states also cut their tax rates in the pre–federal reform portion of the 1980s.

In comparing marginal rates, it is important to recognize that states like Iowa and Montana allow federal income taxes to be deducted, which, as noted above, significantly reduces their actual marginal rates to less than their apparent level. Thus, although Montana appears to have the highest marginal rate (11 percent), that distinction really belongs to Hawaii, which is now the only state with a double-digit tax rate for earned income. (By contrast on January 1, 1976, seven states had double-digit top tax rates—Alaska, California, Delaware, Hawaii, New York, Oregon, and Wisconsin).[10]

Table 12.2 summarizes the changes in top marginal tax rates between 1981 and January 1991. Among the 25 states where federal taxes are not deductible and the state liability is not piggybacked on the federal tax payment, there were 9 decreases and 9 increases between 1981 and 1990. Most of these changes were in the direction of uniformity, with high-tax states tending to reduce their rates and low-tax states tending to increase rates.

The situation is more complicated in the other 15 states. All of the 11 states that allowed federal taxes to be deducted in calculating state tax liability in 1981 implicitly had increases in their top marginal tax rates over the next ten years. As federal marginal rates declined in the 1980s, the implicit value of federal deductibility decreased, resulting in higher implicit state tax rates. Six of these states actually reduced their nominal tax rates during this period, but their implicit marginal rates increased nonetheless. On the other hand, the four states that piggybacked their state income tax on federal liability in 1981 all had effective decreases in their top marginal rates because federal tax rates were reduced, even though three of them increased the percentage of federal liability that went for state taxes.

Here is a summary of what table 12.2 reveals about top marginal tax rates:

□ Number of states without federal deductibility or a piggyback arrangement: 9 reductions, 9 increases, and 7 with no change.
□ Number of states with a piggyback arrangement: 4 decreases in

Table 12.2 CHANGES IN HIGHEST PERSONAL INCOME-TAX RATE IN EACH
STATE BETWEEN 1981 AND JANUARY 1991

(Year shown is when legislation was enacted, not necessarily when change took effect.)

1. States that do not (a) allow federal tax payments to be deducted or (b) piggyback state liability on the federal tax payment.

Decreases (9 states)

California	From 11% to 9.3% (in 1987)
Delaware	From 13.5% to 7.7% (in numerous years)
Hawaii	From 11% to 10% (in 1987)
Maine	From 10% to 8.5% (in 1988 and 1989)
New York	From 10% (on earned income) to 7.875%[a] (in 1987)
Oregon	From 10% to 9% (in 1987)
Pennsylvania	From 2.2% to 2.1% (in 1985; was temporarily higher)
West Virginia	From 9.6% to 6.5% (in 1987; was temporarily higher)
Wisconsin	From 10% to 6.9% (in 1985 and 1987; was temporarily higher)

Increases (9 states)

Idaho	From 7.5% to 8.2% (in 1987)
Illinois	From 2.5% to 3% (in 1989)
Indiana	From 1.9% to 3.4% (in 1982 and 1987)
Massachusetts	From 5.375% to 6.25% (in 1990)
Mississippi	From 4% to 5% (in 1982)
New Jersey	From 2.5% to 7% (in 1982 and 1990)
New Mexico	From 6% to 8% (in 1983 and 1986)
Ohio	From 3.5% to 6.9% (in 1982 and 1983; reduced in 1986)
Oklahoma	From 6% to 7% (in 1990)

No change (7 states)

Arkansas	7%
Georgia	6%
Maryland	5%
Michigan	4.6% (temporarily increased in 1982–83)
North Carolina	7%
South Carolina	7%
Virginia	5.75%

2. States that piggybacked their state tax liability on federal tax payment in 1981. (Calculations are based on a top federal rate of 70% in 1981, which prevailed until the last three months of that year, and a top federal tax rate of 31% in 1991.

Decreased (4 states)

Nebraska	From 10.5% (15% of 70%) to 6.9% (no longer piggybacked)
North Dakota	From 5.25% (7.5% of 70%) to 4.4% (14% of 31%)
Rhode Island	From 13.3% (19% of 70%) to 7.1% (22.96% of 31%)
Vermont	From 16.1% (23% of 70%) to 8.7% (28% of 31%)

3. *States that allowed federal tax payments to be deducted in 1981.* (All 11 of these states had an effective increase in their top marginal rate, although 5 of them had a nominal decrease and 5 had no nominal change, while 1 had a nominal increase. Their 1981 effective top marginal rate was only 30% of the nominal top marginal rate because the top federal rate was 70%. Their 1991 effective top marginal rate was 69% of the nominal top marginal rate because the top federal rate was 31%.)

Decreased nominal rate

Arizona	From 8% to 7% (in 1990); implicit rate increased from 2.4% (8% of 30%) to 7% (no longer allows federal deductibility)
Colorado	From 8% to 5% (in 1987); implicit rate increased from 2.4% (8% of 30%) to 5% (no longer allows federal deductibility)
Iowa	From 13% to 9.98% (in 1987); implicit rate increased from 3.9% (13% of 30%) to 6.9% (9.98% of 69%)
Kansas	From 9% to 5.15% (in 1988);[b] implicit rate increased from 2.7% (9% of 30%) to 5.15% (federal deductibility permitted optionally)
Minnesota	From 16% to 8% (in 1985 and 1987); implicit rate increased from 4.8% (16% of 30%) to 8% (no longer allows federal deductibility)
Utah	From 7.75% to 7.2% (in 1988); implicit rate increased from 2.3% (7.75% of 30%) to 6.1% (7.2% of 85%) (now allows only one-half of federal deductibility)

No change or increase in nominal rate

Alabama	5%; implicit increase from 1.5% (5% of 30%) to 3.5% (5% of 69%)
Kentucky	6%; implicit increase from 1.8% (6% of 30%) to 6% (no longer allows federal deductibility)
Louisiana	6%; implicit increase from 1.8% (6% of 30%) to 4.1% (6% of 69%)
Missouri	6%; implicit increase from 1.8% (6% of 30%) to 4.1% (6% of 69%)
Montana	11%; implicit increase from 3.3% (11% of 30%) to 7.3% (11% of 67%)

Sources: For 1981 tax rates, Council of State Governments, 1982, *The Book of the States: 1982–83* (Lexington: Author), 397; for 1988 tax rates, Steven D. Gold, ed., 1988, *The Unfinished Agenda for State Tax Reform* (Denver: National Conference of State Legislatures), 22–23; updated for later changes.
a. The 1981 tax rate in New York was 10% for labor income and 14% for other income. The 1991 tax rate shown was the one actually in effect; the full 1987 reform called for a lower rate in 1991.
b. The rate shown for Kansas is for joint returns; the top rate for single returns is 5.95%. Federal deductibility was repealed in 1988 and reinstated on an optional basis in 1989; most high-income returns have lower tax liability if they use the rate schedule that does not permit federal deductibility.

effective terms; nominally, 3 increases, and 1 not comparable because its piggyback system was abandoned.

□ States with federal deductibility: 11 increases in effective terms; nominally, 6 decreases and 5 with no change.

Thus, it is true that more states cut their top nominal marginal rates than increased them in the 1980s, with 15 states cutting those rates, 12 increasing rates, and 12 making no change. However, this is misleading because the situation appears different when the effect of lower federal tax rates is taken into account. At least 20 states had increases in *effective* or implicit marginal tax rates, including 9 with nominal increases (Idaho, Illinois, Indiana, Massachusetts, Mississippi, New Jersey, New Mexico, Ohio, and Oklahoma) and 11 others with implicit increases because the value of federal deductibility diminished. By contrast, only 13 states had effective decreases, and 7 did not change.

The conventional wisdom that marginal rates tended to decrease is, however, correct for the states that began the 1980s with the highest rates. All ten states with effective top marginal rates of 10 percent or higher in 1981 did reduce them by 1990.

PROGRESSIVITY

Prior to federal tax reform, some states that formerly had a high degree of progressivity made their tax systems less progressive. Delaware, Minnesota, New York, and Wisconsin are the most prominent examples (Gold 1986: 20–22). This trend was in line with John Shannon's (chapter 6, this volume) metaphor comparing states to ships in a convoy: no ship can get too far out of line with other ships, or it will be exposed to certain dangers (for ships, attack by the enemy; for states, loss of competitiveness). In addition to explicit reductions in progressivity in those states, there was also a gradual implicit reduction in progressivity in many states caused by the failure of exemptions and standard deductions to increase to reflect higher price levels and the limited degree of progression in the nominal tax-rate structures of many states (Cline 1986; Feenberg and Rosen 1986).

This trend was reversed in 1987. Most states conformed to the great majority of the provisions of federal tax reform, so that their tax bases expanded much more at high income levels than at lower income levels, primarily because capital gains were taxed in full and tax shelters were eliminated. Although the federal government reduced tax rates at high income levels by considerably more than it did at lower income levels, few states followed its example in that regard. Most states also chose to rely on increases in standard deductions and personal exemptions as an important method of avoiding the "windfall," thereby targeting relief to the poor and taxpayers with relatively low incomes. Consequently, most state income taxes became more progressive.[11]

This reversal of the previous trend can be attributed to three phenomena: (1) It is more feasible to increase progressivity if many states do so at the same time than if a single state acts unilaterally. (2) The federal policy of providing tax relief for the poor encouraged states to move in the same direction. (3) The economist's concept of progressivity as reflected in increasing effective tax rates as income rises is not well understood by the public or by legislators. Rather, the focus of public attention is usually on nominal rates, which may diverge substantially from effective rates. Although economists tend to assume that taxpayers are fully aware of the tax rates confronting them (and that policymakers are conscious of the implications of their decisions), it is highly questionable that this is so.[12]

CONCLUSION

An important theme of the 1980s was the tendency for the income-tax policies of various states to converge. It was an error to formulate two of the three hypotheses considered here as though they applied to all states, rather than only to states with high income taxes. The hypothesis of a reduction in top marginal tax rates in states with relatively high tax rates was confirmed in this chapter, although when all 40 state income taxes were considered, there were more effective marginal tax rate increases than decreases. Support for the other two hypotheses would also appear stronger if one considered only the states with heavy reliance on a progressive income tax at the start of the 1980s. When the history of the 1980s is finally written, a majority of those high-tax states will probably be found to have reduced progressivity and income-tax reliance compared to other states. At the same time, however, many states that started with less progressivity and reliance on the income tax moved in the opposite direction.

Tannenwald concluded in chapter 11 that competitiveness will not be significantly affected by federal tax reform if states evaluate the competitive standard of their tax systems by comparing top marginal income-tax rates. This is because tax reform did not markedly increase the dispersion of state income-tax rates after considering the federal offset. It may be, however, that federal reform will discourage tax increases even though the dispersion of rates is not changed, because it has increased the burden of paying state taxes.

My conclusion is that it is too soon to predict the eventual effect of federal tax reform. The elimination of sales tax deductibility and the reduced value of state-local income and property tax deductions may have profound effects, but state tax policy tends to evolve slowly, with major changes in tax structures occurring no more than once per decade or less often. The surprising turns of state tax policy in recent years should encourage caution in making predictions.

In any event, interstate competition is likely to intensify even more in the 1990s as the national economic growth rate falls because of the slow increase of the labor force. In past years, states that lagged economically usually had positive growth. In the mid- to late-1990s, many laggard states will have absolute decreases in employment because the national average growth itself will be lower. Confronted by the specter of a contracting economy, states will compete even harder to make themselves attractive places for businesses to locate and grow.[13]

Although interstate competition is an important influence on state tax policy, it does not operate in isolation. Other important factors that may cause shifts in state tax structures are changing concepts of equity, demands for increased services, the legacy of the tax revolt, changes in state economies, and innovations in federal tax policy. Moreover, the state income tax has strong supporters in states that employ it heavily, so significant resistance is encountered when proposals are made to reduce reliance on it.

Notes

1. See, for example, Cline (1986) and Hovey (1986).

2. Support for this view is provided by Wasylenko and McGuire (1985).

3. Gold (1987) lists 16 states that raised the income tax; that tabulation omits Colorado, which should have been included

4. For reviews of reforms enacted by states in response to federal tax reform, see Gold (1988a, b). For a description of how the potential "windfall" was handled, see Gold, Eckl, and Erickson (1987a) and its updated version in Gold, Eckl, and Fabricius (1988b). See also Gold, Eckl, and Erickson (1987b) and Gold, Eckl, and Fabricius 1988a. The estimate of the size of the potential windfall is from the National Association of State Budget Officers (Washington, D.C., 1987), which relied on estimates by state officials.

5. The third and fourth points (as well as, indirectly, the fifth) imply that federal tax reform upset the equilibrium of state income-tax structures. Dennis Zimmerman has argued that the state responses in 1987 and 1988 were efforts to regain the previous equilibrium. Although there is undoubtedly something to this point, it cannot account for many aspects of the outpouring of state tax-reform activity.

6. Several states did not have a potential "windfall," either because their tax base did not conform at all to the federal tax base or because they based their state tax on federal tax liability, which was reduced by federal tax reform.

7. These calculations use estimates of personal income reported in the August 1987 *Survey of Current Business*. Since these personal income estimates are considerably higher than estimates for the years before 1986, they reduce the effective tax rates compared to figures published annually by the U.S. Bureau of the Census (Gold and Zelio 1989).

8. These estimates are for the 12 months ending in June 1988, reported in U.S. Bureau of the Census (1988).

9. For a survey of how states tax retirement income, see Zahn and Gold (1985).

10. This tabulation excludes Iowa, Minnesota, Montana, and North Dakota, which nominally had tax rates of 10 percent or higher but allowed federal deductibility (Council of State Governments 1976: 290). Alaska repealed its income tax in 1979.

11. Galper and Pollock (1988) measured the change in progressivity in six states in 1987, including one that adopted a flat tax in place of one with increasing marginal rates, and another that simply conformed to the new federal tax base. All of these states had an increase in progressivity. Mazerov and Lav (1988) analyzed changes in state tax liability for 16 representative taxpayers and found that progressivity increased in the great majority of cases. As noted in the text, a major reason for the increase in progressivity is conformity to the federal tax treatment of capital gains, which are received primarily by high-income taxpayers. Only six states continued to grant capital gains preferential treatment to most kinds of property—Connecticut, Hawaii, Iowa, Kentucky, Maryland, and Wisconsin (Gold et al. 1987a). By 1991, only Hawaii and Wisconsin did so.

12. Many anecdotes support this view. Several legislators have told me that a major reason why piggybacking of the state income tax on federal liability is unpopular is that the tax rate (e.g., 20 percent of federal liability) sounds high. Likewise, there are many examples of failure to consider how states permitting deductibility of federal taxes really have much lower taxes than it superficially appears. The inattention to the erosion of progressivity over time resulting from inflation and income growth also supports the conclusion that there is no clear perception of the actual degree of progressivity.

13. I am indebted to Donald Walls of McGraw Hill/DRI for this observation.

References

Cline, Robert. 1986. "Personal Income Tax." In *Reforming State Tax Systems*, edited by Steven D. Gold. Denver: National Conference of State Legislatures.

Council of State Governments. 1976. *The Book of the States: 1976–77.* Lexington, Ky.: Author.

Feenberg, Daniel R., and Harvey S. Rosen. 1986. "State Personal Income and Sales Taxes, 1977–1983." In *Studies in State and Local Public Finance*, edited by Harvey S. Rosen. Chicago: University of Chicago Press.

Galper, Harvey, and Stephen Pollock. 1988. "Models of State Income Tax Reform." In *The Unfinished Agenda for State Tax Reform*, edited by Steven D. Gold. Denver: National Conference of State Legislatures.

Gold, Steven D. 1986. *Reforming State Tax Systems.* Denver: National Conference of State Legislatures.

———. 1987. "Developments in State Finances, 1983 to 1986." *Public Budgeting and Finance* 7(1, Spring): 5–23.

———. 1988a. "The Blizzard of 1987: A Year of Tax Reform Activity in the States." *Publius: The Journal of Federalism* 19(Summer): 17–35.

———. 1988b. "The Budding Revolution in State Income Taxes." In *Proceedings of the Eightieth Annual Conference: 1987*, Columbus, Ohio: National Tax Association–Tax Institute of America. 6–11.

Gold, Steven D., and Judy Zelio. 1989. "Interstate Tax Comparisons and How They Have Changed over Time." *Tax Notes* (March 20): 1501–12.

Gold, Steven D., Corina L. Eckl, and Brenda Erickson. 1987a. *State Budget Actions in 1987.* Denver: National Conference of State Legislatures.

———. 1987b. "An Overview of State Tax Legislation in 1987." *Tax Notes* 37(October 19): 301–15.

Gold, Steven D., Corina L. Eckl, and Martha Fabricius. 1988a. *State Budget Actions in 1988.* Denver: National Conference of State Legislatures.

———. 1988b. "State Tax Activity in 1988." *Tax Notes* 41(8, November 21): 863–73.

Hovey, Harold A. 1986. "Interstate Tax Competition and Economic Development." In *Reforming State Tax Systems*, edited by Steven D. Gold. Denver: National Conference of State Legislatures.

Mazerov, Michael, and Iris Lav. 1988. *The Fairest of Them All: A Rating of State Personal Income Taxes for 1987 Returns.* Washington, D.C.: American Federation of State, County and Municipal Employees.

National Association of State Budget Officers. 1987. *Federal Tax Reform: Impact on the States.* Washington, D.C.: Author.

U.S. Bureau of the Census. 1988. *Quarterly Summary of Federal, State, and Local Tax Revenue: April–June 1988.* Washington, D.C.: U.S. Government Printing Office.

Wasylenko, Michael, and Therese McGuire. 1985. "Jobs and Taxes: The Effect of Business Climate on States' Employment Growth Rates." *National Tax Journal* 38(December): 497–512.

Zahn, Mitchell A., and Steven D. Gold. 1985. *State Tax Policy and Senior Citizens: A Legislator's Guide.* Denver: National Conference of State Legislatures.

Part Four

COMPETITION FOR ECONOMIC
DEVELOPMENT

AN EVALUATION OF INTERJURISDICTIONAL COMPETITION THROUGH ECONOMIC DEVELOPMENT INCENTIVES

Dick Netzer

There is not much that state and local governments do that does not affect their economies, for good or for ill. It may well be that the greatest effects stem from policies, actions, practices, and institutions that, at least traditionally, are not governed mainly by concern for their economic consequences. Nonetheless, this chapter concentrates on a narrow band of policies and actions, namely, those undertaken explicitly for their hoped-for economic consequences. I do not focus on policies and actions that are undertaken mainly for other reasons, or that produce outputs that are ends in themselves (like health, education, housing, and the arts), even though these latter policies often have the additional goal of fostering economic growth. Neither do I address general state tax policy, but only tax measures proposed or enacted mainly to foster economic development.

It is tempting to put the term *economic development* in quotes, as something inherently embarrassing. It should be embarrassing, if it is not. A large share of what has been said and written about economic development consists of belaboring the obvious. Of course, no firm will turn down gifts, even ones of small value, and any firm will say that a gift will persuade it to do nice things. Of course, virtually any economic development measure will have some positive effect, at the margin. Of course, given the reality that all of the conceivable tools of state policy cannot amount, in expenditure-equivalent terms, to more than a fraction of 1 percent of gross national product (GNP) in a year,[1] there is no way in which state policies and actions can have really powerful effects on a state's economy. But, of course, officials are right to be concerned about the economic implications of what they do. And, of course, officials will worry in earnest when their regions, states, and cities experience a really bad economic period, and will remain sensitive about that for a long time thereafter—the half-life of the concern being directly related to the severity of the local depression.

The main point explored here is whether interstate competition in this form—incentives for economic development in a given state or part of a state—is a good or a bad thing. Are there ways to make this type of competition more, rather than less, useful? A later section of this chapter examines the difficult, but secondary, question of the empirical efficacy of alternative economic development instruments.

Economic development policy is defined here as efforts to influence decisions on the location of economic activity. The locational decisions that can be affected by public policies include much more than the decision on whether to relocate an existing branch plant or where to put the new General Motors Saturn plant. Economists are concerned, as well, with the expansion or contraction of the scale of existing establishments—businesses, nonprofit groups, and government; with the birth and mortality rates of local firms; with changes in the extent of "import substitution," that is, the provision of consumer goods and services by local, rather than outside, establishments; and with the economic and noneconomic factors that influence household decisions about where to live.

ECONOMIC DEVELOPMENT AS TRADITIONAL STATE POLICY

Although state economic development policy is often said to be a new thing, stemming from a variety of events and changes that began in the mid-1970s (although the changes specified usually began years earlier, and were recognized as such then), state and local governments have, from the earliest days, devoted a great deal of borrowing and capital spending to economic development objectives. Public funds were used to build transportation and other infrastructure that opened land to private development, sometimes in the form of 100 percent publicly owned and operated facilities, sometimes to substitute for privately financed extensions of public systems, and sometimes in the form of capital subsidies for privately operated systems (often the case with transportation). No one called this "economic development"; instead, people spoke of opening up the country and accommodating the purportedly inevitable growth of the population in particular places. Then as today, the effect (and the very lightly disguised objective) was often to increase the value of privately owned land that came to be in the path of development.

Largely because of the wanton thievery typically associated with this type of subsidization, mid- and late-19th-century state constitutions generally contained prohibitions on grants or loans of public funds to private parties. For example, the New York Constitution provided (and still does) that no state money or credit may be "given or loaned to or in aid of any private corporation or association, or private undertaking." Moreover, those constitutions often had sweeping requirements for uniformity in taxation, perhaps honored in the breach by tax administrators, but precluding formal and overt tax preferences. For example, as late as the 1960s, the Illinois constitution's uniformity clause was construed to mean that no type of asset owned by a household or business enterprise could be exempted from property taxation, or taxed at a nominally differential rate.

These constitutional proscriptions necessarily inhibited the emergence of economic development as an explicit goal of state-local policy. Legislators and administrators found ways to circumvent the restraints, but some of the avoidance devices were not developed for years. Local property tax assessors were adept at offering de facto tax preferences early on, but the use of authorities issuing nonguaranteed debt (which was construed not to be state credit), the creation of other intermediaries to launder state money on its way to private beneficiaries, and the amendment of state constitutions to eliminate the proscriptions took longer. Today, the states confront few constitutional obstacles to the use of state money or credit for economic development.

The modern-day version of economic development policy dates from the agricultural distress of the 1920s and, even more, the Great Depression. Early examples include state subsidy of farmers in North Dakota via the operation of a state bank, grain elevators, and other enterprises, and the spread of selective property tax relief for distressed sectors, especially agriculture, but also forestry and mining in a few places.

Explicit "smokestack chasing" began over 50 years ago, in 1936, with the first program in which state-local government borrowing powers were used to raise money to build plants for specific firms— namely, Mississippi's "Balance Agriculture with Industry" program, involving the use of local government general obligation bonds. Kentucky followed, authorizing the use of local revenue in 1946, with Tennessee and Alabama copying that practice in 1951.[2] By the end of the 1950s, industrial revenue bonds were authorized in most of the South and in several New England states as well, not accidentally the only regions of the country then seen as distressed.[3] There was no illusion about the nature of the subsidy: it was recognized that it came from the U.S. Department of the Treasury in the form of exemption of the interest on the bonds from federal income taxation, at a time when federal marginal income tax rates were still very high, other state-local borrowing levels were still modest, and hence the spread between taxable and tax-exempt interest rates was very substantial. Nor was there much illusion that the subsidy was in the national interest.[4]

Daphne A. Kenyon's background paper for the U.S. Advisory Commission on Intergovernmental Relations (ACIR) (1988: 98–102) concisely summarized the wide array of economic development measures now in use. The major types are:

□ Capital subsidies, including:
   Subsidized credit, in the form of direct loans, loan guarantees, and (most commonly) the pass-through of the federal income-tax exemption
   Grants, typically to intermediaries, to finance site preparation costs and other capital costs
   Equity investments in young firms
□ Subsidy of other inputs, including:
   Training costs
   Research and development costs
   Marketing and promotion costs
   Site search costs
□ Tax preferences
□ Enterprise zones, where a variety of incentives are available, often on a more generous basis than elsewhere in the state or city
□ Promotion of the state, region, or city as a good place to locate or visit

It is, of course, possible to label almost any tax or expenditure action as "economic development." Take, for example, a recent compilation of the allocation of funds provided to the City of New York by the Municipal Assistance Corporation to foster "economic development." For the years 1985 through 1988, the total was $365 million—$85 million of which was for education programs, $100 million for housing subsidies, $60 million for completion of the convention center (covering cost overruns), and only $120 million for what would be narrowly defined as economic development, namely, two programs assisting firms locating outside the central business district but within the city.[5]

EFFICIENT AND INEFFICIENT SUBSIDY

In specific cases, any device can be cost-effective from the standpoint of the government that is taking the action. However, what about the efficiency of the various devices from the standpoint of the economy, or society, at large? To deal with this question, one must turn to elementary theory.

Start with the usual abstractions of economists. We assume that private production dumps no important costs on innocent third parties (environmental damages and the like). We also assume that private producers and consumers can realize so large a share of the benefits from private transactions that the composition of production and consumption would not be altered even if third parties could be made to pay for the incidental external benefits generated by private transactions. We assume as well that the United States is a closed economy. Clearly, if markets are competitive, then any action by state and local governments to alter private locational decisions reduces economic welfare—in other words, is inefficient in its effect on resource allocation—whether that action is an investment subsidy, a subsidy of other inputs, or some form of nonneutral taxation.

Thus, competition among states to foster economic development, in this imaginary world, must be not a zero-sum game, but a negative-sum game, until the point is reached at which all states are offering identical treatment of all private-sector firms. Once one state begins to use economic development incentives, the best course is to encourage all others to match those incentives, and the more closely the better. Fortunately, the experience of the past quarter of a century is that the states will do just that—competition among the states, like competition among private producers, tends to produce convergence. Of course, in the imaginary economy discussed here, the ideal regime would prohibit that first state from acting to interfere with the market-determined location of economic activity, because the game becomes zero-sum only in equilibrium; it is negative-sum during the long transition toward equilibrium, which is the normal condition because it is in each state's temporary interest to introduce a new economic development incentive, from which it will gain at others' expense until everyone else has copied the first state. However, it is easier to imagine a world of relatively perfect markets than to imagine a constitutional regime in which American states can be prohibited from competing for the location of economic activity.[6]

In the perfect market, closed-economy scenario, competition will

tend to wipe out the locational distortions. But economic development incentives have sectoral as well as locational distortions, and
these distortions will be worsened, not eliminated, by competitive
emulation. Capital subsidies will tend to make the economy unduly
capital-intensive; training subsidies will yield overinvestment in human capital; research and development (R and D) subsidies will lead
to the absorption of resources in low payoff efforts; and so on. However, just stating these tendencies is to inject a note of caution into
the discussion: the inefficiencies cannot be very large in the aggregate, because the economic development incentives themselves are
not very large.

Under what conditions can economic development efforts and
interstate competition become a positive-sum game? If one relaxes
the assumptions, then it is easy to see that, in the real world, state-
local economic development efforts are not inherently inefficient.
Whether they are inefficient in practice is another issue. First, consider the various real-world departures from the imaginary economy
and the room for maneuver provided for economic development
efforts that are efficient.

1. The United States is not a closed economy, and becomes less
closed every day. This means that an incentive that is successful in
its locational objective may be at the expense of Japan or Taiwan or
Brazil, rather than at the expense of a neighboring state. Such an
outcome increases the probability that the incentive is economically
efficient for the United States (whether or not it is from a worldwide
perspective). However, efficiency is not guaranteed merely by the
fact that a plant locates in Pennsylvania rather than Brazil. The resources used for the subsidy might have been used in numerous
other ways that affect locational competition across international
boundaries, some or most of which might have had higher payoffs—
in terms of total output in the United States—than the subsidy offered and accepted. The point, however, is not that decision makers
need to evaluate an infinity of possible actions, but, instead, that
they ought not to assume that the immediately visible target of opportunity is the best target merely because the competing location
is outside the United States.

There is another possible type of inefficiency in competing internationally with economic development subsidies: state and local
governments could be offering subsidies that undermine international trading rules, even to the point of eliciting retaliation and,
thereby, a loss to the U.S. economy, even as the subsidy-provider
gains.

2. Government in the United States has had limited success in providing for the internalization of all significant externalities of private production and consumption. Because so much of government action along these lines is done by state and local governments, the prevalence of externalities is very uneven geographically. When negative externalities are internalized in some areas but not in others, the pattern of location of economic activity will be suboptimal to the extent that locators respond to the cost savings made possible by not internalizing. It would not improve economic efficiency if all jurisdictions abandoned their efforts to force internalization: there would be geographic uniformity but resource misallocation. Thus, an economic development subsidy that partly offsets the additional cost of the required internalization in the places that do require it may affect locational choice in a way that improves efficiency.[7]

Whether the subsidy has these results depends on the relation between the value of the economic development subsidy being offered to each firm and the cost to each firm of internalizing the externality. It also depends on the extent to which the cost of internalization differs among locations. If the cost of reducing a specific type of environmental damage is $5.00 per unit in City A and $1.00 in City B, but the firm is not required to reduce the damage and incur the cost at all in City A, then an economic development subsidy that costs anything less than $1.00 per unit and induces the firm to move to City B must be efficient, everything else being equal.

3. The public sector's impact on the location of activity is marked not only by sins of omission—in the failure to require that all important externalities are internalized—but also by sins of commission that parallel the negative externalities case. One obvious sin is the common, but not universal, use by state and local governments of particular types of inefficient taxes.[8]

The problem here is not taxes that are inefficient in distorting locational choice; the solution to that problem is with the state tax system, not in finding offsetting subsidies. Instead, the issue concerns taxes that are sectorally distorting, but not used everywhere or not used equally. We would not want uniform and universal use of bad taxes. Economic development subsidies might offset the distorting effects of the tax in question. But, other things being equal, the subsidy would tend to correct a sectoral inefficiency while increasing locational inefficiency. The resolution should be determined by which is the more costly form of inefficiency, in the specific case.

For example, when regulated telephone companies had a pervasive monopoly of telecommunications (from about 1925, when telegraph use began declining sharply, to the late 1960s), the price elasticity of demand for the services of those companies was so low that the distortions in heavy taxation of that input (for business customers) and that type of consumer expenditure (for residential customers) were minimal. Such heavy taxation became widespread, but was and is far from uniform in severity. Technological change and regulatory developments have greatly increased the price elasticity of the demand for the services of local telephone companies and of AT&T Communications, the main objects of the heavy taxation, so that heavy taxation is now distorting the choices of telecommunications users. Because much of the distorting taxation of telephone companies is embedded in major components of the tax system in ways that are hard to disentangle, the obvious solution, reforming the taxation of telephone service, is not a simple undertaking.[9] A city or state might offer some offsetting subsidy to businesses that are heavy users of telephone services, like a credit against other taxes. This, like any other reduction in the level of distorting taxes, would make the whole national tax system more efficient, but it might also inefficiently tilt locational choice toward the city offering that subsidy.

Another relevant type of tax distortion known to occur is the locational distortion that is an incidental by-product of a specific provision of federal tax law. The locational distortion may be seen as a small price to pay for the wonderful primary effects of the provision and, therefore, the locational distortion persists. A state or local subsidy designed to offset this particular distortion could be an efficient one. To offer an example, for much of the history of the federal investment tax credit, it appeared that the credit was structured in a way that encouraged firms to invest in new "greenfields" plants, rather than reequip older plants. If the point was valid, then the credit was fostering locational shifts from central cities to outlying parts of urban areas, and from the Rust Belt to the Sun Belt.

A similar sin of commission by government that poses similar questions is economically inefficient regulation. Uniformity at the level of the lowest common denominator is hardly desirable. Offsetting subsidies, in the places where the distorting regulation is worst, like capital subsidies to offset especially onerous zoning and building code restrictions, could be a net contribution to efficiency, but not necessarily.

At times, economic development subsidies may be the only practical way to offset distortions that are the product of a succession of historical accidents, but almost impossible to remedy. A spectacular example is the case of the conversion of the old Commodore Vanderbilt Hotel in New York to the Hyatt Grand Hotel, entailing the complete reconstruction of the building. The obstacle to the Hyatt investment was the impossibly tangled ownership claims to the site, including federal claims related to the Penn Central bankruptcy, and claims by Penn Central, Conrail, and New York State, the latter as the owner of the commuter lines into Grand Central. Settlement of the claims was delaying the project and was raising costs; the solution was an arrangement in which the project was subsidized, to offset those costs, by property tax exemption and by the state government's assumption of substantial litigation costs. Absent the ownership mess, the conversion could have been done without subsidy, suggesting that the Hyatt venture was an efficient investment that would have been killed off without the government subsidy.

There is also the reality that competing jurisdictions do subsidize economic development. As already noted, the implication of this reality is that competition improves, rather than detracts from, locational efficiency if the jurisdictions that do not offer subsidies match the ones that do make such offers. The flaw in this argument is the contribution of such competition to sectoral distortions. That, of course, is the common defect of the second-best argument about parallel subsidies in other arenas—for example, the traditional argument for subsidies of a given mode of transportation. Highways had to be subsidized, or so it was said, because the railroads had been subsidized years earlier; the inland waterways and the airlines because the highways were subsidized; and most recently, urban mass transportation because of the parallel subsidy to urban automobile use. The goal of neutrality in public policy toward competing transportation modes was laudable, but the price of the strategy has been excess capacity in the old modes, like the railroads and inland waterways, as their newly subsidized competitors matured, and excess demand for other modes where the subsidies take the form of underpricing the publicly provided facilities that private vehicles must use—notably, urban highways and airports.

4. Finally, even if governments tried to conduct their business in ways that minimized the distorting impact of their actions, markets would not function perfectly. Information is far from costless; therefore, market participants have incomplete and uneven information. Because shifts of resources from one place or use to another can be very costly, inertia interferes with the mobility of resources that is required for perfect markets. There are economies and diseconomies

of scale in production (including economies of agglomeration and diseconomies of congestion), which violate the requirements of perfect markets. Consequently, if markets are not functioning perfectly, economic development policy instruments that offset the imperfections can move toward, rather than away from, efficiency in resource allocation.

Thus, an early rationalization of credit subsidies for economic development, especially the use of tax-exempt bonds, began with the conviction that there were important barriers to the interregional mobility of investment funds. The South was held to be a region of capital scarcity (barriers to mobility meant that the low income and meager savings of the region could not be overcome by an equilibrating inflow of funds from richer regions), where firms confronted high interest rates and onerous loan conditions. At least since the 1950s, it has been asserted, time and again, that the credit and capital markets inefficiently restrict access by new and small enterprises, justifying intervention with subsidized credit and capital by all levels of government. To the extent that the identified capital-access problems are a product of capital market imperfections (rather than the correct pricing of risky loans), then economic development incentives in the form of credit and capital subsidies may be efficient.

There is little question that the market for human capital is highly imperfect, and inherently so. The imperfections result in underinvestment by many individuals and households in their own capital, or misdirected investment, as well as in mistakes in investment in training by firms (mistakes from the standpoint of the economy). In principle, it is possible to devise training subsidies that efficiently offset the imperfections. As with training costs, firms may not always be able to fully capture the benefits of their own expenditure for research and development; the smaller and more specialized the firm, the more this is likely to be true. Not everything can be patented, especially failed experiments, from which others, including competitors, may learn a great deal. Thus, economic development subsidies aimed at R and D costs could be efficient.

There is a market imperfection rationale for economic development subsidies for marketing and promotion. Marketing and promotion are, in essence, getting information to potential buyers, investors, visitors, and the like. There can be major economies of scale in the dissemination of information; this is certainly true of advertising. A state agency that aggregates information for consumers, thus lowering the unit costs of providing information, can provide an efficient mode of economic development subsidy.

DIFFERENTIAL EFFECTIVENESS OF POLICY
INSTRUMENTS

No doubt governors, mayors, legislators, and other state and local officials would prefer to do good for the country while their states and localities are doing well from economic development policy initiatives. Hence, they should be quite willing to choose economically efficient instruments, provided the instruments are equally effective in promoting local development. But they surely are concerned first of all with what works in practice, with how much economic bang there is for the subsidy or tax abatement buck. That calls for measurement of cost-effectiveness, which is troublesome. As hard as measurement is with regard to the locational effects of differentials and changes in the level and nature of general state-local taxes, it is even harder with regard to the mixed bag of nontax incentives and customized tax incentive provisions. The analysis is difficult in individual cases, and it is even more difficult to make persuasive generalizations.

Studies of individual cases and aggregative studies confront the same obstacle: separating the effects of the economic development incentive itself from the effects of the numerous other variables that affect locational decisions. Surveys of participants are done frequently, despite the obvious problem that the participants have every reason to dissemble publicly, and may not even tell the truth to themselves. Local economic development officials have every reason to exaggerate the effectiveness of their wares, so as to assure the continuance of the program and their continuance in office. The firm receiving the subsidy can gain the most favorable terms only by strenuously claiming that the subsidy will be *the* decisive factor. Like taxpayers with the Internal Revenue Service, grantors and grantees will give their interests, not the skeptical claims of the opposition, the benefit of any doubts about the central importance of generous economic development subsidies.

Nor is it possible, except in rare instances, to get objective data on the individual cases that can shed much light on just what stimulus causes how much response. The rare instances include real estate development projects, separately incorporated with sale of the equity interest fairly soon after the physical investment has been put in place. In such cases, rates of return with and without the subsidy can be calculated, and one can confidently draw conclusions from the rate-of-return data about the causal role of the subsidy.[10]

There is an approach that finesses the problem of isolating the effects of the subsidy, which can be of use in individual cases and specific programs: calculating the break-even point, that is, the proportion of the increase in investment or employment experienced (or promised) by the firms receiving the subsidy that must be induced by the subsidy, if the benefits are to equal the costs of the subsidy. If the break-even point is very low, then one need not worry about the other causes for the new investment; if the break-even point is very high, then one must surmise that the program will not be cost-effective. Investment tax credits have been appraised, and found wanting, by this approach.[11]

There is, of course, a statistical method of isolating the effects of separate variables that avoids surmise, deception, and bad memory: multiple regression analysis. For years, economists have used regression analysis to estimate the locational effects of differentials in the levels and composition of state-local tax systems. Results have been contradictory and often implausible, and the modal coefficient has been without statistical significance. There are good reasons for this, which I have explored elsewhere.[12] But the inherent difficulties are much greater for the bundle of measures called economic development policies. Regression analysis works only if there are numerous observations and if the independent variables can be defined reasonably well. Both of these requirements pose special problems for the analysis of economic development policies.

This is because there is considerable interstate variation in the specific provisions of similar-sounding measures, and rates of participation in similar programs differ greatly over time and place, with resulting variation in the composition of those firms that do participate. Consider a widely used instrument like direct loans to small firms. No two states have identical provisions, and the programs vary along a number of dimensions, including interest rates and maturities, required private-lender participation percentages, permissible uses of the funds, and the nature of the backing for the loans required. It would be silly to use the volume of loans extended as the independent variable, but as the variable is made more complex, or subdivided into several separate variables, one loses degrees of freedom. Moreover, with the variation in the terms of the programs, one would expect participation by different types of businesses, calling for a more elaborate set of control variables to explain borrower behavior, again reducing the degrees of freedom. One would expect also that the geographic dispersion of participation within a given state would be influenced by the specific character of the program, which might require that elaborate control variables depicting intrastate conditions be substituted for simple variables applying statewide (for locational factors like wage rates, effective property tax rates, or even climate).

This is very unlike a typical state tax policy regression study that uses straightforward tax policy variables, such as effective rates of the major taxes, top marginal rates, and measures of the total tax burden, and that can rely on the fact that the major taxes apply more or less uniformly to a vast number of firms. In contrast, economic development incentives typically reach a tiny fraction of firms. In New York State, the major business tax incentives features are each used by only a few hundred firms, and in any one year, state and local business loan closings probably number less than 1,000 of the million or so business establishments in the state.

So, one should not take seriously the occasional regression study that purports to measure the effectiveness of economic development policies by examining the relation between a dependent variable for economic growth and independent policy variables like the number of economic development programs a state uses, or the dollars it spends for things labeled economic development, or the number of firms taking advantage of the state programs.[13]

There have been more worthwhile efforts to evaluate the cost-effectiveness of economic development measures. One recent effort, reported in Rasmussen, Bendick, and Ledebur (1984) and in Ledebur and Hamilton (1986), found that the cost to the government providing the subsidy exceeds the benefit to the firm being subsidized for every type of incentive examined, except for state loan guarantee programs. Typically, the excess of cost over benefit is substantial. For example, the federal cost of industrial revenue bonds is more than twice the benefit to the firm (the cost to state governments is far less than the benefit, but the state is not the unit providing the subsidy in this case). State costs exceed firm benefits by a ratio of 1.4:1 or more for subsidized direct loans, subsidies for equipment, plant and site acquisition, and tax abatements. In these cases, the federal government actually gains from the incentive program, via higher federal tax liabilities, so that the overall ratio of costs for all levels of government compared to firm benefits is close to 1.0.

However, a ratio of 1.0 does not dispose of the question, either way. Advocates of economic development incentives will argue that this is an unduly narrow way to evaluate the programs, that one should also consider benefits other than those that accrue to the firm itself. On the other hand, it is not self-evident that benefits that extend beyond the firm and its employees are real benefits. It should be noted that in benefit-cost studies conventionally done for public works projects and in housing policy analysis, a ratio of benefits to the immediate user of the facility to governmental cost of 1.0 is considered low. For example, in highway project analysis, projects with ratios of user savings to governmental costs of 2.0 are treated as low-priority projects, unlikely to be funded; funded projects have ratios of 4.0 or higher.

One can quarrel with the way the benefits of tax abatement programs were measured in the study reported in Ledebur and Hamilton (1986). Alternative approaches can show much higher potential benefits, including the break-even point approach noted earlier and the simulation studies using the AFTAX model developed by the Papkes (1984), which show that some tax measures can produce substantial differences in after-tax rates of return, which presumably is the variable to which business decision makers pay the most attention.[14]

McGahey (1986) reported that the studies he examined of the effects of specific policy initiatives rarely found any "measurable impact on variables like employment and economic development" (66). He also reported on two 1984 papers that examined the impact of entire packages of state economic policies (that is, the aggregation of all economic development initiatives within a state) on unemployment; the packages had no effect, but there were statistically significant effects from some policy instruments, apparently canceled by the effects of other instruments—for example, job training support.[15]

Many states and even some large local governments regularly publish reports containing a compendium of economic development programs and estimates of the direct fiscal costs. Coverage varies; tax incentives receive the most frequent and comprehensive treatment, often as part of a larger report on tax expenditures that includes programs that do not have economic development objectives, like housing tax preferences. Typically, the fiscal costs are estimated on the basis of the assumption that none of the investment or activity that is tax-favored would have occurred in the absence of the tax preference.

Still, the empirical evidence on what works in economic development is thin or unpersuasive. When the empirical evidence fails, one can fall back on logic. What does logic tell us? First, for a firm faced with a locational decision, a dollar is a dollar at the margin of indifference when everything but the development incentive is equal. The firm will respond to the incentive feature that provides the most dollars. But, second, other things are never equal. The costs of capital are likely to be least unequal among alternative locations—capital is more mobile than other factors, and capital markets, for all their imperfections, are less imperfect than most other markets—and the costs of capital are likely to be small relative to operating costs. The opposite conditions apply to operating costs.

State and local governments can affect operating costs by influencing factors, such as the quality of the labor supply, the extent to which labor costs are increased by regulatory and social insurance requirements, the condition of infrastructure services, and the severity of environmental protection rules. Economic development efforts designed to influence any of those factors conceivably could have strong effects on operating costs, and in some cases, at relatively low monetary costs. However, important problems and conflicts are involved, including conflicts with equity and other goals, as well as the frequent difficulty of designing programs that offer the desired incentives selectively and, therefore, effectively.

Consider, for example, a policy of trying to reduce labor costs for small enterprises by relieving them of part of the usual social insurance obligations. Under the experience rating system of setting unemployment insurance tax rates (and analogous arrangements for workers' compensation and temporary disability insurance programs), new enterprises begin by paying the maximum statutory tax rate and, unless they are extraordinarily lucky, are likely to continue at the maximum for some years (a single former employee making a successful claim can assure that result, for small firms). It would be clearly inequitable to exclude employees of small firms from coverage, so an incentive program that waives unemployment insurance taxes for new enterprises for, say, the first three years of their lives could be financed (within the unemployment insurance system) only by raising the rates for other firms—not a great idea from the standpoint of the state's competitive position. Or, states could do away with experience rating entirely, which some observers would applaud. However, experience rating is an entrenched practice (dating back to the first U.S. unemployment insurance system, Wisconsin's, more than 50 years ago) with passionate defenders, especially within the business community.

Some programs affecting operating costs involve few conflicts with other goals. Who really objects to more and better education and training, for example? However, there are serious problems of program design. For 20 years, governments have experimented with education and training programs aimed at improving the quality of the labor force in places that need economic development. The formal evaluations of most of the programs have not been particularly favorable, suggesting not that this is a bad idea, but, instead, that it is difficult to implement successfully.

As a result, state and local economic development programs tend to look for the lost key under the lamp post, rather than where it was dropped. These programs focus on capital and credit subsidies, despite the likelihood that such subsidies will not be terribly cost-effective, unless another government, such as the U.S. Department of the Treasury, pays for them.

SOME POLICY CONCLUSIONS

Ideally, state and local governments should use approaches to economic development that combine the national concern for efficiency in resource allocation with the local concern for program effectiveness. What measures do that best?

One approach that clearly is wrong, on both counts, is the *subsidization of capital and credit*, whether by loans, grants, or tax abatements tied to capital investment.[16] As noted earlier, the empirical evidence suggests that such subsidies—aside from the use of tax-exempt bonds—are not cost-effective from the state-local perspective. This is not surprising. Thirty years ago, the first large-scale study of small business finance, done by the Federal Reserve System (U.S. Congress 1958) concluded that the availability of capital and credit was not a major obstacle to the development of new businesses and the expansion of old ones,[17] a conclusion that analysts have not disputed subsequently. True, risky enterprises must pay high premiums for loans and must share the equity interest with investors, both of which entrepreneurs hate to do. It is also true that, if state and local government lenders and equity-capital-providing agencies make the subsidies very substantial, economic activity that would not otherwise have occurred will be elicited. But the cost would be large per unit of economic benefit because of the high failure rate of the subsidized enterprises.

If the availability of capital is not a real obstacle to economic development, then subsidies of this type must be economically inefficient from a national standpoint, as well as cost-ineffective from the local standpoint. Such subsidies encourage an inefficient substitution of capital for labor. The fact that governments have been extraordinarily generous with capital and credit subsidies, most of them highly inefficient, does not make these capital and credit subsidies any better.

A special note of condemnation is necessary for the use of tax-exempt bonds for economic development purposes. There is no possible case for the continued use of what are now called "small-issue industrial development bonds." They are so widely used that they must largely cancel out the locational effects—for good or for ill. The cost to the federal treasury is large relative to user benefits. There is no conceivable national interest in a program that randomly distributes interest-rate subsidies to firms; if anything, the program is worse from this standpoint with quantitative caps than it was without caps, because the caps make the distribution of the subsidy among firms even more chancy and erratic than when any sufficiently aggressive firm could find a way to get the subsidy. Like any other inefficient use of tax-exempt borrowing, such a subsidy raises the costs (marginally) of borrowing for state and local capital projects that are efficient resource uses.

There is considerable dispute about some other types of tax-exempt borrowing, or rather about the appropriateness of extending the tax-exemption privilege to those types. Thirty years ago, some economists began pointing out how poor a policy tax-exempt borrowing was as a form of federal aid to state and local governments.[18] Although everything that has transpired since then would seem to support that proposition, during the past decade the federal government's "house position" has changed, and it now sees merit in some uses of tax exemption, while seeing terrible mischief in other uses. The federal budget document now distinguishes between "public purpose" state and local debt and "private purpose" tax-exempt borrowing, and the U.S. Congress has enacted restrictions on the latter in the tax legislation of the 1980s. An even more obscurantist practice has been the use of the label "IDB" (for industrial development bonds) for any type of borrowing the observer finds objectionable.

I have argued elsewhere (Netzer 1985, 1987) that the distinction is wholly spurious on both historical grounds (there is nothing untraditional about state-local borrowing to finance facilities owned by private parties) and economic grounds. Virtually all services and facilities financed by state-local funds are mixed public and private goods, typically more private than public: surely, an undergraduate dormitory at the University of California, Los Angeles (UCLA), is more of a private good than a means-tested rental housing development in East Los Angeles. (Federal officials object to the latter, but not to the former; however, they would object to the dormitory if it were at the University of Southern California, rather than UCLA, which is a distinction without merit.)

Most of the allegedly "private purpose" tax-exempt borrowing has nothing much to do with economic development. The Office of Management and Budget (OMB), Executive Office of the President, estimated the federal costs of "private purpose" state-local debt except for "small-issue IDBs" in fiscal year 1988 at about $20 billion (see table 3 in Kenyon 1988). Under $1 billion of this represents subsidies to private investment that are related to economic development, such as debt for sports and convention facilities and some IDBs for industrial pollution control and energy facilities. If state-local borrowing continues to be tax-exempt in general, this borrowing, like that for "small-issue IDBs," should be eliminated, not capped, however modest the subsidy amounts.[19]

Reducing Information Costs

Although, as noted earlier, most subsidies related to operating costs are not cost-effective, either inherently or because it is difficult to design programs that work well, quite a few small efforts have proved effective for the reason that modest public expenditure seems to have a good deal of leverage. These programs in one way or another reduce information costs for firms, and thus are likely to be efficient in the larger sense, as well as cost-effective. McGahey (1986) has provided a good discussion of this genre of program, which includes certain types of training programs, as well as technology transfer and new product development efforts. He concluded by urging systemization of this type of work in the form of state government strategic planning and economic extension services.

Efficient and Effective Tax Policy Measures

If many of the special tax incentives offered for economic development are not cost-effective, and if tax incentives designed to lower the cost of capital vis-à-vis other inputs are economically inefficient, are there tax reforms that can do good? More precisely, are there efficiency-enhancing tax reforms that can have positive local effects? State-local tax systems contain numerous departures from economic neutrality, whose correction can satisfy both requirements.[20]

One such departure is the long-standing differentially heavy taxation of railroads, other transportation industries, and public utilities. Another is the inclusion in the sales tax base of items that are not final purchases of goods and services by consumers, but are intermediate business purchases. Such purchases are treated differently among the states (see Mikesell 1986). Obviously, a state sales tax that narrowly covers consumer purchases but broadly covers intermediate business purchases will be locationally harmful, at the margin. The efficiency cost is in the erratic nature of what is taxed and what is not, depending on fine definitions in the regulations and in the extent of vertical integration.

The nonuniformity in coverage and effective rates, by type of asset, that marks the American property tax is another source of distortion, whose correction would be efficient and locationally helpful to the states whose property tax systems are most distorting. The instruments of nonuniformity include not only the legendary departures in assessment practices from the standards specified by statute but also partial exemptions, formal classification for taxation at different rates (a spreading practice), and idiosyncratic coverage of business equipment and inventories. The corporate income tax is still another opportunity for efficiency-improving reform. As McLure (1980) has shown, the state corporate income tax is not a profits tax at all, but, instead, separate taxes on payrolls, property, and sales within the taxing state, the combined height of which is proportional to the nationwide profits earned by the firm. Such a tax package affects the mix of capital and labor inputs; depending on how each of the states differently defines and measures "payrolls," "property" and "sales," it can be locationally distorting; and it is highly uneven among industries and firms. The obvious move toward neutrality, if business as such has to be taxed at all by state and local governments, is to replace the tax with one on value added.

How Much Competition?

How, then, does one answer the initial questions: Is interstate competition in this form good or bad, and to the extent bad, what should be done about it? The answer seems to be that economic development incentives are, for the most part, neither very good nor very bad from the standpoint of efficient resource allocation in the economy. Despite all the imperfections, the offering of incentives does not represent a fall from grace, but neither does competition in this form operate in ways that truly parallel the efficiency-creating operations of private competitive markets. Given the low cost-effectiveness of most instruments, there is little national impact, only a waste of local resources in most cases.

Thus, we should urge state and local governments to concentrate on the few types of policy that do make sense for them. As for the federal government, it should withdraw the most egregiously inefficient and ineffective of economic development subsidies, particularly subsidies provided through tax-exempt borrowing. The federal government also should ensure against the direct local exporting, across state lines, of costs, or cartel-like exercises of market power (for example, the use of discriminatory severance taxes), or the undermining of national policies in order to lower costs locally (for example, in regard to equal opportunity requirements). Also, the background conditions for efficient interstate competition would be improved greatly if the federal safety net for the poor were more real than imaginary.[21]

AMENITY AS ECONOMIC DEVELOPMENT

The following postscript should not be necessary, but is. It has long been obvious that a great deal of household relocation within the country is in response to perceived differences in amenities, rather than to narrower economic considerations. Inevitably, this means that some of those who decide on firm locations will also be responsive to amenities because, generally, they will not locate their enterprises in places where they do not want to live. In addition, and more importantly, economic activity will be responsive to household location and consumer demand. Recently, it has become an article of faith among many economic development specialists that amenity is the key factor in locational choice by business, and that, therefore, the improvement of amenities should be the top priority in economic development policy. Specifically, we are told, more public money should be spent for education, housing, cultural and recreational facilities, and services, not for themselves but for their supposed effect on economic growth.

Because all of these factors are good things, it would be ridiculous—and actually inefficient, according to public finance theory—

for the federal government to attempt to restrain competition in this form. But it is also inefficient for state and local decision makers to spend more for these purposes than they would have, if they had not been persuaded of the incremental economic development advantages. This is because, in my opinion, those economic development advantages are bogus.

There are at least four reasons for saying so. The first is that, although amenity obviously has been important in locational choice, much of the location-decision-conditioning amenity is beyond the reach of state and local government action, either for years or forever. Climate seems the most important of all variables. Scenery and outdoor recreation opportunities based on natural features also are largely beyond the reach of public policy. It takes decades to convert a Stanford from a pleasant college to a locational magnet for high-tech activities, and generations to create one from scratch.

Second, it is often not clear how to make a real difference in those variables that are within the reach of state and local governments, at least without spending amounts of money that are certainly not within reach. Housing is an obvious case. If high housing costs really are a deterrent to economic development in the Northeast and in California, then so be it. There is no way that governments are going to spend enough to reduce the difference in housing costs between those areas and the rest of the country by $50,000–100,000 per unit. The schools are another case, to some extent. Many areas with schools that are perceived to be inferior do not spend much for them, but others—like New York, Washington, D.C., and other large cities— spend a great deal. No doubt were New York City to double its expenditure per pupil, from its already very high level, great improvements would result, but no one is sure that an increase in expenditure in a more plausible range would make much difference.

Third, evidence is not strong that the amenity variables that state and local governments can influence by greater expenditure have much impact on the rate of economic growth. As Kenyon (1988) has reported, econometric studies have shown significant positive coefficients for education spending and economic growth. But there is no such evidence for other types of state-local spending, and one has to be skeptical about the pull of even education spending in the light of the extremely strong growth rates over the years of so many states with notoriously bad schools and other inferior services too. If the pull of climate and other features of nature is so powerful, it may be that a statistically significant coefficient for education still does not lead to cost-effectiveness.

Strangely enough, given the very small amount of public expenditure involved (state and local government expenditure for culture probably is only about $750 million annually in all states combined), there has been a great deal of empirical study of the purported local economic impact of the arts, leading to some strident and thoroughly implausible claims. Most of the work has been of poor quality, with the better work putting forth rather modest claims.[22]

Finally, the extent of differentiation is quite small for some amenity variables. Furthermore, differentiation may not matter much once a certain threshold has been reached. For example, most places have a decent supply of local park and recreation facilities, and short of recreating Denver's Front Range or San Diego's Pacific beaches, states and cities cannot do much to distinguish themselves from the pack in this regard. So, this cannot be a factor in locational choice. Similarly, once every mid-sized city has a full range of professional cultural attractions—a symphony orchestra, a regional theater group, a regional ballet company, one or two good museums—the cultural dimension also ceases to be a factor in choice of location among those cities.

To have an attractive city with good services is a worthwhile goal; if cities and states want to compete about which is most attractive, that is surely to the good. Moreover, if cities and states abandon the forms of competition that are ineffective, or even harmful, in favor of competing over high-quality schools and infrastructure that is in good repair and adequate to serve businesses and residents, that, too, is a step forward in state and local government policy. The advance is especially welcome to the extent that state and local governments have been underinvesting in human capital and physical infrastructure. Even if the local economic development payoffs from this approach are modest in any particular community, both the nation and local residents may benefit substantially.

Notes

1. U.S. Advisory Commission on Intergovernmental Relations has estimated in the past that taxes with an initial impact on business amount to about 30 percent of total state-local tax collections. Suppose that the combined value of all explicit economic development measures is equal to 10 percent of taxes with an initial impact on business. In calendar year 1986, that would have been $11.6 billion, using National Income and Product Accounts government finance data (*Survey of Current Business*, July 1987, p. 39), or 0.27 percent of gross national product.

2. See Federal Reserve Bank of Chicago (1952).

3. In the late 1950s, Senator Paul Douglas of Illinois sponsored legislation providing federal assistance to "distressed areas"; the examples used included Appalachia, some other parts of the South, industrial New England, and isolated areas with used-up forests and mines, like southern Illinois.

4. In the 1952 publication by the Federal Reserve Bank of Chicago (see note 2), all the arguments used against the device in subsequent years appear, apparently for the first time.

5. Letter certifying the allocation of Municipal Assistance Corporation (MAC) funds from Paul L. Kickstein, New York City budget director, to Governor Mario M. Cuomo and Felix Rohatyn, MAC board chairman, January 19, 1988. The funds were derived from debt service savings from the refinancing of MAC debt and the release of debt service reserves in excess of those contractually required. The MAC was established in 1975 to borrow on behalf of the city government, at the timeof the fiscal crisis. At the end of 1984, its role was restricted to refinancing its outstanding debt and paying off its debt.

6. See L. White (1986) on this point.

7. This parallels the Baumol and Bradford (1970) argument on optimal departures from marginal cost-pricing neutrality.

8. With the possible exception of land value taxes, all state-local taxes are inefficient, to some degree; the issue here, of course, concerns tax instruments that are relatively more inefficient than others.

9. One approach to reform might be to apply similar taxes to telephone company competitors and alternative technologies. The long distance companies have proven very adroit at avoiding state taxation, and the taxation of customer-owned equipment goes against the trend of exempting personal property from taxation.

10. This approach has more promise with housing subsidies than with economic development subsidies. For an application to a housing subsidy program in which many projects involved condominium conversion, and hence a sale, on completion, see M. White (1983).

11. See New York State Legislative Tax Study Commission (1985) for an example.

12. See Netzer (1986) for a summary and critique of the results.

13. This discussion stresses regressions that use political jurisdictions, usually states, as the unit of observation, because jurisdictional boundaries *do* coincide with clear-cut policy differences and the goal is to illuminate the impact of different policies.

14. See Papke and Papke (1984), where the model is explained and applied.

15. McGahey's (1986) description of the methods used in the 1984 studies makes one suspect that none of the results may be reliable.

16. Some tax incentives that are nominally triggered by investment decisions may not really be so conditioned—for example, an investment tax credit conditioned on an increase in employment within the state, which will affect the net cost of capital to the firm only if the level of investment planned (in the absence of the credit) would not reduce the firm's tax liability to zero. Otherwise, the credit is a subsidy of labor costs, not capital.

17. Indeed, some commentators on the 1958 study asserted that the observed high mortality rate among small businesses indicated that credit was too easily available (see Federal Reserve Bank of Chicago 1958).

18. See Robinson (1960) for an early example of the genre.

19. An efffective way of doing so is to deny the deductibility of any payments, whether

as interest or lease payments, made by a taxable entity (firm or household) to service tax-exempt debt.

20. The following is based on the discussion in Netzer (1986: 30–32).

21. See L. White (1986) for an excellent discussion of appropriate and inappropriate limits on competition.

22. In a volume of essays published by the National Conference of State Legislatures, designed to convince state governments of the powerful economic impact of the arts, most of the authors were highly skeptical and devoted themselves to keeping the claims modest (Radich 1987, especially the essay by Bruce Seaman).

References

Baumol, William J., and David F. Bradford. 1970. "Optimal Departures from Marginal Cost Pricing." *American Economic Review* 60(3): 265–283.

Federal Reserve Bank of Chicago. 1952. "City-Financed New Factories." *Business Conditions* (Federal Reserve Bank review), (September): 12–14.

————. 1958. "Financing Small Businesses—A Review." *Business Conditions*, (July): 9–16.

Kenyon, Daphne A. 1988. "Interjurisdictional Tax and Policy Competition: Good or Bad for the Federal System?" Washington, D.C.: U.S. Advisory Commission on Intergovernmental Relations, January. Draft.

Ledebur, Larry C., and William W. Hamilton. 1986. "The Failure of Tax Concessions as Economic Development Incentives." In *Reforming State Tax Systems*, edited by Steven D. Gold. Denver: National Conference of State Legislatures.

McGahey, Richard M. 1986. "State Economic Development in a Changing World Economy: Strategic Planning and Economic Extension Services." *New York Affairs* 9(3): 63–80.

McLure, Charles E. 1980. "The State Corporate Income Tax: Lambs in Wolves' Clothing." In *The Economics of Taxation*, edited by Henry J. Aaron and Michael J. Boskin. Washington: Brookings Institution.

Mikesell, John L. 1986. "General Sales Tax." In *Reforming State Tax Systems*, edited by Steven D. Gold. Denver: National Conference of State Legislatures.

Netzer, Dick. 1985. "The Effect of Tax Simplification on State and Local Governments." In *Economic Consequences of Tax Simplification*, edited by Alicia H. Munnell. Federal Reserve Bank of Boston, Conference Series No. 29. Boston: Federal Reserve Bank of Boston.

————. 1986. "State Tax Policy and Economic Development: What Should Governors Do when Economists Tell Them Nothing Works?" *New York Affairs* 9(3): 19–36.

————. 1987. "Federal Tax Reform and State-Local Economic Development Policy." *Review of Law & Social Change* 15(1): 147–165.

New York State Legislative Tax Study Commission. 1985. "The New York State Investment Tax Credit." Staff working paper. Albany: Author.

Papke, James A., and Leslie E. Papke. 1984. "State Tax Incentives and Investment Location Decisions: Microanalytic Simulations." In *Indiana's Revenue Structure: Major Components and Issues, Part II*, edited by James A. Papke. Lafayette, Ind.: Purdue University Center for Tax Policy Studies.

Radich, Anthony J. 1987. *Economic Impact of the Arts: A Sourcebook.* Denver: National Conference of State Legislatures.

Rasmussen, David, Marc Bendick, and Larry Ledebur. 1984. "A Methodology for Selecting Economic Development Incentives." *Growth and Change* 15: 18–25.

Robinson, Roland I. 1960. *Postwar Market for State and Local Government Securities.* Princeton, N.J.: Princeton University Press, for the National Bureau of Economic Research.

U.S. Congress. House. Committee on Banking and Currency and Select Committee on Small Business. 1958. *Financing Small Business.* 85th Cong., 2d sess.

White, Lawrence J. 1986. "The Role of the States in Promoting Economic Development: Should Competition to Attract New Investment Be Restricted?" *New York Affairs* 9(3): 6–18.

White, Michelle J. 1983. "J51: Incentive, Subsidy, or Windfall?" *New York Affairs* 7(4): 112–125.

Chapter Fourteen

DOES ECONOMIC THEORY CAPTURE THE EFFECTS OF NEW AND TRADITIONAL STATE POLICIES ON ECONOMIC DEVELOPMENT?

R. Scott Fosler

In the previous chapter, Dick Netzer addresses a limited group of state and local activities, principally those dealing with subsidies, tax breaks, and other incentives, which have been conventionally defined as "economic development programs." He concludes that, although economic theory would view this form of interstate competition as a distortion of markets and therefore as likely to reduce national output and economic welfare, in a world of imperfect markets and imperfect governments, such interventions may improve economic efficiency from a national standpoint. Netzer's conclusion is well founded, and his analysis of the methodological and analytical limitations in assessing state and local economic development efforts is especially valuable.

However, conventional economic theory and, for that matter, conventional economic development practice, are being outpaced by economic change and by a new conception of economic development that is emerging among state and local policymakers. The key here is Netzer's opening proposition that "there is not much that state and local governments do that does not affect their economies, for good or for ill. It may well be that the greatest effects stem from policies, actions, practices, and institutions that, at least traditionally, are not governed mainly by concern for their economic consequences." This is an accurate and important statement, and it warrants going beyond the "narrow band of policies and actions . . . undertaken explicitly for their hoped-for economic consequences" that are the focus of Netzer's paper.

State and local governments currently spend about $625 billion per year, or nearly 14 percent of our gross national product. Thus, the sheer magnitude of their spending is economically consequential. Moreover, state and local governments account for about 84 percent of the public sector's total nondefense purchases of goods and services. These governments, not the federal government, are responsible for the vast majority of the nation's civilian public-service delivery expenditures, aside from transfer payments.

The content of those public services has economic importance, both in its own right and as key inputs to business. In a highly competitive economy heavily weighted toward knowledge-based activities, many state and local programs are of special importance, particularly primary, secondary, and higher education; training; technological development; and the regulation of capital markets. Numerous other services also have economic impact, including physical infrastructure, business and environmental regulation, the development and management of natural resources, and land-use regulation.

Many state and local strategists now recognize the economic importance of these and other government functions that are not part of the conventional economic development package of tax abatements and financial incentives. State and local officials have gone far beyond the traditional emphasis on industrial recruitment, or "smokestack chasing," and are now concerned more broadly with the internal development of the regional or local economy.

Until the 1970s, conventional economic development practice was characterized by the efforts of some southern states to attract manufacturing plants from the North, beginning with Mississippi's "Balance Agriculture with Industry" program, which offered tax abatements to northern manufacturers in the 1930s. However, a new generation of state economic initiatives began in the 1970s, stimulated largely by the restructuring of the world economy.

The first region to feel the stress was New England, and so it is no surprise that one of the first states to experiment with new economic formulas was Massachusetts. Leaders in both the private and public sectors at first responded in the conventional manner by trying to recruit industry from outside the state to replace lost jobs. When they were unsuccessful in convincing out-of-state businesses that Massachusetts was a good place to locate, they turned their attention to developing the resources within the state that could nurture the business and entrepreneurial potential already present. Thereupon began experimentation with a wide variety of new programs—in providing capital, improving workforce skills, regenerating mature industry, developing and applying new technology, guiding growth to depressed areas, and reducing tax burdens. These programs laid the foundation for a new generation of state economic initiatives that have little to do with direct recruitment. The closer attention to the economic impact of state actions also underscored the importance of traditional services, such as education and physical infrastructure.

Other states have followed a similar path. As economic hardship visited the manufacturing states of the Midwest, the agricultural states of the Great Plains, the natural-resource states of the West and South, and even high-technology states, such as California, each responded first by stepping up its recruitment efforts and then by adopting a wide range of new economic initiatives directed toward internal development. Virtually all states have begun to explore the economic importance of traditional government services, especially education. No longer do any of the states concentrate exclusively on recruitment (even though most still recruit aggressively). Nearly all are now concerned with business start-ups, expansion, retention, and regeneration, as well as relocation.

The increasing economic importance of state and local government services has tended to blur the lines and conceptual distinctions between the economic roles of the public and private sectors. In the conventional model, the private sector, for all intents and purposes, *is* the economy. Government's role is limited to interventions to correct market failures and to provide a limited menu of public goods. The new state and local strategies conceive of a state or local jurisdiction as a far more complex unit of production, in which numerous parts—social and political, as well as those strictly defined as economic—are integrally related to one another. Such a conception not only accepts the blurred line between public and private sectors but also views the relationship between the two sectors less as a set of distinct responsibilities—sometimes supportive, sometimes antagonistic—and more as a web of interdependent and mutually reinforcing functions. Numerous new state programs, such as enterprise zones, product development funds, small business incubation, technology development, skills training, and the provision of seed and venture capital, are administered by quasi-public corporations, further blurring the public-private distinction.

Social institutions are also increasingly seen as being economically important. For example, the role of the family and of other community influences in preparing students for school and productive employment is now recognized as having major economic significance. The failure of large numbers of American families to participate in the education of their children stands in sharp contrast to the family structures in competing nations that nurture literate, productive workers. The growing number of educationally disadvantaged children in the United States has placed an enormous strain on the private sector. Businesses are unable to find adequate numbers of workers capable of performing in competitive economic enterprises. Firms are confronted with a massive training bill to overcome this deficiency, and will also have to pay higher taxes to equip public schools to try to remedy these deficiencies, or to finance preventive programs in an effort to forestall such problems in the future.

Recognition of such interdependencies has fostered a new respect for cooperation in many jurisdictions. Key actors who once saw themselves as adversaries (e.g., business, labor, government, and civic groups) have begun to recognize that they are all in the same vulnerable boat, and that only cooperative action can likely save them. Thus, through "public-private partnerships," Baltimore rebuilt its inner harbor, New York pulled back from imminent bankruptcy in the 1970's, and Kansas created a new strategic planning capability.

Cooperative efforts have been undertaken among the functional agencies of government, between the executive and legislative branches of government, and between government and the private sector. There is also increased cooperation among governments and private-sector organizations within state, regional, county, municipal, and neighborhood arenas. In each of these instances, however, the relative tendency toward cooperation is tenuous, and could easily retreat in the other direction toward competition.

Cooperation and competition, of course, are opposite sides of the same coin. The southern states invented "smokestack chasing" and actively competed among themselves for northern branch plants, even as they worked cooperatively through such regional institutions as the Southern Growth Policies Board. Within a given jurisdiction, the systematic structuring of competition—for example, in the contracting out of public services to businesses—is viewed as a way to strengthen the service capacity or efficiency of government, and hence as a form of "cooperative competition."

In short, the experience of state and local development efforts reflects a series of economic relationships that is both broader and richer than those captured in conventional economic theory. Perhaps that is why practitioners so infrequently look to theory for guidance, and why theory adapted to these changing circumstances could be invaluable to economic policymaking.

Chapter Fifteen

TRYING TO UNDERSTAND THE ECONOMIC DEVELOPMENT OFFICIAL'S DILEMMA

Nonna A. Noto

In Dick Netzer's long career of research and experience, he has heard nearly every economic subsidy excuse in the book. In chapter 13, he attempts to sort out in a positive sense those economic development incentives that are least wasteful and, preferably, that may even generate positive economic returns. His frank opinion is that these subsidies generally do not work: most lead to inefficient resource allocation from a national standpoint, and those few that may be efficient in concept are often implemented ineffectively by state and local governments. His candidate for worst offender is capital subsidies, particularly tax-exempt bonds issued by state and local governments. He suggests that state and local governments should get back to the basics by removing egregious differentials in the tax treatment of different economic activities, reducing regulatory burdens when such reductions do not mean unduly sacrificing equity or environmental goals, and enhancing labor-force quality and public infrastructure within reasonable cost limits.[1]

One is left, however, to ponder several questions. If research fails to indicate that economic development incentives generate positive returns, what explains policymakers' continued reliance on these concessions to businesses? What can be done to discourage the use of wasteful economic development subsidies?

This chapter offers three lines of explanation for why state and local officials offer subsidies to businesses: (1) the early-bird model, (2) the immobility model, and (3) the political accountability model. It mentions several legislative and administrative remedies that encourage cost-effectiveness in economic development programs. Finally, it considers what researchers might do to communicate their findings more effectively to policymakers and the general public.

The views expressed in this paper are mine and do not represent the position of the Congressional Research Service.

We live in a world of dramatically fluctuating fortunes for individual economic sectors and their host regions (Markusen 1985, 1987). To better explain the behavior of state and local officials as they deal with business, researchers may need to adapt their models to acknowledge these dynamic forces and accompanying local political concerns. Under the traditional economic model, economic rents are competed away, factors are assumed to be mobile, and there are no political considerations. In addition, the long-run model seems to view the community as being at a relatively steady state of acceptable economic activity, in a relatively equal bargaining position vis-à-vis firms, and, consequently, as not really needing to make concessions to business.

What happens to our analysis and policy recommendations if we change some of these assumptions to reflect the shorter-run time-frame of the economic development official who is concerned about keeping his or her job? What if we take an aggressive view of communities going after the big payoff or, in economists' terms, trying to capture the short-term economic rent? What if we acknowledge that a large fraction of the population and capital investment in the community is not mobile in the short run?

If we think of business and the community as being engaged in a game of brinkmanship, it seems reasonable that local officials would adapt their economic development strategy, depending on the strength of the community's bargaining position with respect to firms. The steady-state, equal-bargaining scenario of the mainstream economic model represents but the middle of the full bargaining spectrum.

At one extreme is a growing community in a strong bargaining position. This community is unlikely to receive many requests for concessions, let alone consider them. Quite the reverse. If it can, a jurisdiction will levy exportable taxes (e.g., severance taxes, taxes on hotel rooms and restaurant meals, and gambling taxes) and other taxes on seemingly immobile residents and businesses.[2] Localities may also demand developer exactions (requiring private developers to provide certain infrastructure and public amenities in exchange for permission to build) or charge development impact fees (Nelson et al. 1988).

At the other extreme is a community with a depressed economy. This community is in a weak bargaining position and has to make concessions in some form, through either generalized deflation or subsidies targeted to specific firms.

Consider three alternative models that help to explain the persistence of local subsidy efforts. The early-bird model acknowledges that for some period of time, at least, economic development officials may be right to think that the subsidy will work. Both Netzer (chapter 13) and Ronald C. Fisher (chapter 16) point out that alert communities can take advantage of temporary opportunities to capture from other communities the fiscal dividend generated by businesses (for example, communities that were among the first to offer subsidized credit or tax abatement, before the rest of the pack caught on). The problem is that neither the latecomers nor the early-birds seem to acknowledge when widespread competition has eliminated the economic return—the point at which the subsidies benefit businesses alone because the net returns to communities as a group have been driven to zero.

The immobility model acknowledges boom-and-bust cycles in local economies. For the down side of the cycle in particular, the model challenges the assumption of mobile factors. It helps to explain the willingness of community members to accept a lower standard of living to protect a way of life. State and local economic development incentives are, above all, a demonstration of loyalty to a particular geographic place.[3]

From the outsider's viewpoint, the risk of loss or chance for gain may seem low relative to the size of the economic development concessions being made. But consider what citizens stand to lose if a major employer follows up on its threat to move out of their locale. In directly measurable terms, the move signals the loss of the citizens' major source of labor income, compounded by the decline in value of a major asset, their houses. In less easily measured terms, it is the loss of their community. Not every person is willing to migrate to places of purported greater economic opportunity. How else can one explain the continuation, throughout history and today, of many different societies marked by inferior economic performance?

Warren T. Brookes of the *Detroit News* has dubbed the scenario of subsidies to salvage immobile factors as the hospice model— simply easing the pain of a slow death. However, there are sufficient examples to provide communities with some hope of recovery. In our own time, many of us have witnessed the rise and fall of energy and farm states. We have also seen the New York City and Boston regions fall as manufacturing centers but rise again as financial, service, and high-tech centers. In some cases, subsidies may help to speed the turnaround.[4]

In the immobility scenario, members of the community are willing to give away some of their economic rent to attract or retain business. The question is, what form of concession is most effective and efficient? Within the United States during the 1980s, we had evidence of workers accepting lower wages to protect their jobs in the face of strong international competition and in the aftermath of deregulation. What is the difference between broad-based concessions offered by community members in the form of generalized deflation of wages and property values, and concessions channeled through government and targeted to a specific firm?

Economists have a bias against offering concessions to a particular firm. Netzer (chapter 13) joins those who recommend that a community concentrate instead on bolstering its basic infrastructure in a way that could benefit many types of residents and firms. But what if the community finds itself in a monopsony bargaining situation, facing one very large employer who is shopping for a location? The phenomenon of the one-company town is not entirely a thing of the past. There may not be a long line of other employers waiting to bid for the location. More rigorous economic analysis is needed to identify the conditions under which concessions to an individual firm, channeled through the government, may be an efficient alternative to the generalized, cost-lowering approach.

The political accountability model introduces the role of public officials concerned with preserving the viability of the communities they steward or, at a minimum, holding onto their own jobs. Elsewhere, Netzer (1986:28) has raised the question of who should bear the burden of proof in the argument over the effectiveness of economic development strategies. Should it be the academic naysayer who argues "the firm would have moved in anyway" or the state or local official granting the concession? Consider what personal responsibility these two individuals bear for the consequences of their decision or advice. What does the academic stand to lose if his or her judgment is wrong—anything more than the approval of his or her peer group of fellow researchers?

What about the state or local official? He or she is open to criticism for two types of errors. If the official does not grant the concession, and the firm moves away or does not locate there in the first place, the official stands to lose the election or be fired. On the other hand, if the official grants the concession, and a new firm moves in, or an old firm stays put or expands, the official can be accused of spending too much, wastefully and unnecessarily. From the economic development official's point of view, which error holds the greater risk of loss? At present, it would seem the first, erroneously not making the concession.[5]

Critics frustrated with the inefficiencies and losses they perceive in the competitive economic subsidy game sometimes express the wish that state and local governments could be legally or constitutionally forbidden to make such concessions to business so as to protect them from themselves, as it were. The imagined laws would serve as a shield that economic development officials could raise in their own defense when being bullied into making concessions.

As Netzer (chapter 13) points out, U.S. constitutional prohibitions are unlikely to be imposed on subsidies funded by state and local governments. There are, however, legislative and administrative options available to federal, state, and local officials that could be pursued more seriously. These policies embody the theme of making the government granting the subsidy accept greater economic accountability for spending taxpayers' money on these incentives. The intent is to encourage greater public cost-effectiveness in economic development programs.

As an example of such a policy, the U.S. Congress has placed restrictions on the use of tax-exempt bonds in an effort to curtail the perceived misuse of a federal subsidy by state and local governments.[6] Many states, in turn, legislate the rules governing local bond issuance and tax abatement programs and could raise accountability standards to encourage greater cost-effectiveness.

State and federal aid formulas could also be designed not to subsidize the incentive programs of states and localities. Tax-base capacity measures could be adjusted upward by the amount of the abated tax bases. Otherwise, state school finance formulas, for example, wind up subsidizing local property tax abatement programs, even if this is unintended by state taxpayers.[7]

More budgetary discipline could be imposed, if not by the local governments themselves, then by the states. Cities frequently grant property tax abatements without any guiding constraints on the cost side from a total abatement budget or economic development budget (Wolkoff 1983).

Edward V. Regan, comptroller of New York State, has endorsed a formal tax-expenditure accounting of the costs of economic development policies. He had such a provision incorporated into the 1987 legislation that amended New York's economic development zones act (1987 N.Y. Laws, ch. 442). His office also developed legislation[8] that would require the state government, all local governments, and any authority that has the power to grant tax abatements to report annually to New York's director of the budget the value of every abatement and exemption granted.[9] Regan also requested the Government Accounting Standards Board (GASB) to investigate setting national standards for financial reporting of economic development programs (Regan 1988: 33–35).

In addition, the type of research evidence summarized by Netzer (chapter 13) needs to be communicated more effectively and translated into workable policy guidelines, understandable to both government officials and the public at large. Potentially, research findings could help build citizen pressure against wasteful state and local economic development concessions, stiffen the spines of local officials, and embarrass businesses who attempt to make heavy-handed demands on communities.

Because of the highly unique circumstances surrounding each subsidy, Netzer (chapter 13) emphasizes the difficulty of making any believable econometric estimate of the effectiveness of incentives. Perhaps simpler measures of effectiveness are called for at this stage. Publicizing even basic facts about the tax expenditure costs of subsidy programs would be a start. Public finance researchers accustomed to taking the aggregate community view may need to work with methods more typical of corporate financial analysis. Rasmussen, Bendick, and Ledebur's (1984) cost-benefit framework provocatively points out a basic tax-accounting phenomenon: that state-provided subsidies are partially offset by the higher federal income taxes (similarly, federal subsidies by higher state taxes) that result from lower deductions for interest, taxes, and other expenses.

Netzer (chapter 13) mentions calculating for the community a break-even point for the increase in investment or employment that needs to be induced by the subsidy. Similarly, Morse and Farmer (1986) established an expected value for the percentage of investment that needs to be influenced for the community to break even on its subsidy program; actual behavior can then be measured against this criterion to determine if the program seems rational. Wolkoff (1983, 1987) and Regan (1988) encouraged attempting to distinguish the likely payoffs from assisting different types of firms, by estimating the likelihood that their location will be influenced by the subsidy, and by assessing both the benefits (tax base, types of jobs) and costs (such as environmental damage and public service needs) that the firms are likely to bring to the community.

Whether good or bad for the federal system, competition between jurisdictions to attract economic activity is probably inevitable. No matter how much academics protest, state and local officials are likely to want to have some economic development cards they can play. If nothing else, subsidies allow politicians to take some decisive action and demonstrate that they care about attracting business to their jurisdiction. Consequently, rather than only discrediting techniques they believe do not work, it behooves other researchers to follow Netzer's example of trying also to sort out which economic development incentives might help, and under what conditions.

Notes

1. For those interested in following up on Netzer's arguments in more detail, see Netzer (1986) on state tax systems and Netzer (1987: 157–65) on tax-exempt bonds.

2. Baum (1987: 354–56) has pointed out that fiscal exploitation (defined as levying taxes on nonresidential properties at a rate that exceeds the cost of providing them local services) is analytically the converse of subsidies.

3. See Elazar (1984), Markusen (1987), and Hagstrom (1988) for extensive discussions of the deep-rooted economic, cultural, and political phenomena that differentiate regions of the United States.

4. See Baum (1987) for a theoretical exploration of the conditions under which local subsidies from immobile to mobile factors may increase local welfare, and a few cases where they may even increase national economic welfare. Unemployment attributable to downward wage rigidities (caused in his example by a national minimum wage) is one possible justification for subsidy. Another is the argument that, for a declining community, a subsidy may speed up the economic adjustment process and cause less pain than relying on the normal market processes of declining wages and prices for local goods.

5. Wolkoff (1983, 1987) explicitly addressed the political costs of a firm locating elsewhere.

6. See Zimmerman (1990), ch. 11.

7. Wolkoff (1983: 83) identified this subsidy from school aid in Michigan, and Morse and Farmer (1986: 332) in Ohio.

8. S. 6943 was introduced in the New York State Senate on February 8, 1988, but was not enacted.

9. The governor, in turn, would be required to include the economic development tax expenditure report in New York State's executive budget. In addition, any local authority granting an abatement would be required to notify all other affected local governments with a statement of the associated tax expenditures expected to affect those governments. The proposed legislation also required that each report on tax abatements include a statement of the benefits achieved by the program, such as the number of jobs created (Regan 1988: 30–33).

References

Baum, Donald N. 1987. "The Economic Effects of State and Local Business Incentives." *Land Economics* 63(4, November): 348–60.

Elazar, Daniel J. 1984. *American Federalism: A View from the States*. New York: Harper & Row.

Hagstrom, Jerry. 1988. *Beyond Reagan: The New Landscape of American Politics*. New York: W. W. Norton.

Markusen, Ann. 1985. *Profit Cycles, Oligopoly, and Regional Development*. Cambridge, Mass.: MIT Press.

————. 1987. *Regions: The Economics and Politics of Territory*. Totowa, N.J.: Rowman & Littlefield.

Morse, George W., and Michael C. Farmer. 1986. "Location and Investment Effects of a Tax Abatement Program." *National Tax Journal* 39(2, June): 229–36.

Nelson, Arthur C., et al. 1988. "Symposium: Development Impact Fees." *Journal of the American Planning Association* 54(1, Winter): 3–78.

Netzer, Dick. 1985. "State Tax Policy and Economic Development: What Should Governors Do when Economists Tell Them Nothing Works?" *New York Affairs* 9(3): 19–36.

————. 1986. "Federal Tax Reform and State-Local Economic Development Policy." *Review of Law & Social Change* 15(1): 147–65; responses, 167–79.

Rasmussen, David W., Marc Bendick, Jr., and Larry C. Ledebur. 1984. "A Methodology for Selecting Economic Development Incentives." *Growth and Change* 15(January): 18–25.

Regan, Edward V. 1988. "Government, Inc.: Creating Accountability for Economic Development Programs." Research Report. Washington, D.C.: Government Finance Research Center of the Government Finance Officers Association.

Wolkoff, Michael J. 1983. "The Nature of Property Tax Abatement Awards." *Journal of the American Planning Association* 49(1, Winter): 77–84.

————. 1987. "Economic Development as a Signaling Game." University of Rochester Public Policy Analysis Program, Rochester, N.Y., April. Photocopy.

Zimmerman, Dennis. 1990. *The Private Use of Tax-Exempt Bonds: Controlling Public Subsidy of Private Activity*. Washington, D.C.: The Urban Institute.

SUMMARY VIEW

Chapter Sixteen

INTERJURISDICTIONAL COMPETITION: A SUMMARY PERSPECTIVE AND AGENDA FOR RESEARCH

Ronald C. Fisher

In what ways do governments in the American federal system compete with each other? Has that competition been increasing or become more aggressive? What, generally, are the economic effects of that perceived competition? These questions have received substantial public attention in recent years—both in the journalistic press and broadcast media—but increasingly, they also have been the focus of academic inquiry. In part, this academic work reflects an expanded awareness and interest in the state and local government sector, where most interjurisdictional competition occurs and has its greatest effect.

The objective in this final chapter is to review some of the recent academic inquiry into interjurisdictional competition and, in the process, to both summarize and build upon the other chapters in this volume. As such, I am not attempting to survey all the issues or research on the topic; indeed, the U.S. Advisory Commission on Intergovernmental Relations (ACIR) (1991) has already provided a complete and up-to-date review. Nor do I explore any specific aspect of interjurisdictional competition in detail. Rather, the approach here is to pose some basic but fundamental questions, examine the answers suggested by this volume's authors and others, and then suggest some appropriate directions for additional research.

WHAT IS INTERJURISDICTIONAL COMPETITION?

In a federal system, governments compete in at least two major ways using a variety of policy tools. The more familiar form is horizontal (or interjurisdictional) competition, which refers to interaction among governments at the same general level of the federal system—competition among states or among localities within a region or metropolitan area. Jurisdictions compete for population in general, for residents with specific characteristics, for investment, employment, sales, and intergovernmental aid. This competition is carried out with the various tools of government fiscal policy (taxes, expenditures, debt) and government regulatory authority (labor markets, commerce, contracts, property rights).

In contrast, vertical (or intergovernmental) competition refers essentially to the allocation of responsibilities and resources among the federal, state, and local governments in the federal structure. For instance, how should the responsibility for income redistribution be divided or shared among the national and subnational governments? Although perhaps a less familiar form, these allocation issues involve competition none the less. Governments compete to have more or less responsibility for both the right to set the characteristics of a service or function as well as the responsibility for financing that service. In that regard, Daniel J. Elazar, in chapter 4, argues that what he calls "cooperative federalism" (all governments and the private sector interact in providing goods and services) comes closer to characterizing the nature of vertical competition in the United States than "dual federalism" (each type of government carries out separate functions) or "hierarchical federalism" (higher-level governments impose decisions on subordinate jurisdictions).

Why do governments compete in these ways, or perhaps more accurately, what induces government officials to act competitively? Albert Breton (chapter 2) and John E. Chubb (chapter 3) suggest three possibilities: (1) governments act to prevent the exit of individuals, firms, or tax base, (2) public officials seek to retain elected office, and (3) governments acquire information about other jurisdictions' actions (i.e., one jurisdiction's good idea tends to be adopted by others).

I want to offer a fourth perspective. In a sense, *interjurisdictional* competition is a misnomer, because much of what we categorize in that vein is really competition among people using government as an agent. Further, this competition among people is largely distributive; that is, the objective of people in this competition is to get "more" for themselves (of course, "more" means more "goods" and less "bads"). From this perspective, competition is not the result of a federal system of government; instead, the desire of people to compete with each other is one reason why governments are created.

For instance, the local jurisdictions that provide primary and secondary education—whether single-purpose school districts or multipurpose municipalities—compete for tax base, state and federal financial aid, students, athletes, and teachers, among other things. Interjurisdictional competition for those things would undoubtedly exist or arise even if decentralized governments did not provide the service. In Hawaii, where education is provided by the state government, surely there is competition among individual schools for many of the same things that independent school districts compete for. As another example, there is often competition among residents at different locations within jurisdictions over the spatial distribution of public service benefits, and residents may form neighborhood associations or substate regional commissions to assist with that competition. Similarly, some states formed regional groups to compete for the location of the proposed "supercollider" research facility in 1988. As Wallace E. Oates (1972) has explained elsewhere, the optimal size government is different for different purposes. In attempting to gain more resources for themselves through competition, individuals may use existing governments in the federal system or effectively create new ones when the existing structure does not serve the immediate purpose.

If the objective of interjurisdictional competition is to acquire more resources for some individuals, the appropriate policy is sometimes to use or encourage the operation of markets toward that end, such as publicizing the availability of fiscal incentives and encouraging mobility to take advantage of those incentives, whereas sometimes the objective can be served by blocking the operation of markets— for instance, by using regulations to restrict market entry or exit. Although the chapters in this volume focus on fiscal incentives, regulations may be equally important. As Wagner and colleagues (1982: 48) have argued, "anything that can be accomplished through the taxing and spending aspects of the budget can be accomplished instead through government regulation."

Perhaps the best known and most often analyzed form of regulation used for competitive purposes is zoning. As explained by Hamilton (1975) and others, some form of fiscal zoning is necessary to ensure stability in a world of Tiebout-type competition for residents. In the case of industrial and commercial activity, exclusionary zoning effectively imposes prohibitive tax rates on activities deemed to have too high a cost by some people. There is less research on the effects of other types of regulations on interjurisdictional competition. There have been examinations of the monopoly aspects of licensing, but usually not in the context of interjurisdictional competition. Recently, Craig and Sailors (1988) examined the effect of state government laws that favor in-state firms in competitive bidding. Their results suggest that these regulations increase the costs of state government purchases without substantially increasing economic activity in the state. That is, the bids likely would have gone to in-state firms anyway, but at lower prices. If true, the regulation affects the distribution of resources within the state perhaps more than among states. Without commenting on the specifics of that research, my suggestion is that more attention to competition through regulation seems warranted.

IS INTERJURISDICTIONAL COMPETITION INCREASING?

Although there always has been interjurisdictional competition in the United States, the perception seems to be that this competition is increasing, or at least is receiving more attention by officials. However, Dick Netzer, in chapter 13, explains that state competition for economic development existed from the earliest days of the union. The notion of an economic "war between the states" dates from a 1963 article by Gooding, not from the 1970s or 1980s. And Break's classic book on intergovernmental relations noted that "state and local governments have been engaged for some time in an *increasingly* [my emphasis] active competition among themselves for new business" (1967: 23). Although it is possible that interjurisdictional competition is continually increasing, it may be more likely that it just seems that way as states and localities adopt new competitive techniques and abandon old ones.

There probably is no direct way to test whether interjurisdictional competition has been increasing, but John Shannon's analogy (chapter 6) that fiscal differences among jurisdictions are similar to the length of a convoy suggests a possible indirect test. The ACIR (1991) notes that "competitive behavior can imply either a move toward diversity or a move toward conformity." Shannon argues that competition "appears to set the outer limits on interjurisdictional fiscal diversity." What has been happening to the fiscal differences among states and localities in recent years? Has the effect of either an actual increase in competition or an increased awareness of competitive activity altered the distribution of jurisdictions in terms of spending and revenues?

Some evidence on that issue is reported here in table 16.1, which shows the coefficient of variation among states for per-capita state-

Table 16.1 COEFFICIENT OF VARIATION FOR STATE-LOCAL FISCAL
CHARACTERISTICS, BY STATE, VARIOUS YEARS

Fiscal Year	Per-Capita Expenditures	Per-Capita Own-Source Revenue	Per-Capita Taxes	Per-Capita Income
1971	.29 (.20)[a]	.23 (.20)	.21 (.22)	.14 (.14)
1975	.32 (.23)	.22 (.19)	.21 (.21)	.15 (.13)
1980	.41 (.16)	.68 (.19)	.50 (.21)	.14 (.13)
1986	.42 (.19)	.61 (.23)	.36 (.23)	.16 (.15)

Source: U.S. Advisory Commission on Intergovernmental Relations, various years,
Significant Features of Fiscal Federalism (Washington, D.C.: Author).
Note: Data in parentheses exclude Alaska.
a. The coefficient of variation is the standard deviation divided by the mean value.

local expenditures, own-source revenues, and taxes for various years over the past 15 years. For comparison, the coefficient of variation for state per-capita personal income is also shown. If Alaska is excluded (and Alaska is a clear outlier recently), the distribution of per-capita fiscal characteristics among the states has not changed appreciably since 1971. If anything, the interstate variation in per-capita taxes and own-source revenue has become a bit larger. Similar to the fiscal characteristics, there also has been no obvious pattern of change in the distribution of state per-capita incomes. So, in a period when it is perceived that there was an increasing amount of interstate economic and fiscal competition, the differences among states in revenues and spending have not narrowed. For Shannon's analogy, the length of the convoy has remained remarkably stable. Of course, it is true that some states substantially changed their positions in the distribution during this period, but within a constant overall distribution.[1]

Although I do not report similar general data here, results in the education literature show that the variation in per-pupil expenditures on elementary and secondary education among localities within states also has not been declining. What these facts tell us about interjurisdictional competition is not clear. If the pattern of state and local spending and taxes reflects differences in consumer demand, then competition should not narrow those differences without changes in that underlying demand. Interjurisdictional competition may alter the costs that individuals face for satisfying their demand, but if behavior is relatively price inelastic, as the evidence shows, then even an increase in the cost of "being different" will not alter actual differences much. In any case, worries or hopes that competition will eliminate or greatly reduce interjurisdictional fiscal differences seem unfounded.

WHAT ARE THE ECONOMIC EFFECTS OF INTERJURISDICTIONAL COMPETITION?

The natural inclination of economists is to analyze interjurisdictional interaction with the same tools used to analyze private markets. As Wallace E. Oates and Robert W. Schwab explain in chapter 7, if there is mobility among jurisdictions, no information costs, and no interjurisdictional externalities, then fiscal differences will be capitalized into the prices faced by immobile factors and consumers, all local taxes will become benefit taxes at the margin, and interjurisdictional competition will lead to an efficient allocation of resources. These results follow essentially the seminal concept suggested by Tiebout (1956), that the spatial equivalent of private-market perfect competition generates the same result—economic efficiency.[2]

The usual concerns about the use of the perfect competition model also arise here. First, if the assumptions (no transaction costs or externalities) are violated in practice, to what degree is the outcome also affected? Second, do governments interact on the assumption that changes in their own behavior will not bring reactions by other governments, as the perfect competition model requires, or do governments recognize the interdependency among jurisdictions and react to the actions of others in a strategic way, perhaps even to the point of collusion?

On the first issue, it is clear that transaction costs can be substantial, both in private markets and in interjurisdictional interaction. The "law of one price" has been long discredited because information and moving costs clearly allow a distribution of prices for identical products. Consequently, economists have developed elaborate models of search behavior on the assumption that both sides of the market do not have equal information. There is similarly ample evidence of less-than-perfect information and mobility regarding governmental differences. Simple gravity models (in which interaction is largely a function of distance) have been successful in explaining everything from the choice of shopping locations to whom one marries. Interstate and interlocal unemployment differences persist. Both of these observations are consistent with the idea of relatively high transaction costs, a result also borne out by the existing studies of moving decisions. It seems reasonable, therefore, that not all fiscal differences among governments would be bid away or capitalized either. It might even be that some consumers exhibit a type of "brand loyalty," preferring to stick with a jurisdiction because of familiarity.

Less-than-perfect mobility helps explain why state and local governments set general nominal tax rates on capital and then selectively offer fiscal incentives, which have the effect of lowering effective rates for certain types of businesses. Those governments are trying to "tax discriminate" based on the perceived mobility of the business activity. Another aspect of transaction costs in competitive markets—that it may take some time to achieve equilibrium—also helps to explain the observed behavior of governments. On the one hand, a government may choose to set relatively high tax rates on capital and earn fiscal rents for a while, until the investors react by moving elsewhere. On the other hand, a government offering fiscal incentives may realize that those incentives eventually will be offset by capitalization, although again, there are short-run fiscal rents to be earned.[3]

It seems important to emphasize these latter points because of the commonly perceived "lack of reality" of the competitive model and its implications. If interjurisdictional fiscal differences are capitalized so that it is impossible for governments to maintain a cost advantage, why do governments pursue fiscal incentives so aggressively? As already noted, one answer is that capitalization may not fully offset cost differences or that the capitalization process occurs slowly. The other answer may be capitalization itself. If one government offers a fiscal incentive that attracts economic activity from other jurisdictions, the expected effect is an increase in the price of immobile goods in the jurisdiction, most particularly of land. Although the increase in land prices serves to offset the fiscal advantage for new entrants, the increase in land values is a capital gain to existing landowners—a gain that might have been the objective of the fiscal incentives to begin with. As Netzer notes in chapter 13, "the effect (and the very lightly disguised objective) was often to increase the value of privately owned land that came to be in the path of development."

Oligopoly, or game theory, is the alternative to perfect competition for conceptualizing interjurisdictional interaction. In those models, it is well known that collusion can dominate other strategies, in the sense that all parties can be better off. The implication of this theoretical point for policy matters has been explored by Gramlich (1987), who demonstrated how cooperation—horizontally among subnational governments, vertically between the levels of the federal system and among providers and recipients—can improve public welfare policy results compared to competition. As Gramlich noted, "Game theory elements exist whenever there are small independent groups that can either compete or cooperate in some activity" (1987: 418). If the decisions of one agent (a state government, for instance) depend on the behavior of others, then planning actions jointly can improve the welfare of all. It seems relatively straightforward to apply Gramlich's reasoning about governmental interaction on welfare policy to governmental interaction on other issues as well.

The concern about cooperation or collusion in an oligopoly model, stressed by Breton in chapter 2, is the potential instability. How are cooperative agreements to be enforced? Breton suggests that self-enforcement cannot work, and that, consequently, stability is the responsibility of the national government. Contrary to that viewpoint, however, some interstate agreements, mostly on tax matters, seem to have been relatively successful. Agreements about the apportionment of interstate business tax bases and enforcement of state excise taxes come to mind. Still, the role of the national government is important. On this point Gramlich (1987) agreed, although he argued that matching grants are a stabilizing device because the participation of all (recipient) governments is encouraged and achieved, and no one jurisdiction can free ride on the actions of others. In a way, then, matching grants create a type of intergovernmental cooperation.

WHAT IS THE FEDERAL GOVERNMENT'S ROLE?

There seems to be general agreement among the authors in this volume that the national government has an important role to play concerning interjurisdictional competition in a federal system, but there is less agreement on what that role should be. Oates and Schwab (chapter 7) take the traditional position that the national government's role is that of altering the distribution of resources. There is no reason to talk about efficiency and competition, of course, unless there is some mechanism to achieve society's distributional objectives, an action particularly required of the national government if mobility limits the opportunity for state and local governments to engage in redistribution.

Breton (chapter 2) argues that the primary and necessary role of the national government is to introduce and maintain some stability in the competitive process among state and local jurisdictions. However, the potential for instability seems to stem from an unequal distribution of resources coupled with mobility. Breton argues that "instability. . .may come about because some jurisdictions do not have the resources . . . to compete with other wealthier jurisdictions." Such distributional differences can be exacerbated by mobility. Breton concludes that "well-designed intergovernmental grants programs are among the most effective instruments available to deal with competitive instability." Thus, he is concerned with distributional policy for reasons of efficiency rather than equity.

As explained by Therese J. McGuire in chapter 9, the traditional efficiency argument for grants is to offset the effect of interjurisdictional benefit spillovers. Open-ended matching categorical grants can accomplish this by reducing local tax prices and thus inducing communities to select the efficient amount of public goods. In practice, however, it is difficult to justify the actual level of matching rates based on the apparent magnitude of spillovers.

A second efficiency reason for grants is provided by the possibility that mobility may not lead to the optimal allocation of population among jurisdictions. Buchanan and Wagner (1970), Buchanan and Goetz (1972), and Flatters, Henderson, and Mieszkowski (1974) have shown that mobility can impose external costs on existing jurisdiction members due to public goods congestion or labor market effects. For instance, if one jurisdiction's fiscal or economic conditions make it attractive for immigration, the existing public facilities, such as roads and school systems, may become overcrowded, reducing the benefits to residents. Similarly, an influx of new workers may reduce wages for all. In deciding whether to make the move, potential new residents have no reason to consider such costs that will be imposed on current residents. In the absence of mobility restrictions (such as zoning), Flatters et al. (1974: 112) concluded that "decentralized migration and movement of population will result in a Pareto-optimal distribution of population only under very special circumstances." Without those circumstances, "free migration will be inefficient and a federation should be set up in order to induce workers to move from the overpopulated to the underpopulated region by subsidizing those residents in the latter region and taxing those residing in the former region" (Flatters et al. 1974: 106).

In other words, lump-sum redistributional grants—for instance, per-capita grants to offset income or wealth differences—are necessary to preserve the efficiency that results from competition. In considering moves, individuals and firms consider only their average cost in the new jurisdiction and not the marginal cost, the effect of their move on the cost for existing residents. In general, too much moving around occurs, governments are led to offer too many inducements to prevent the loss of residents, and inefficiency—what Breton calls instability—results. Regional or interjurisdictional resource differences do matter then, and need to be addressed by the federal government, a fact that Breton suggests has been better recognized and achieved in Canada than in the United States.

WHAT ISSUES DESERVE ADDITIONAL INQUIRY?

Three general issues merit additional research: (1) development of a general theory of interjurisdictional interaction, (2) empirical examination of the degree to which the conditions of the standard competitive model apply to governments, and (3) examination of how state and local governments make decisions about governmental interactions (rather than examination of the effects of those decisions).

On the first issue, there is no doubt that much of the existing research on interjurisdictional competition is directed at specific aspects of the subject. No one general framework or model underlies all of this work. Chubb (chapter 3) favors the development of such a general theory, perhaps based on recent applications of game theory. Although there has been a resurgence of interest in game theory in economics, I am not convinced that such a model can be more general or applicable than the perfectly competitive model, with its limitations. Of course, as Gramlich (1987) has noted, oligopoly models can provide different policy perspectives than competition, and may be more appropriate for some cases, but no such model may apply to all cases.[4]

If one does settle on a model, such as perfect competition, then it is important to have some sense of the degree to which the theoretical conditions are satisfied in practice. For interjurisdictional competition, questions arise concerning the actual degree and nature of mobility and spillovers of taxes and benefits among jurisdictions. Both aspects are crucial to the positive and efficiency properties of the competitive model, and yet there has been little specific examination of mobility or of the benefit side of spillovers.[5] There is room for more work along the lines of Gramlich and Laren (1984), who explicitly examined the mobility of income-support recipients, and Wheaton (1984), who did not assume some degree of mobility to predict the effects of policy but inferred what mobility conditions are consistent with observed effects. Wheaton reported that commercial office rents in the Boston metropolitan area are not higher in higher tax jurisdictions, a result requiring that consumers of office-building capital be more mobile than the suppliers. This is opposite to what is commonly assumed. Similarly, the degree of competition may be influenced by the number of governments in the federal structure (at least in some geographic areas). Although there has been some examination of the effect of the number and type of governments on fiscal decisions, there has been little analysis of how that government structure comes to be. This seems to be another promising topic.

   In addition to examining the conditions of competition, empirical examination of some predicted results of governmental interactions in a competitive model also seems warranted. For instance, as Oates and Schwab (chapter 7) explain, competition among jurisdictions will cause any potential fiscal gains to the governments from development to be bid away; as a result, the revenue from any new investment is expected to be just sufficient to cover the costs of services required by that investment. However, it has been difficult to test this hypothesis empirically because so little is known about the distribution of benefits from state and local government services. Development of an improved method for estimating the fiscal residuals for business taxpayers from state and local government services and application of that method to some specific cases could be very illuminating.

   Finally, it is important to focus more research on why and how state and local governments make decisions about competition or interaction. In Chubb's words (chapter 3), it is necessary to look inside the "black box" and focus on the behavior of the competitors, rather than just on the effects of competition. As Netzer (chapter 13) explains, there are a number of reasons why econometric analysis may not be able to identify the marginal effect of various tax or financial development incentives, and, in addition, there have already been quite a number of those studies. However, there has been much less (in some cases no) empirical analysis of what factors influence governments in selecting a tax structure or how governments decide to offer development incentives, to sell tax-exempt revenue bonds, or to use zoning to control or limit economic development.

Taking these government decisions as exogenous and concentrating only on the responses of individuals and firms is equivalent, in traditional market analysis, to ignoring supply while focusing on demand. This generally makes no sense and wastes, in addition, the substantial investment that economists and others have made over the past 25 years in developing models of fiscal decision making by governments (i.e., the median voter, monopoly bureaucrat, or Tiebout models). Application of these concepts explicitly to fiscal decisions about interjurisdictional competition appears to be a natural extension, as well as one that pays off in the sense that "new" results are obtained. For instance, the econometric results about the effectiveness of development-tax incentives change when allowance is made for communities that act to block development altogether (see Wasylenko 1986). It is important to begin to focus on the supply of development incentives and on the ways in which interjurisdictional competitive concerns influence general fiscal decisions.

Notes

1. Even changes in the relative positions of individual states were not that substantial. Only two states went from above average in per-capita spending in 1971 to below average in 1986, and only four states changed from below average in 1971 to above average in 1986.

2. If one jurisdiction has higher taxes relative to services than other jurisdictions, residential and business activity will leave that jurisdiction, reducing demand for immobile factors such as land and perhaps labor. As a result, the higher taxes are offset by the lower prices of land, labor, and other immobile factors.

3. Suppose one jurisdiction offers tax abatements for new investment. The tax incentive may attract investment that would otherwise not occur, providing additional economic benefits to the community and tax revenue to the government in the short run. But the increased investment will eventually increase the prices of immobile factors such as land. Those higher land costs will deter additional investment in the long run, mitigating the incentive.

4. Indeed, this has been the experience of those who examine interfirm competition. It is not clear why interjurisdictional competition should be any different.

5. In contrast, the interjurisdictional effects of taxes have been examined rather extensively by McLure and others (for instance, see McLure 1964, 1967).

References

Buchanan, James M., and Charles Goetz. 1972. "Efficiency Limits of Fiscal Mobility: An Assessment of the Tiebout Model." *Journal of Public Economics* 1: 25–45.

Buchanan, James M., and Richard Wagner. 1970. "An Efficiency Basis for Federal Fiscal Equalization." In *The Analysis of Public Output*, edited by Julius Margolis. New York: Columbia University Press.

Craig, Steven G., and Joel W. Sailors. 1988. "State Government Purchases in a Federalist Economy." *Public Choice* 56: 121–130.

Fisher, Ronald C. 1989. *State and Local Public Finance.* Glenview, Ill.: Scott, Foresman.

Flatters, Frank, Vernon Henderson, and Peter Mieszkowski. 1974. "Public Goods, Efficiency, and Regional Fiscal Equalization." *Journal of Public Economics* 3: 99–112.

Gooding, Edwin C. 1963, 1964. "New War Between the States." *New England Business Review*, October and December 1963, July and October 1964.

Gramlich, Edward M. 1985. "Reforming U.S. Federal Fiscal Arrangements." In *American Domestic Priorities: An Economic Appraisal*, edited by John M. Quigley and Daniel L. Rubinfeld. Berkeley: University of California Press.

————. 1987. "Cooperation and Competition in Public Welfare Policies." *Journal of Policy Analysis and Management* 6: 417–431.

Gramlich, Edward M., and Deborah S. Laren. 1984. "Migration and Income Redistribution Responsibilities." *Journal of Human Resources* 19: 489–511.

Hamilton, Bruce W. 1975. "Zoning and Property Taxation in a System of Local Governments." *Urban Studies* 12: 205–211.

McLure, Charles E. Jr. 1964. "Community Tax Incidence in Open Economies." *National Tax Journal* 17: 187–204.

————. 1967. "Tax Exporting in the U.S.: Estimates for 1962." *National Tax Journal* 20: 49–77.

Oates, Wallace, E. 1972. *Fiscal Federalism.* New York: Harcourt Brace Jovanovich.

Tiebout, Charles M. 1956. "A Pure Theory of Local Expenditures." *Journal of Political Economy* 64: 416–24.

U.S. Advisory Commission on Intergovernmental Relations. 1991. *Interjurisdictional Tax and Policy Competition: Good or Bad for the Federal System?* Washington, D.C.: Author.

Wagner, Richard E., Robert D. Tollison, Alvin Rabushka, and John T. Noonan. 1982. *Balanced Budgets, Fiscal Responsibility, and the Constitution.* Washington, D.C.: Cato Institute.

Wasylenko, Michael. 1986. "Local Tax Policy and Industry Location: A Review of the Evidence." In *Proceedings of the Seventy-Eighth Annual Conference*. Columbus, Ohio: National Tax Association–Tax Institute of America.

Wheaton, William C. 1984. "The Incidence of Interjurisdictional Differences in Commercial Property Taxes." *National Tax Journal* 37: 515–528.

ABOUT THE CONTRIBUTORS

Albert Breton is professor of economics at the University of Toronto. His research field is public economics. He has taught at the Université de Montréal, Carleton University, Université Catholique de Louvain, The London School of Economics, Harvard University, the Università di Perugia, the Université de Paris I (Panthéon-Sorbonne) and the Institute de Sciences Politiques de Paris. He is past President of the Canadian Economics Association. He has recently published (with Ronald Wintrobe) a paper on "The Bureaucracy of Murder Revisited" and one on "The Growth of Competitive Governments."

John E. Chubb has been a senior fellow in the Governmental Studies Program at the Brookings Institution since 1984. He is the author of numerous books and articles on American government and public policy. His most recent book, coauthored with Terry M. Moe, is *Politics, Markets, and America's Schools*.

Daniel J. Elazar is director of the Center for the Study of Federalism at Temple University, Senator N.P. Paterson Professor of Intergovernmental Relations at Bar Ilan University, Israel, President of the Jerusalem Center for Public Affairs and a member of the Advisory Commission on Intergovernmental Relations. He is the author of *American Federalism: A View from the States*, *Exploring Federalism*, *The American Constitutional Tradition*, and many other works on federalism and intergovernmental relations. He is also co-editor of *Publius: The Journal of Federalism*.

Ronald C. Fisher is professor and chairperson of the department of economics at Michigan State University. He served as Deputy Treasurer for the State of Michigan from 1983–85, specializing in taxation and economic policy. He specializes in the study of government finance and taxation, particularly regarding state and local governments. His publications include *State and Local Public Finance* and numerous professional articles and research reports on public finance topics.

R. Scott Fosler is vice president and director of government studies for the Committee for Economic Development (CED), and a senior fellow of the Johns Hopkins Institute for Policy Studies. His most recent books are *Demographic Change and the American Future* (co-author) and *The New Economic Role of American States* (editor), and he is currently editing a book on local economic development. He is a former elected official in county and municipal government, and has advised numerous state, regional and municipal governments in the United States and abroad.

Steven D. Gold is director of the Center for the Study of the States at the Rockefeller Institute of Government, the public research arm of the State University of New York. He is also on the faculty of SUNY Albany's Graduate School of Public Affairs. Before moving to Albany in 1990, he was director of Fiscal Studies for the National Conference of State Legislatures. He has written or edited many books, the most recent of which is *The State Fiscal Agenda in the 1990s.*

Therese J. McGuire is assistant professor of economics and public policy at the University of Illinois at Chicago. In 1989, she directed the Arizona state tax and expenditure review project, which resulted in recommendations being made to the governor and legislature for reform of the state's fiscal system. She has published several articles on state and local public finance and economic development and she has been active in state tax reform projects around the country.

Dick Netzer is professor of economics and public administration and senior fellow at the Urban Research Center of New York University. He has written and done research in urban economics and pubic finance for more than 40 years, and has had extensive experience as a member of governmental policymaking and advisory boards and commissions, especially in New York City and state.

Nonna A. Noto is a specialist in public finance at the Congressional Research Service, U.S. Library of Congress. Formerly, she was an urban-regional economist at the Federal Reserve Bank of Philadelphia where she wrote about Philadelphia's city and school district budgets and regional employment patterns for the bank's *Business*

Review. She has published several articles on intergovernmental fiscal relations and written numerous Congressional Research Service reports on federal taxes and tax expenditures.

Wallace E. Oates is professor of economics at the University of Maryland. He joined the faculty at Maryland in 1979, following a Ph.D. from Stanford in 1965 and 14 years at Princeton University. His primary research interests are in public finance (with a focus on state and local government) and in environmental economics. In public finance, he published *Fiscal Federalism* and has explored issues in intergovernmental finance. In environmental economics, his publications include *The Theory of Environmental Policy* with William Baumol and other books and papers.

Robert W. Rafuse, Jr. is a senior fellow at the U.S. Advisory Commission on Intergovernmental Relations. He was Deputy Assistant Secretary of the Treasury for State and Local Finance from 1979–87. He has taught public finance at Princeton University, the University of Illinois at Champaign-Urbana, and The George Washington University. He recently authored the ACIR report, *Representative Expenditures: Addressing the Neglected Dimension of Fiscal Capacity*.

Andrew Reschovsky is professor of agricultural economics and public affairs at the University of Wisconsin-Madison. His research is primarily in the area of state and local public finance. He has written numerous articles in professional journals and is the principal author of *State Tax Policy: Evaluating the Issues*. He is currently conducting research on long-term tax burdens.

Robert M. Schwab is associate professor of economics at the University of Maryland. He received his Ph.D. from Johns Hopkins University in 1980. He recently served as a consultant to the Maryland Commission on State Taxes and Tax Structure. Most of his research focuses on state and local public economics and includes studies of intergovernmental competition, optimal community structure, and tax amnesties.

John Shannon is a senior fellow at The Urban Institute. Before that, he served on the staff of the Advisory Commission on Intergovernmental Relations for 24 years. He has also served at the local level with the Detroit Bureau of Governmental Research, at the state level with the Kentucky Department of Revenue, and at the federal level on the White House staff. He has taught at several universities and has published over 100 articles dealing with public finance and intergovernmental issues.

Robert Tannenwald is an economist in the research department of the Federal Reserve Bank of Boston, where he supervises the Banking Structure Unit. From 1984 through 1986 he served as executive director of the Massachusetts Special Commission on Tax Reform. He has published extensively in the field of public finance.

ABOUT THE EDITORS

Daphne A. Kenyon is an associate professor of Economics at Simmons College. From 1983–88 she was a researcher and public policy analyst specializing in issues of state and local public finance at the U.S. Advisory Commission on Intergovernmental Relations, the U.S. Treasury, and The Urban Institute. She is the author of studies of federal deductibility of state and local taxes, state fiscal discipline mechanisms, and limitations on issuance of state and local debt. She is editor, with Michael Fix, of *Coping with Mandates: What Are the Alternatives?*

John Kincaid is Executive Director of the U.S. Advisory Commission on Intergovernmental Relations, Washington, D.C., and associate professor of Political Science (on leave) at the University of North Texas, Denton, where he was founder and first director of the Classic Learning Core of the College of Arts and Sciences. He is also co-editor of *Publius: The Journal of Federalism* and general editor of a 50-book series on "Governments and Politics of the American States" being published by the University of Nebraska Press. He recently edited and contributed to two issues of *The Annals* of the American Academy of Political and Social Science entitled "American Federalism: The Third Century" and "State Constitutions in a Federal System." He also is co-editor and contributor with Daniel J. Elazar of *The Covenant Connection: Federal Theology and the Origins of Modern Politics* (forthcoming). He has written in the fields of federalism, intergovernmental relations, and political theory.

DATE DUE

HIGHSMITH 45-220